The Art of Literary Biography

The Art of Literary Biography

Edited by

John Batchelor

CLARENDON PRESS · OXFORD

1995

Oxford University Press, Walton Street, Oxford OX2 6DP
Oxford New York
Athens Auckland Bangkok Bombay
Calcutta Cape Town Dar es Salaam Delhi
Florence Hong Kong Istanbul Karachi
Kuala Lumpur Madras Madrid Melbourne
Mexico City Nairobi Paris Singapore
Taipei Tokyo Toronto
and associated companies in
Berlin Ibadan

Oxford is a trade mark of Oxford University Press

Published in the United States
by Oxford University Press Inc., New York

British Library Cataloguing in Publication Data
Data available

Library of Congress Cataloging in Publication Data
The art of literary biography / edited by John Batchelor. p. cm.
1. Authors, English—Biography—History and criticism—Theory, etc.
2. English prose literature—History and criticism—Theory, etc.
3. Biography as a literary form. I. Batchelor, John, 1942–
PR756.B56A75 1995
820.9'492—dc20   94-30502
ISBN 0-19-818289-9

1 3 5 7 9 10 8 6 4 2

Typeset by Datix International Limited, Bungay, Suffolk
Printed in Great Britain
on acid-free paper by
Biddles Ltd.,
Guildford and King's Lynn

for Claire Lamont

ACKNOWLEDGEMENTS

The editor would like to express his gratitude to Claire Lamont, who was joint host of the conference on the 'The Art of Literary Biography' at the University of Newcastle upon Tyne, 1–3 April 1993, and to Rowena Bryson, whose dedication and expertise contributed greatly both to the smooth running of the conference and to the preparation of the present book. Acknowledgements are due for permission to quote in Jon Stallworthy's essay an unpublished poem, an unpublished letter and an extract from the *Autobiography* by Louis MacNeice (by permission of David Higham Associates for the estate of Louis MacNeice and Faber and Faber Ltd.). Acknowledgements are due for permission to quote in Linda Anderson's essay on Elizabeth Bishop from the unpublished 'Travel Diaries', 'Recorded Observations', and 'Three American Poets' by Elizabeth Bishop (by permission of Vassar Library and the Bishop Estate: copyright © 1994 Alice Helen Methfessel); from 'Giant Snail', 'The End of March', and 'In the Waiting Room' from *The Complete Poems 1927–1979* (Farrar, Strauss & Giroux, Inc., copyright © 1979, 1983 Alice Helen Methfessel); and from 'In the Village', from *The Collected Prose* (copyright © 1984 Alice Helen Methfessel), and are also due to the Curator of Rare Books and Manuscripts at Vassar College, Nancy MacKechnie, for her assistance, and to Newcastle University Research Committee for a grant in aid of research. Acknowledgements are due for permission to quote in Hermione Lee's essay on Virginia Woolf unpublished material by Ben Nicolson (Mrs Vanessa Davidson and the University of Sussex Manuscript Collection) and unpublished material by Fredegond Shove (King's College Cambridge Modern Archive). Hermione Lee's essay was first given as a paper at a conference on Virginia Woolf, organized by Julia Briggs and Jeri Johnson, at Hertford College, Oxford, September 1992. Acknowledgements are due for permission to quote in Ann Thwaite's essay in Chapter 13 from 'Mrs Alfred Tennyson . . .' (part II of 'The Literary World' by Philip Larkin) from *Collected Poems* (the Estate of Philip Larkin). Acknowledgements are due for permission to use in David Bradshaw's essay unpublished materials in the possession of the following libraries, institutions and individuals: British Library of Political and Economic Science, London School of Economics and Political Science; Mrs Anne Charlton; Galton Institute, London; Lady Huxley; Mr Max Nicholson; The Poetry/Rare Books Collection, University Libraries, State University of New York at Buffalo; Contemporary Medical Archives Centre, Wellcome Institute for the History of Medicine, London; Wellcome Unit for the History of Medicine, University of Oxford.

CONTENTS

List of Illustrations   xi

Introduction   I
  JOHN BATCHELOR

PART I: Theory, Culture, and Context: The Nature
        of Literary Biography

 1. Biography: Inventing the Truth   15
     RICHARD HOLMES

 2. A Life for a Life   27
     JON STALLWORTHY

 3. Secondary Lives: Biography in Context   43
     CATHERINE PETERS

 4. Biography: Cult as Culture   57
     JÜRGEN SCHLAEGER

 5. Psychiatry and Literary Biography   73
     ANTHONY STORR

 6. Women's Lives: The Unmapped Country   87
     LYNDALL GORDON

PART II: Some Individual Studies

 7. John Wilmot, Earl of Rochester: An Author
    in Search of a Character   101
     KEN ROBINSON

 8. Conrad's Truancy   115
     JOHN BATCHELOR

 9. Virginia Woolf and Offence   129
     HERMIONE LEE

10. Huxley's Slump: Planning, Eugenics, and the
    'Ultimate Need' of Stability   151
     DAVID BRADSHAW

Contents

11. Elizabeth Bishop: The Secret Life of a Poet 173
    LINDA ANDERSON

PART III: Life and Art: The Biographer at Work and
         the Writer as Biographer

12. Jane Austen, Matthew Arnold, Shakespeare:
    The Problem of the *Opus* 187
    PARK HONAN

13. Starting Again: One of the Problems of the
    Biographer 201
    ANN THWAITE

14. Pieties and Literary Biography 213
    NORMAN WHITE

15. The Necessary Ignorance of a Biographer 227
    JOHN WORTHEN

16. Virginia Woolf and 'The Proper Writing of
    Lives' 245
    JULIA BRIGGS

17. Learning about Ourselves: Biography as
    Autobiography 267
    HUMPHREY CARPENTER
    (in conversation with Lyndall Gordon)

    Notes on Contributors 281
    Index 285

LIST OF ILLUSTRATIONS

between pp. 116–117

1. Louis MacNeice.
   © Camera Press Ltd.

2. William Wilkie Collins, by Sir John Everett Millais, 1850.
   © National Portrait Gallery, London.

3. Lord Rochester, attributed to J. Huysmans.
   © National Portrait Gallery, London.

4. Sigmund Freud at his desk. Etching by Max Pollak, 1914.
   Mary Evans/Sigmund Freud Copyrights.

5. Joseph Conrad.
   © Hulton Deutsch Collection Ltd.

6. Virginia Woolf, London 1939. Photo Gisèle Freund.
   © John Hillelson Agency.

7. Aldous Huxley.
   © Hulton Deutsch Collection Ltd.

8. Matthew Arnold. Photograph by Camille Silvy, 1861.
   © National Portrait Gallery, London.

9. Emily Tennyson, by G. F. Watts.
   © Lincolnshire Library Service.

10. D. H. Lawrence, *c*. December 1908.
    Courtesy of Mrs Joan King.

❧ *Introduction* ❧

Terry Eagleton has remarked recently that 'there would seem no end to the peculiar English mania for the Individual Life'.[1] It was partially in acknowledgement of this mania that two conferences on literary biography were held, one at the University of Newcastle upon Tyne from 1 to 3 April 1993 and the other at Schloss Hofen on Lake Constance, also in April 1993. Most of the contributions to this book are selected from the Newcastle conference, whose subject was 'The Art of Literary Biography', and which was hosted by John Batchelor and Claire Lamont. The following essays in the book are lectures or papers given at the Newcastle conference: those by Linda Anderson, David Bradshaw, Julia Briggs, Lyndall Gordon, Richard Holmes, Park Honan, Hermione Lee, Catherine Peters, Jon Stallworthy, Anthony Storr, Ann Thwaite, Norman White, and John Worthen. Humphrey Carpenter decided not to publish his paper given at the Newcastle conference and has instead contributed his instructive and entertaining 'conversation' (with Lyndall Gordon) which appears as the final item in this book. Ken Robinson, one of the organizers of the Newcastle conference, was unable to attend because of ill health: his proposed paper on Rochester is published here. The essays by John Batchelor and Jürgen Schlaeger were papers given at the conference entitled 'British Biographical Writing: Truth, Subversion, Gender, Ethics', at Schloss Hofen. This conference was hosted by Professor Schlaeger and organized jointly by the University of Konstanz and the British Council (Germany), 14–17 April 1993.

The organizers of the Newcastle conference wanted to bring together freelance biographers, such as Humphrey Carpenter, Richard Holmes, and Ann Thwaite, with biographers who work from within universities, such as Lyndall Gordon, Park Honan, Hermione Lee, and Jon Stallworthy, with a view to sharing ideas about the form and exploring the professional experience common to these two slightly different kinds of writer. Literary biography can be regarded as a bridge between the academy and the common reader (Michael Holroyd and the late Richard Ellmann can be regarded as major examples of writers who cross the bridge from opposite directions, from the market-place and the academy respectively). It is good for English literature, as a university subject, not to be sealed into the academy, and the writing and reading of literary biography can be welcomed as activities which can operate at a high and intellectually responsible level.

There seems no doubt that the writing of biography is in some sense a 'conservative' activity in that it celebrates a known life of the past. Catherine Peters in her essay on 'Secondary Lives' says that literary biography is 'a traditional, rather old-fashioned form, evolving slowly rather than by great imaginative leaps and profound intellectual discoveries'. Jürgen Schlaeger, in 'Biography: Cult as Culture', agrees:

Compared with the images of our culture which post-modernism projects, biography is, in spite of its intertextual construction, fundamentally reactionary, conservative, perpetually accommodating new models of man, new theories of the inner self, into a personality-oriented cultural mainstream, thus always helping to defuse their subversive potential.

Biography in this view is 'immune' from deconstruction. This is not to say that theory has no place in the biographer's activity. There will be theory, either consciously or by default, informing the nature of the biographer's relationship with his/her material. Ken Robinson, in his essay on the problems confronting a biographer of Rochester, remarks that while biographers 'strive for the degree of accuracy that their art will allow' their work is 'in an important sense invention'. Richard Holmes's essay, 'Biography: Inventing the Truth', takes the fictive nature of the biographer's enterprise as its focus. Park Honan, who has taken up the ultimate challenge to a literary biographer—that of writing a life of Shakespeare—has addressed this issue in his recent book of essays on biography, *Authors' Lives*. He agrees that a biographer needs theoretical self-awareness but adds—from the pragmatist's workshop, so to speak—that when the biographer is actually writing his/her narrative, practical problems, at once 'vast and pokey' and 'involving countless bits of paper, marked-up Xeroxes, and references in microfilms', tend to shoulder theory aside by forcing the writer to give priority to immediate problems of organization, 'to adopt complex filing systems and simple working theories'.[2] Also, as Terry Eagleton says, biography has a robust and simple shape forced on it by its subject-matter: 'The structure of biography is biology: even the most wayward of geniuses have to get themselves born and educated, fight with their parents, fall in love and die.'[3]

The working theories include, crucially, such things as selection of material and the biographer's distance from the life of his/her subject. The problem of selection is a problem that biographers share with novelists. In the Preface to *Roderick Hudson* Henry James wrote that 'really, universally, relations stop nowhere, and the exquisite problem of the artist is eternally but to draw, by a geometry of his own, the circle within which they shall happily *appear* to do so'. Catherine Peters's account of the repeated rewritings of parts of her recent *King of Inventors: A Life of Wilkie Collins* focuses the practical difficulties: how to give enough space to minor figures in the story without obscuring the central figure. One solution is to write at great length (Edel's *James* showed how tedious such inclusiveness can be, while Ellmann's *Joyce*, by contrast, showed how it could be done without sacrificing narrative impetus); another is to give information about the secondary lives in a kind of 'Who's Who' published as an appendix (Richard Holmes adopts this solution in his life of Coleridge), or to give very condensed notes on minor figures against their entries in the index, as Robert DeMaria, jun. does in his recent biography of Johnson.[4]

The problem of selectivity and the problem of objectivity are linked; is the central figure to be given heroic presence in the biographer's dramatic organization? Jon Stallworthy, in 'A Life for a Life', remarks that 'once upon a time there were heroes'. Norman White, in 'Pieties and Literary Biography', takes up Stallworthy's title to address the question of objectivity:

There is that word 'Life', meaning a person's existence between birth and death; but there is also the word 'Life' meaning what a biographer tells you was another person's existence. In spite of scholarly notes about sources and authorial limitations you can't get away from the fact that biography claims the two are the same, though plainly they are not.

Jürgen Schlaeger says that from a German perspective the cult of personality and the fondness for heroes that accompany the ascendancy of biography look peculiarly English. For him England 'oozes biography from every pore. . . . for a person with my non-English sensibilities a visit to the National Portrait Gallery is traumatic. The existence of such an institution is in itself a strong indicator of a personality-centred culture.' Biography in England is enjoying high prestige because of a current 'pressing need for a reassertion of individualism.' German traditions are different and less empirical:

Germans generally expect redress not from ancestor-worship or from a biographical restaging of other people's lives but from hard work, from devotion to a cause, from systematic thinking, from the philosophical tradition, in short, from practices that are as far removed from what biography does as can be.

Biographical argument can also be carefully judged philosophical and political—and forensic—argument, as Hermione Lee shows in her essay, 'Virginia Woolf and Offence', where she confronts recent attacks on Woolf (by critics such as John Carey) as snobbish, anti-Semitic, elitist, and politically rotten. Hermione Lee's position on this is summed up, with ringing conviction, in her claim that 'in Virginia Woolf's lifelong argument with herself and others about the effect of class on her imagination, she excoriates and defends herself better than anyone else can'. As Julia Briggs says in her essay on 'Virginia Woolf and "The Proper Writing of Lives"', biography was the early model for Virginia Woolf's thinking about the nature of imaginative writing. In her later work she abandoned this model, but it raised issues which remained potent for her to the end of her career.

The literary biographer must perform a balancing act. He/she must keep the balance between objectivity and personal engagement, between reliance on documentary evidence (letters, journals, and memoirs) and intuitive re-creation, between the subject's under-documented childhood and his/her well-monitored but perhaps tedious years of elderly distinction. The literary biographer needs the skills of an intellectual and cultural historian, a literary critic, a novelist, and a psychiatrist. Where the record is fragmentary he/she should add to that list the abilities of an archivist, an archaeologist, and a sleuth. There are strong examples of these qualities in this volume, especially in Linda Anderson's sensitive use of archive material relating to Elizabeth Bishop's lesbianism in her essay 'Elizabeth Bishop: The Secret Life of a Poet', and in David Bradshaw's research in primary material which suggests, in his essay 'Huxley's Slump: Planning, Eugenics, and the "Ultimate Need" of Stability', that Aldous Huxley's political sympathies in the 1930s were quite different from those commonly attributed to him on the basis of *Brave New World*.

Keeping the balance between love and detachment is the most obvious problem and perhaps the most difficult. In his autobiographical book, *Footsteps: Adventures of a Romantic Biographer*, Richard Holmes speaks of self-identification as 'the first crime in biography' but also as something which is sometimes inevitable and necessary, and sometimes the biographer's last resort.[5] *Footsteps* is in effect a personal meditation on the practice and theory of a biographer, following his subjects from place to place, imagining himself back into their skins and their lives, abnegating the self in service of the subject: 'There is something frequently comic about the trailing figure of the biographer: a sort of tramp permanently knocking at the kitchen window and secretly hoping he might be invited in for supper.'[6] In the first volume of his biography of Coleridge he illustrates the pleasures and the limitations of the method, and acknowledges, in particular, that however scrupulous a researcher may be, he/she will be very lucky to find first-hand access to unmediated material in the case of a famous life. The lives of the great come to us overlaid by interpretation. As a child Coleridge visited a cave called the Pixies' Parlour, which was about a mile to the south of St Mary Ottery where he lived. Coleridge carved his initials at the back of the cave. Richard Holmes adds:

In 1986 I crawled [into the cave] and was astonished to discover the initials S T C carved at the very back of the cave. It took me a moment to realize

5

that the sandstone walls are so porous and flaky that these could not possibly be Coleridge's original graffiti, but some later act of piety. Such carvings and re-carvings of his initials, ceremoniously repeated by generation after generation of unknown memorialists, suddenly seemed to me like a symbol of the essentially cumulative process of biography itself.[7]

I have mentioned psychiatry: Anthony Storr, a contributor to this volume, has thought long and hard about the relationship between biography and his own profession. In his paper on 'Psychiatry and Literary Biography' he sees a dilemma which can only partially be resolved. It is impossible to understand the lives of some writers (Kafka is his chosen example) without recourse to psychiatry, yet the attempts to use the methods of psychiatry in writing about the famous dead are doomed to approximation: 'detailed causal psychoanalytic interpretations of the character and behaviour of deceased persons in terms of what may have happened to them in early childhood are intrinsically unreliable.' In an earlier paper on 'Writers and Recurrent Depression', given to the Royal Society of Literature, Anthony Storr reported research among forty-seven contemporary British writers and artists which found that 38 per cent of these successful and well-known people had been treated for depression. Practitioners of the art of biography, including contributors to this volume, will be encouraged to learn that 'biographers were less susceptible'.

One of the functions of this volume is to contribute to a small but growing literature, that of a modern poetics of biography. Recent contributions to this literature have included (in chronological order) books by Leon Edel, Richard Ellmann, A. O. J. Cockshut, Jeffrey Meyers, Ira Bruce Nadel, Richard Holmes, and Park Honan, and two volumes of conference papers from earlier conferences on biography from the University of East Anglia and the Australian National University.[8] The authors of and contributors to these volumes agree that one of the limitations facing a biographer is that he/she will be forced to compromise—that the perfect biography is less achievable than the perfect novel or (still less) the perfect poem. A biographer is limited by the amount of time and money he/she has for research, travel, and (in the case of the recently dead subject) interviews, by the degree of access to the archive and the degree of co-operation from the executors that he/ she has managed to negotiate.

Questions of co-operation and access can become delicate and thorny. In their contributions to the University of East Anglia conference on biography Hugh Brogan and Hilary Spurling record how embarrassed they were to find that they were both working on biographies of Ivy Compton-Burnett, each being 'strung along' by Compton-Burnett's executors and friends (Hugh Brogan honourably withdrew from this contest).[9] Ian Hamilton and Michael Millgate have written intelligent and *engagé* studies of the (occasionally) enlightened but (more often) power-loving and self-interested behaviour of literary executors.[10] As Jon Stallworthy shows in his essay, 'A Life for a Life', the biographer's struggle to gain access to the archive makes excellent—and painful—material for fiction: witness James's *The Aspern Papers*, Golding's *The Paper Men*, and A. S. Byatt's *Possession*.

In a contribution to the Australian conference on biography Philip Ziegler argues forcibly that, whatever the obstructions, total immersion in all available archive material is an indispensable stage in the biographer's task. What appears in the finished book should never be more than the tip of the iceberg. The biographer must undergo a

monstrous accumulation of unprocessed detail, most of which will eventually be discarded, but none of which is valueless. I cannot express too strongly my belief that biographers must aim to embrace the totality of the subjects' life. This aim is, of course, unattainable, but that is no excuse for not seeking to attain it. Biographers must never lose their hunger for the minutiae of their subjects' everyday existence.[11]

Lyndall Gordon, in a contribution to *The Craft of Literary Biography*, proposes a contrasting view. She says that, for her life of T. S. Eliot, Eliot's refusal to have a biography, and the Eliot estate's consequent embargo on quotation from copyright material, were beneficial: 'the impossibility of official biography may be, far from a handicap, an actual advantage, not because of the licence this offers but because of the chance to invent a new form.'[12]

'Read no history: nothing but biography, for that is life without theory' (Disraeli). A. O. J. Cockshut, in his study of nineteenth-century biography published twenty years ago, quoted Disraeli's remark as a preface to his own observation that 'for nearly two centuries we have been living in a golden age of biographical writing', from Johnson to Ellmann, and yet the form is something of a Cinderella: 'Everyone seems to know that the two centuries from Richardson to Lawrence constitute a great age of the novel; those who are aware that the same is true of biography have been curiously, perhaps even culpably, reticent.'[13]

Cockshut's account reminds us that the 'poetics' of biography goes back at least to Carlyle. For Carlyle, biography is good in so far as it is hero-worship:

[Boswell] passes for a mean, inflated, gluttonous creature; and was so in many senses. Yet the fact of his reverence for Johnson will ever remain noteworthy. The foolish conceited Scotch Laird, the most conceited man of his time, approaching in such awestruck attitude the great dusty irascible Pedagogue in his mean garret there: it is a genuine reverence for Excellence; a *worship* for Heroes, at a time when neither Heroes nor worship were surmised to exist. Heroes, it would seem, exist always, and a certain worship of them![14]

Froude's life of Carlyle (4 vols., 1882–4) was both an act of immersion and an act of truth-telling in the cause of love. As Lytton Strachey said, 'it shrank with horror from the notion of omitting a single wart from the portrait.'[15] Robert Skidelsky, in a paper for the East Anglia conference, remarks that with Strachey's *Eminent Victorians* (1918) debunking biography became the norm, but that since then, because of the power of literary executors, biography has again become a somewhat Victorian form, displaying 'a hero-worship that shares much in common with Froude's.'[16]

Because literary biography is a pragmatic and historical form, its relationship with literary theory will always be open to negotiation. Park Honan, in his essay on Austen, Arnold, Shakespeare, and the 'problem of the *opus*', sees the current 'storm of theory' as conferring freedom on the biographer. 'As for the theories, I may be naïve. I'm not worried. What are they good for, if not for an easy, free play of mind?' Some university teachers of English literature may be bothered by biography's messy reluctance to keep in separate compartments the author and the work. John Carey in a recent article notes what he perceives as a paradox. The huge current readership for literary biography seems to be working against the trend of English studies: 'should we bother to read literary biographies? . . . Most new thinking in English studies over the last few decades has encouraged a presupposition that the answer to this question is "No".'

'Deconstruction' has popularised the idea that what an author actually meant in a text is not discoverable, or anyway not provable, so readers not only can but must construct the meaning of texts as they go along. The author is dead, Roland Barthes has announced, and the reader is free. If so, there is not much point in knowing about authors.[17]

The New Criticism in the 1950s and the critical orthodoxies that have followed it hold that the situation can arise where an author states an intention while the work, in the opinion of literate readers, says something else. The New Critics, following Lawrence's 'Never trust the artist. Trust the tale',[18] argued, very plausibly, that in such cases the work is the higher authority, and, if this is the case, in instances of conflict it follows that biographical information can never add to or modify our literary assessment and understanding of the work. The present buoyancy of literary biography supports the case for a contrasting view, a view which seems to me implicit in the work of all literary biographers: namely, that in practice the reading of literary biography gives us a different intellectual process from that indicated by the New Critics, one in which literary understanding is progressive. We read the work. Then we read the biography. Then we read the work again and we see more.

In the book that follows I have divided the essays into three groups under the following headings: 'Theory, Culture and Context: The Nature of Literary Biography', 'Some Individual Studies', and 'Life and Art: The Biographer at Work and the Writer as Biographer'. These divisions reflect the fact that some of the essays address theoretical questions, some are on single authors, and some deal with specific problems that come up in the course of writing biographies. The divisions are not watertight: the essays addressing

9

theoretical questions also have a lot to say about the biographer's practice (and vice versa) and the essays on individual lives contain consideration of theoretical and practical matters. Literary biography resists the splitting up of intellectual activity into compartments, and I hope that readers of this book will agree that it is fitting that our discussions of literary biography, recorded in this book, tended to display the same kind of pragmatism as does biography itself.

JOHN BATCHELOR

Notes

1. Terry Eagleton, reviewing *Patrick Hamilton: A Life*, by Sean French, *London Review of Books*, 2 Dec. 1993, 12.
2. Park Honan, *Authors' Lives: On Literary Biography and the Arts of Language* (New York, 1990), 5.
3. Eagleton, *London Review of Books*, 12.
4. Richard Holmes, *Coleridge: Early Visions* (London, 1989), 365–71; Robert DeMaria, jun., *The Life of Samuel Johnson: A Critical Biography* (Oxford, 1993), 339–56.
5. Richard Holmes, *Footsteps: Adventures of a Romantic Biographer* (1985; repr. Harmondsworth, 1986), 264.
6. Ibid. 144.
7. Holmes, *Coleridge: Early Visions*, 12 n.
8. Leon Edel, *Literary Biography* (London, 1957), Richard Ellmann, *Golden Codgers: Biographical Speculations* (London, 1973), A. O. J. Cockshut, *Truth to Life: The Art of Biography in the Nineteenth Century* (London, 1974), Jeffrey Meyers (ed.), *The Craft of Literary Biography* (New York, 1985), Ira Bruce Nadel, *Biography: Fiction, Fact and Form* (London, 1985), Eric Homberger and John Charmley (eds.), *The Troubled Face of Biography* (London, 1988), Ian Donaldson, Peter Read, and James Walter (eds.), *Shaping Lives: Reflections on Biography* (Canberra, 1992).
9. Hugh Brogan, 'The Biographer's Chains', and Hilary Spurling, 'Neither Morbid nor Ordinary', *The Troubled Face of Biography*, 104–12, 113–30.
10. Ian Hamilton, *Keepers of the Flame: Literary Estates and the Rise of Biography* (London, 1992); Michael Millgate, *Testamentary Acts: Browning, Tennyson, James, Hardy* (Oxford, 1992).
11. Philip Ziegler, 'Biography: The Narrative', *Shaping Lives*, 225–6.
12. Lyndall Gordon, 'T. S. Eliot', *The Craft of Literary Biography*, 180–1, 184.
13. A. O. J. Cockshut, *Truth to Life*, epigraph and p. 11.
14. Thomas Carlyle, *On Heroes, Hero-Worship and the Heroic in History* (1841; repr. London, 1897), 183.
15. Quoted in Robert Skidelsky, 'Only Connect: Biography and Truth', *The Troubled Face of Biography*, 5; Lytton Strachey quotation from *Portraits in Miniature* (London, 1931), 199.

16. Skidelsky, 'Only Connect', 8.
17. John Carey, 'Literary Biographies', *English Review*, 1/1 (Sept. 1990), 11.
18. D. H. Lawrence, *Studies in Classic American Literature* (London, 1924), 9.

❧ PART I ❧

Theory, Culture, and Context:
The Nature of Literary Biography

❧ I ❧

Biography: Inventing the Truth

RICHARD HOLMES

What I want to suggest is that biography—the form that I have loved and struggled with for nearly thirty years—is essentially, and by its very origins, disreputable. Its genius, and indeed its very genealogy, is impure. It was relished and attacked during its first popular flowering in the eighteenth-century, just as it is relished and attacked today. It has always had the doubtful status of a maverick or mongrel art, and that is precisely why it remains so alive, so adaptable, so dangerous for all concerned: writers, subjects, readers, and most of all for its critics who want it to behave.

Let me propose a simple myth of its genesis, a sort of Origin of the Species. The problematic, delightful, and disputed nature of biography derives from its original two forebears, who one secret, sultry morning formed an Unholy Alliance. Fiction married Fact, without benefit of clergy. Or as I prefer to say, Invention formed a love-match with Truth. These are the Adam and Eve of our subject. The result was a brilliant, bastard form—Biography—which has been causing trouble ever since.

Consider for a moment the extraordinary divergence in the offspring produced. The two most successful biographies in the English language to date are probably James Boswell's *Life of Samuel Johnson Lld* (1791), which has never been out of print for 200 years; and Andrew Morton's *Diana: Her True Story* (1992), 'including a new chapter and 28 new photographs', which has sold two and a half million copies world-wide and whose sales will be clicking upwards as we annotate our footnotes.

Consider too the different kinds of portraiture, the different modes of inward life, achieved in those two works. Here is Boswell, entering with unforgettable empathy and metaphoric daring into Johnson's inner world of moral struggle.

His mind resembled the vast amphitheatre, the Colisaeum at Rome. In the centre stood his judgement, which, like a mighty gladiator, combated those apprehensions that, like the wild beasts of the Arena, were all around in cells, ready to be let out upon him. After a conflict, he drove them back to their dens; but not killing them, they were still assailing him. (*Life*, p. 427)

Boswell animates in Johnson's life a quality of moral epic. The extended gladiatorial simile is worthy of, and indeed perhaps inspired by, the poetic similes of Milton's *Paradise Lost*. Boswell defines a classical hero, an Augustan Everyman, doing battle against the hirsute monsters of doubt, subjectivity, and irrationality which will become in due course the great powers of Romanticism. Through Johnson's inner life, he dramatizes a historic conflict of cultural sensibilities. He makes biography imaginative, large, generous: even at moments sublime.

The biography that Andrew Morton writes is influenced less by John Milton than by Barbara Cartland. But the tradition of gossip, of aristocratic scandal, of piquant anecdote, also runs deep in the form and arguably goes back to John Aubrey's *Brief Lives*. It is useless to pretend it does not exist. Morton has been much mocked, both for his success and for his novelettish style. But consider the skill—which includes the circumvention of libel—with which he presents this peculiarly modern image of domestic suspicion and jealousy. 'Diana has long been concerned about the influence of the Highgrove Set on her husband. When she is at their Gloucestershire retreat she routinely presses the "last number redial" button on his portable telephone. Invariably she is connected to Middlewich House, the Parker-Bowles's Wiltshire home.' It is interesting that the telephone, long thought to herald the demise of modern biography by replacing letters, here becomes the instrument of intimacy and romantic suggestion. (Indeed it could be argued that in all the circumstances the mobile telephone has given scandal-biography its most powerful relaunch in history.) Morton hardly makes biography sublime; but he confirms its capacity for sublime triviality and domestic tattle.

The diversity of the biographic form, and the range of inventive power with which it can render both the external details and the inward nature of a life—its power to reconstruct and to intrude—have always posed certain problematic questions. I should like to raise four of these, which each reflect something of the controversial nature of the form we have inherited. They concern ethics, authenticity, celebrity, and the principle of empathy.

The ethics of research into another person's life have always been questionable. By what right, by what contract, does a biographer enter into another's zone of activity and privacy? Even an actual legal contract with a dead author's estate does not necessarily cover this issue. The idea of the biographer as a pursuing hound—James Joyce's 'biografiend'—has been present from the start. Dr Arbuthnot, writing in the eighteenth century of the innumerable biographical pamphlets produced by the 'unspeakable' Edmund Curll, gloomily remarked that biography had 'added a new Terror to Death'. Henry James in his famous story about Shelley's love-letters, *The Aspern Papers*, characterized the young American researcher as a 'publishing scoundrel'. The biographer has appeared in a similar role in recent novels by William Golding and A. S. Byatt. Ian Hamilton has vividly dramatized the case in his study of J. D. Salinger, where the novelist resorts to law to defend his privacy. The long saga of Ted Hughes's battles against Sylvia Plath's biographers puts the question in its most anguished, immediate form, while Diane Wood Middlebrook's biography of Anne Sexton (1991) presses it into new areas of intimate exposure, by using the tape-recordings of some 300 psychotherapy sessions undertaken by Sexton towards the end of her life before committing suicide. All these should give us pause for reflection.

Next there is the problem of authenticity. Biographers base their work on sources which are inherently unreliable. Memory itself is fallible; memoirs are inevitably biased; letters are always slanted towards their recipients; even private diaries and intimate journals have to be recognized as literary forms of self-invention rather than an 'ultimate' truth of private fact or feeling. The biographer has always had to construct or orchestrate a factual pattern out of materials that already have a fictional or reinvented element. Perhaps the most insidious lies in the apparently established ground of earlier or 'authorized' works: Moore's life of Byron, or Forster's life of Dickens being cases in point. A remarkable example appeared recently in Christopher Benfey's intriguing work *The Double Life of Stephen Crane* (1993), in which Benfey shows that Crane's early standard biography by Thomas Beer (1923) was in fact a tissue of inventions. Much of Benfey's effort is concentrated on discovering the inauthentic, the romancing of a life performed both by Crane and by his friends. He writes wryly:

> As for the extraordinary letters Beer quotes at length, containing some of Crane's most bracing, and most often quoted, literary and philosophical opinions, they too are apparently forgeries. . . . We must now forget that Crane claimed he got his artistic education on the Bowery, that he thought *War and Peace* went on and on like Texas, that he said that while Robert Louis Stevenson had passed away, he hadn't passed away far enough. (Benfey, p. 8)

Truth, in this sense, is always something of a floating currency; and the exchange rates alter through history.

Third comes the peculiar magnetism of celebrity. Biography has always been drawn towards the famous, the glamorous, the notorious. It is pulled, unnaturally perhaps, out of the orbit of the ordinary, the average, the everyday lives that most of us lead and need to understand. Instead it typically tells the stories of great saints and great sinners; kings, actors, criminals, generals, Romantic poets, mad novelists, promiscuous painters. There are over 200 lives of Lord Byron. The 'minor' character, the faithful spouse, the loyal companion, the intelligent sensible friend, are so often reduced to footnotes, the unmarked grave at the foot of the page. This can be seen as a fundamental distortion within the form's capacity to deal with life in its largest, broadest sense as we mostly experience it. Freud defined this as the problem of 'hero-worship' inherent in the genre, with its concomitant but suppressed desire to devalue greatness, to find the feet of clay and the rattling skeleton in the cupboard.

Of course there is a tradition of the great 'minor' life—itself a suggestive paradox—of which Johnson's *Life of Richard Savage*

(1744) seems to me a crucial, and singularly revealing example and to which I shall return. Biography indeed can alter our fundamental assumptions about what lives have been significant, and why. The contemporary influence of feminism has been a notable force for justice and revaluation in this respect: we now have admirable lives of Mary Wollstonecraft as well as her husband William Godwin; of Dorothy Wordsworth as well as brother William; of Zelda Fitzgerald as well as Scott; of Caitlin Thomas as well as Dylan; of Ellen Ternan as well as Dickens. Yet even some of these remain pale, moonlight satellites around the planetary celebrity. Biography finds it difficult to deal imaginatively with the mundane. And where the mundane, in its richest sense, is central to a life—as in a happy marriage, or a long and constant friendship—it is often peculiarly impotent, both in its sources (what house companions write letters to each other?) and in its narrative invention (how to describe twenty years of tender, ruminative breakfasts?).

Lastly, there is the complicated and subtle question of empathy. Why is a biographer drawn to particular subjects, what element of suppressed autobiography is involved, and how does this affect the possibilities of an 'objectively' truthful account? I have tried to examine some of these delicate, self-reflexive issues in a book called *Footsteps* (1985), but I am still deeply puzzled and fascinated by them. The power of certain lives to draw endlessly repeated reassessments—Johnson, Byron, Napoleon, Queen Victoria, D. H. Lawrence, Plath—is a peculiar mystery. It suggests that they hold particular mirrors up to each succeeding generation of biographers, almost as the classical myths were endlessly retold by the Greek dramatists, to renew their own versions of contemporary identity. Each generation sees itself anew in its chosen subjects.

But in this sense a final, truthful, 'definitive' account must always be something of a chimera. We get back the answers only to the questions we ask of a life. The picture lives only within the frame we have invented for it. Andrew Motion's recent fine and mournful life of Philip Larkin (1993) is everywhere shaped by its anxious, intelligent liberalism trying to make sense of political and sexual views that are currently unacceptable. It is, as a newspaper headline puckishly put it, 'the Life of Mr Nasty told by Mr Nice'. But it is also brought alive—a fact not sufficiently noted—by its gentle, ironic humour which suggests the comedy of absurdity which almost defines our contemporary way of making sense of English-ness. If it also makes us question the sources of Larkin's art, the 'pretty dismal' ground from which his poetry grew, then it perfectly expresses the self-doubting spirit of the age. One can only say that a later age will certainly see Larkin differently.

These four problems that I have outlined (there are of course plenty of others) do not devalue the modern form of biography, in my view. But they make it complicated, provisional, and to some degree perilous. Because of its current popularity, and the tremen-dous impact made by the work of Richard Ellmann, Michael Holroyd, Peter Ackroyd, Victoria Glendinning, Claire Tomalin, and Margaret Forster, among others, this is easily overlooked. It is arguably the most successful, and intellectually stimulating, literary form which has held a general readership in Britain since 1960. But this may not last. If biography is to have a future, it has to face up to the problems it has inherited.

All these seem to express the original, underlying tension found in its genealogy: Invention marrying Truth. The fluid, imaginative powers of re-creation pull against the hard body of discoverable fact. The inventive, shaping instinct of the story-teller struggles with the ideal of a permanent, historical, and objective document. Sylvia Plath once said that if poetry is like a closed fist, then fiction is like an open hand. On that marvellous analogy, then biography is something like a handshake, a handshake across time. But it is also an arm-wrestle, even if a friendly one, like most lively marriages.

If we go back to the eighteenth century, where popular English biography began, we can learn something about the terms of the original contract from our great master-biographer, Samuel John-son. The term 'biographer' incidentally first becomes current in 1715, when it replaces the more antiquarian 'biographist'. From this time collections of 'Lives', or 'True Histories', become widely available through the productions—disreputable of course—of Edmund Curll, Robert Shiel, and the editors of *The Newgate Calendar*. It is a crucial period of transition where the novel and the biography first begin to move in separate, but not immediately distinguishable, directions. Daniel Defoe, and his female counterpart Eliza Haywood, mixed both forms with a fine lack of discrimination.

There is an interesting sociological argument that the novel developed as a result of private study-rooms, withdrawing-rooms, and small libraries and boudoirs, increasingly built in middle-class and well-to-do homes at this period. The novel began to flourish in an architecture of growing privacy, and solitary fantasy. By contrast biography may partly have developed from the enormous growth in congenial coffee-houses, companionable taverns, and clubs, where gossip, anecdote, and the telling of 'the latest story' became a premium. Biography could thus be seen as a coffee-house form, both talkative and reflective, where the liveliness of a tale—its power to amuse, provoke, or cause solemn meditation—was finely balanced against its veracity or 'intelligence'.

If there is anything in this idea, then it is hardly surprising that Johnson, the author of *The Lives of the Poets*, was the clubman and coffee-house talker *par excellence*. When he first came to London in 1737, abandoning the schoolmasterly solitudes of Lichfield and domestic life with his wife 'Tetty', he soon embarked on a series of short biographies (of scholars, scientists, men of action) which bore fruit in his early masterpiece, the life of his raffish friend, the poet and murderer Richard Savage, in 1744.

The Life of Savage is, I think, the first great literary biography in English, and it does many surprising things. It chooses a subject who is essentially a failure in life. It takes scandalous materials—an adultery case among the aristocracy, a birthright claim, a blackmail campaign, a murder trial, an obscenity charge, a backstreet night-life existence, and a prison death—and turns them into a meditation on virtue.

By examining and quoting at length Savage's forgotten poetry —the witty, scabrous 'Bastard' and the visionary, confessional 'Wanderer'—it invents critical biography: the attempt to relate a particular art to a particular life, and to see one growing out of the conditions of the other. Finally, by setting the love of a friend against the judgement of a moralist, it brilliantly dramatizes the whole issue of empathy. To this day it is impossible to decide how far young Johnson was taken in by Savage, his Outcast Poet; or how far he was deliberately taking up his cause.

Unlike Defoe or Haywood, Johnson was very clear that the new biography was a form in conflict with fiction. When he announced the forthcoming work in the pages of the *Gentleman's Magazine* in August 1743, he made a historic declaration of independence.

It may be reasonably imagined that others may have the same Design, but as it is not credible that they can obtain the same Materials, it must be expected they will supply from Invention the want of Intelligence, and that under the Title of the *Life of Savage* they will publish only a Novel filled with romantick Adventures, and imaginary Amours.

This biography will be committed to an ideal of human truth, moral truth. Its readership will be 'the Lovers of Truth and Wit': the readership that biography has sought ever since.

Yet Johnson's theoretical claims are not entirely borne out by the wonderful, biased, blackly humorous and moving story that he finally wrote. As with all great biographers, he was in some sense dissolved or transmuted by the life he brought back to life. Something in him became Savage, and lived him out with the force of fiction.

Looking back several years later in *Rambler* essay no. 60, Johnson seems to reflect on what had occurred. 'If the biographer writes from personal knowledge, and makes haste to gratify the public curiosity, there is a danger lest his interest, his fear, his gratitude, or his tenderness, overpower his fidelity, and tempt him to conceal, if not to invent.'

Johnson certainly concealed and invented a great deal in his *Life of Savage*. What has been taken as a model of judicious impartiality is in fact a work of passionate advocacy and special pleading. He disguises documentation which tends to disprove Savage's birth-claims; hides evidence concerning political subversion and semi-pornographic writing; covers up testimony against Savage during his trial for murder; slides over dates and events which reveal Savage as something close to a blackmailer; and consistently distorts or dismisses the efforts of numerous kindly and long-suffering patrons—Sir Richard Steele, Ann Oldfield the actress, Lord Tyrconnel, and Alexander Pope—to help Savage in the teeth of his unfailing profligacy and ingratitude. But these are detailed issues of historical evidence that I have examined elsewhere in a book called *Dr Johnson and Mr Savage* (1993).

What concerns me here is the larger issue of biographical invention, in terms of narrative forms and contemporary image-making. Despite his disclaimers, Johnson set out to tell a story as melodramatic as any novel by Defoe. His protagonist is a proto-Romantic figure, the Outcast Poet, the Accuser, the Enemy of social injustice. The 'materials' and 'Intelligence' he drew upon were often semi-fictional as sources, and became more imaginative and emotive as he handled them. His primary source was a 'Newgate pamphlet' dating from the trial of 1727, whose specific purpose was to exculpate Savage by romancing his 'misfortunes'. The aristocrat whom Savage claimed as a mother, the luckless Lady Macclesfield, is cast by Johnson in the role of female villain, a woman of 'implacable hatred', exactly along the lines of a scandal-novel written about her by Eliza Haywood in 1724.

Johnson's image of his poor poet, 'Hopeless, abandoned, aimless, and oppress'd', is partly based on popular ballads written about him (though, characteristically, *signed* by Savage) in coffee-house magazines of the day. The many memorable anecdotes he tells of Savage's picaresque life in the backstreets of London—such as the story of Savage's tattered poet's cloak and haughty refusal to accept a replacement made for him by a city tailor—depend, however, upon the neat, ironic conventions of theatrical comedy, as in John Gay's *Beggar's Opera* (1728) and James Miller's Grub-Street farces. (One play by Miller, *The Coffee-House* (1734), specifically features Savage.) In other words, it can be shown that Johnson's version of Richard Savage's 'true history' is constantly shaped by the 'invented history' of the day. Johnson tells Savage's biography, and relates its facts, *through* fictional forms. This classic of eighteenth-century biography is also a brilliant patchwork of eighteenth-century prison confessional, scandal novel, balladmongering, courtroom melodrama, and theatrical farce. It is a weave or wedlock of truth and invention.

Far from denying the varied narrative excitements within the form, Johnson saw that literary biography had epic possibilities of story-telling. (And it was his protégé Boswell who would fulfil these.) In a little-known paper, *Idler* no. 102, Johnson first defined them.

Nothing detains the Reader's attention more powerfully than deep Involutions of distress, or sudden Vicissitudes of Fortune, and these might be abundantly afforded by the memoirs of the Sons of Literature. They are entangled in Contracts which they do not know how to fulfill, and obliged to write on Subjects which they do not understand. Every Publication is a new period of Time, from which some Increase or Declension of Fame is to be reckoned. The gradations of a *Hero's* life are from Battle to Battle, and of an Author's from Book to Book.

This is, of course, partly a benign Johnsonian reflection on the proverbial modesty of authors. But the themes of 'distress', and sudden shifts in worldly 'fortune', are as central to the plotting of his Life of Savage as they are, say, to Defoe's *Moll Flanders*. They are both told as adventure stories, from which certain moral—or immoral—conclusions may be drawn.

Finally, it can be observed that Johnson's biography of his friend is also a form of displaced autobiography. Johnson is using his own experiences as a young man in Grub Street to give authenticity, and indeed pathos, to those of Savage, especially during the period of night-walking which they famously shared between 1737 and 1739. It is as if the clear, glass window of 'objective' narrative suddenly becomes reflective and mirror-like, so we continually glimpse a 'subjective' image of Johnson himself superimposed upon the story-surface. We find this even in tiny turns of phrase and explanation.

Savage's method of Life particularly qualified him for Conversation. . . . He was generally censured for not knowing when to retire, but that was not the defect of his Judgement, but of his Fortune. When he left his Company he was frequently to spend the remaining part of his Night in the Street, or at least abandoned to gloomy Reflections. (*Life*, p. 137)

In this sense the biography invents Savage as a kind of demonic *alter ego*, a version of what Johnson himself might have become had he been less resolute or less intellectually gifted in those harsh, early years of literary apprenticeship. Here, most remarkably, is the shadow or projection of a fictional form which in other hands would become *Dr Jekyll and Mr Hyde*.

Let me end by emphasizing, as I began, that for all its problems —of ethics, authenticity, celebrity, and empathy—this seems to me the most *lovable* of modern English literary forms. Like Johnson, I believe that it helps us the better to enjoy life or to endure it. It is possible for a good biography to *tell* the truth, and to enlighten and encourage us in so doing. Being essentially the product of an eighteenth-century Age of Enlightenment, it insists that the proper study of mankind is man. In a post-Freudian age we have to face up to the complications of this process, but we cannot possibly shirk them. If I had to define biography in a single phrase, I would call it an art of human understanding, and a celebration of human nature. We should, I am sure, be proud of it.

❧ 2 ❧

A Life for a Life

JON STALLWORTHY

Once upon a time there were heroes. Some time later, some of those who recounted the lives of heroes were themselves accorded heroic status: Homer and Shakespeare became heroes of the second order. And in our own century, some who have recounted the lives of second-order heroes seem themselves to be emerging as heroes of a third order: Lytton Strachey, Richard Ellmann, Michael Holroyd. Dust-jacket typography makes little or no distinction between biographer and subject, author and author: *Oscar Wilde: Richard Ellmann; Bernard Shaw: Michael Holroyd.* This may seem no different from what has come to be called 'Boswell's Life of Johnson', but that was a shared Life, as none of its major successors have been. Literary biographers today write books that sometimes outsell their subjects' books, a fact reflected in the size of their advances and royalties. Novelists have been known to comment on this phenomenon: none more wittily than A. S. Byatt, the biographer of whose novel, *Possession*, is said to have

persuaded the Vicar, whom he had met at an episcopal tea party, that biography was just as much a spiritual hunger of modern man as sex or political activity. Look at the sales, he had urged, look at the column space in the Sundays, people need to know how other people lived, it helps them to live, it's human. A form of religion, said the Vicar. A form of ancestor worship, said [the biographer]. Or more. What are the Gospels but a series of varying attempts at the art of biography?[1]

Notwithstanding the irony, notwithstanding the recession, this is a good time for biographers.

But—I have recently been butted by some disquieting reflections. In the course of writing my Life of MacNeice, I ran into a problem of the dark lady (or dark gentleman). I came upon a letter in which MacNeice wrote that he had 'as good as decided to set up with a girl' but found himself 'being emotionally dishonest' and broke off the relationship 'rather brutally, I'm afraid'. I had no idea who this was, and wrote to a woman who had given me a vivid and generous account of her own friendship with MacNeice at a time when he was courting someone else. She was devoted to them both. I asked her if she could identify this dark lady, who was presumably to be seen with the poet in the early days of her own acquaintance with him. Answer came there none. I wrote again, saying that since my last letter had not been returned, I assumed that—like Noah's dove—it had arrived. This suggested one of three things: that she was ill, or that she was fed up with MacNeice's dilatory biographer, or that she was herself the dark lady and wished to remain in the dark. While waiting for an answer, I reread (what else?) *The Aspern Papers*.

I found it more shocking than I had remembered. I had forgotten the elaborate deceit of Aspern's biographer—that he had 'a visiting-card neatly engraved with a well-chosen *nom de guerre*'— or the terms in which he presents the failure of his campaign: 'I was grateful to [Miss Tina] for not treating me as if I had killed her aunt.'[2] This was, of course, precisely what he *had* done. My sense that *The Aspern Papers* represented a pre-emptive strike against prospective biographers of Henry James was confirmed by Michael Millgate's excellent book, *Testamentary Acts*. From this I learnt that the Master followed Miss Tina's example, making 'a gigantic bonfire' of his personal papers in the very year her story was first published in book form. Some years later, he wrote to his nephew:

My sole wish is to frustrate as utterly as possible the postmortem exploiter —which, I know, is but so imperfectly possible. Still, one can do something, & I have long thought of launching, by a provision in my will, a curse not less explicit than Shakespeare's own on any such as try to move my bones. Your question determines me definitely to advert to the matter in my will—that is to declare my utter & absolute abhorrence of any attempted biography or the giving to the world by 'the family', or by any person for whom my disapproval has any sanctity, of any part or parts of my private correspondence.[3]

The biographer as 'postmortem exploiter' is a disturbing concept —to both biographers and their subjects—but even more disturbing is that of the biographer as homicide. I might have dismissed it as a figment of the inflamed imagination of a neurotic novelist, had not an ingrained professional rigour caused me to search and compare the computer files of the Society of Authors and New Scotland Yard. The results were not reassuring.

Consider the case of L. P. Hartley. His novel, *The Betrayal*, is the second part of a diptych, but sufficiently self-contained to be reviewed without reference to the first part, *The Brickfield*. An ageing novelist, Richard Mardick, has appointed his younger companion and secretary, Denys Aspin, as his literary executor and biographer. There are hints in both books that they have, or have had, a homosexual relationship, but the central event of Mardick's life—an event to be masked in Aspin's Life of Mardick—is his adolescent heterosexual love-affair with Lucy Soames that ended with her drowning (whether by accident or suicide is never established).

The memoir [Mardick reflects] would be a compromise with Truth, but it would be a gesture to Justice which posterity could interpret as it liked. *Toute vérité n'est pas bonne à dire*; some truths were better unspoken; nor, except in the law-court, was it essential to tell the truth, the whole truth, and nothing but the truth.[4]

Mardick, whose best-known novel is called *The Imperfect Witness*, has given Aspin (in the earlier novel) his version of the whole truth of Lucy's tragedy. The whole truth of his present predicament dawns on him when his biographer says:

'I'm not used to writing. I shall find it so difficult—I mean, deciding what to put in and to leave out.'

'I told you I relied on your discretion, Denys.'

'But I'm not very discreet—I might put in something that you wouldn't like.'

Somewhere below Richard's conscious mind a warning bell sounded, but he didn't heed it.

'You can show me what you've written and I'll vet it for you.'

'But how could you, Richard? I hate to say it, but by that time you would be . . . well, you wouldn't be, I mean, anywhere where you could use a blue pencil.'

Richard smiled.

'My ghost might perhaps direct you, Denys.'

'But are ghosts punctual? Hamlet's father, so I seem to remember, spoke too late in the day.'

'Yes, but what he said went. Anyhow, he had been murdered. You won't have murdered me—at least I hope not.'

'You never can tell, Richard. You never can tell. You mustn't try me too far. At any rate I don't want to murder your reputation—I could, you know.' (p. 115)

The biographer as blackmailer becomes the biographer as incubus. The ineffectual Mardick is unable to prevent Aspin—appallingly injured in a fight—from being billeted on him, and the strain precipitates a fatal heart-attack. Hartley shows us the biographer as criminal and, once again, as inadvertent homicide.

Consider, then, the case of William Golding, whose novel, *The Paper Men*, opens with a scene that must derive from the climax of *The Aspern Papers*. Wilfred Barclay, novelist, is woken at night by what he takes to be a badger rifling his dustbin, but discovers to be his house-guest, Professor Rick L. Tucker, in search of discarded manuscripts. Seven years later—on another sabbatical—Tucker runs Barclay to earth, in the Swiss mountains, to say: 'Wilf. I want you to appoint me your official biographer.'[5] Wilf refuses, as he also refuses an inducement—the favours of Rick's girlfriend Mary Lou. He almost signs the proferred document beginning '*I hereby appoint Professor Rick L. Tucker*' after Tucker rescues him from what seems like certain death on a mountain walk. 'It seems I owe you my life' (p. 92), he ruefully concedes. Discovering, then, that he has been tricked, that Tucker had prevented him from falling a foot or two in the fog rather than the hundreds of feet he had supposed, Barclay takes his revenge in an appropriate form:

I shall make you my literary executor [he says], probably in association with my agent. . . . I shall authorize you to write my biography while I am still alive but with reservations. . . . I'll mention the principal one so that you can think it over. I shall give you a full and free account of my life without concealment and you can write what you like about that. But you will also give a clear account of the time you offered me Mary Lou. . . . In fact the biography will be a duet, Rick. We'll show the world what we are—paper men, you can call us. How about that for a title? Think Rick —all the people who get lice like you in their hair, all the people spied on, followed, lied about, all the people offered up to the great public—we'll be revenged, Rick, I'll be revenged on the whole lot of them, ha et cetera. . . . It's a trade, my son. Me for you. My life for yours. (p. 152)

That is only the start of the novelist's revenge. He withdraws this agreement—because, unknown to his would-be biographer, he is writing the duet, *The Paper Men*, himself—and plans a Hardyesque finale. As he confides to his typescript:

I have taken all the papers from the chests and built them into a bonfire down by the river. As I sit at this desk I have only to lift my head and over the typewriter I can see the pile, a positive mountain of mostly white paper waiting there—startlingly white against the dark woods on the other side of the river. When I've rounded off this manuscript I shall take a can of paraffin down there, drench the lot and set fire to it—a rite of passage made out of the detritus, the nail clippings, cut hair, the worn-away time, unnecessary correspondence, reviews, theses, financial statements, manuscripts, interlinears, proofs, the paperweight of a whole life!

Then I shall find Rick and give him this small sheaf of papers, all that is necessary, all that will be left, all that means anything to set over against the lying stories, the partial journals and all the rest. It will be a kind of dying. (p. 190)

He savours the prospect with an almost orgasmic pleasure, knowing it will be another kind of death for Rick: the death of his obsession and of his hopes for advancement in his profession. Both Paper Men are in at the death. The novelist's typescript records the *coup de grâce*:

Rick is a hundred yards away across the river, flitting from tree to tree like playing Indians. I shall have an audience for my ritual. Now he is leaning against a tree and peering at me through some instrument or other.

How the devil did Rick L. Tucker manage to get hold of a gu   (p. 191)

Attempting to save his Life (with a capital L), Wilfred Barclay loses his life (with a lower-case l) to Rick L. Tucker, who must take it if he is to save the Life (with a capital L) in which he has invested *his* life (with a lower-case l). The harsh light of Golding's satire strips away the shadows to reveal the biographer as murderer.

Consider, then, the case of A. S. Byatt, who casts the biographer, Professor Mortimer P. Cropper (Mort for Short), as the villain of *Possession: A Romance*. His Life of the poet Randolph Henry Ash is called *The Great Ventriloquist*, a title that would do very well for Jake Balokowsky's Life of Byatt. *Possession* is a ventriloquial *tour de force*. Not the least of its delights is the way it moves with seldom a false note from voice to voice, genre to genre, mode to mode. Like Golding and Larkin, Byatt reserves her fiercest satire for the American—and it is significant that he *is* American— academic biographer. If there is a satiric American novel, if there is *any* American novel, about a British biographer, I do not know it.

Byatt's American is more villainous than Henry James's. He may not carry a false visiting-card, but he travels with something no less disreputable,

his black box, a device he had invented and perfected in the 1950s, and was now reluctant to abandon in favour of newer or slicker machines since it had served him well over the decades. He was adept at acquiring invitations into the most unlikely houses where some relic of Ash's hand might be found; once there he had come to the conclusion that it was necessary to make some record, privately, for himself, of what he found, in case the owner subsequently proved reluctant to sell, or even to allow copies to be made, as had been known, once or twice, most detrimentally to the cause of scholarship.[6]

We see him first in the bathroom of such a house. It is 3 a.m. Wearing the 'long black silk dressing-gown' one would expect of the villain of a Victorian melodrama, he and his black box are advancing the cause of scholarship. Next day, he will put the black box into the black Mercedes one of his rivals calls a hearse, and continue his quest for those manuscripts and memorabilia of Randolph Henry Ash that have so far eluded his cheque-book. Hearse and quest will end in a graveyard, where Professor Mortimer P. Cropper comes a cropper. Planning not murder but the next worst thing, Ash's biographer is caught in the act of robbing his subject's grave of the letter that unlocks the central secret of the novel.

Consider, then, the case of Julian Barnes. *Flaubert's Parrot* is an obsessive would-be biographer's meditation on the impossibility of biography, punctuated by references to another subject that he cannot at first confront: 'What does the fiancée feel when she snaps open the box and sees the ring set in purple velvet? I never asked my wife; and it's too late now.'[7] Or thirty-six pages later: 'Look, writers aren't *perfect*, I want to cry; any more than husbands and wives are perfect. The only unfailing rule is, if they seem so, they can't be. I never thought my wife was perfect. I loved her, but I never deceived myself. I remember . . . But I'll keep that for another time' (p. 70). Or twenty-one pages later: 'When I was a doctor I never killed a single patient. . . . No, I didn't kill my wife. I might have known you'd think that' (p. 47). Later still, we're told he loved his wife; she didn't love him; she took lovers; she took an overdose; she was brain-dead on a life-support machine; he switched her off. Are we to believe him, this biographer who writes (in a Flaubertian context): 'Demand violently: how can we know anybody?' (p. 155) The answer to the first question must be No. What are we to believe then? Perhaps that the biographer's obsessive interest in Flaubert and his mistresses was greater than his interest in his own wife and her lovers; that he was more attuned to the aspirations of the dead than to the despair of the living.

The representation of the biographer as homicide, murderer, or grave-robber in the work of five leading twentieth-century novelists must worry a twentieth-century biographer and prompt the question 'Why?' There are probably several answers. One lies behind a question asked by Julian Barnes: 'What novelist, given the choice, wouldn't prefer you to reread one of his novels rather than read his biography?'[8] Tennyson had made the same point in a more extreme form. 'Why does one want to know about a man's life?' he asked. 'The less you know about a man's life the better. He gives you his best in his writings. I thank God day and night that we know nothing about Shakespeare.'[9] Recognizing—however much he might deplore—the public interest in his own life, Tennyson authorized his son Hallam to give an account of that life 'full enough to preclude the chance of further and unauthentic biographies'.[10] Many other authors have adopted this strategy of the pre-emptive strike: Hardy ghost-writing his own biography, and many in their *auto*biographies exploiting the rich seams of their lives, either to deflect or to direct post-mortem exploiters.

Not only authors are concerned with authenticity. We know ourselves, but accept that others may be unknowable. So the narrator of *Flaubert's Parrot* describes Louis Colet as

a) Tedious, importunate, promiscuous woman, lacking talent of her own or understanding of the genius of others, who tried to trap Gustave into marriage. . . .
b) Brave, passionate, deeply misunderstood woman crucified by her love for the heartless, impossible, provincial Flaubert.[11]

The most sustained exploration of this theme in recent fiction—and another novelist's advance-guard action against prospective biographers—is *The Truth About Lorin Jones*. Alison Lurie's opening sentence introduces us to her biographer: 'Polly Alter used to like men, but she didn't trust them any more, or have very much to do with them.'[12] She has *altered* and will alter again (as Mortimer Cropper will come a cropper). Her name rings other bells when we overhear her thinking:

Though Polly had never met Lorin Jones [the painter], she'd been following in Lorin's path all her life. Lorin had grown up in a New York suburb; Polly (twenty years later) in a neighbouring suburb. Both of them went to school in Westchester; both, after college, lived on Bank Street in the West Village. Their paths must have crossed, probably many times. When Polly was a toddler she and her mother might have passed Lorin and hers on the street in White Plains. . . . Later, when she began to visit museums and galleries in New York, Lorin might have been among the other spectators; she could have been buying pantyhose at the same counter of Bloomingdales, or sitting next to her future biographer on the Eighth Avenue bus or at a Modern Museum film showing.

Photographs of Lorin Jones from that period showed a strikingly beautiful young woman, in the French Beatnik fashion popularised after World War II by Juliette Greco. . . . Whenever Polly looked at these photos she had a sense of *déjà vu*. Damn it, she knew she'd seen this woman somewhere, at some time. If only there had been a sign: some loud clanging bell, some flash of light to warn her that their lives would be intimately connected! (p. 2)

Here we have the biographer as *alter ego*—with the emphasis on the *ego*. Polly Alter, who has suffered at the hands of men, begins her quest for the Truth About Lorin Jones by interviewing the four men who, she says, 'had discouraged and denigrated and exploited and neglected' her (p. 4). The truth about Lorin's relations with these—her dealer, half-brother, ex-husband, and lover—proves quite other than Polly had supposed; as does the truth about Polly herself:

Without lifting a finger, just by being born twenty years sooner, Lorin Jones had destroyed Polly Alter as a painter.

And Polly couldn't do anything about it. She couldn't paint any more, and she couldn't even the score; she couldn't hurt Lorin Jones, because she was already dead. Instead, she had contracted to exalt her rival, to make her even more famous and admired.

Or—the possibility hissed in her ear like a snake—she could write her book to show that Lorin Jones, however gifted, was a cold, selfish, vengeful, secretive person and a complete neurotic. She could suggest that there is a choice sometimes between being a good person and a good painter, and that Jones had chosen the darker path. (p. 196)

As in Woolf's *To the Lighthouse*, for 'paint' and 'painter', read 'write' and 'writer'. Here we have a portrait of the failed artist as biographer. Byatt's Mortimer Cropper is another artist's *alter ego*: he wears his subject's watch and signet ring. 'Like many biographies,' we are told, his Life of Ash 'was as much about its author as its subject'.[13] Reading this book, Maud, the critic heroine of *Possession*, concludes that Cropper

had a peculiarly vicious version of reverse hagiography; the desire to cut his subject down to size. She indulged herself in a pleasant thought about the general ambiguity of the word 'subject' in this connection. Was Ash subject to Cropper's research methods and laws of thought? Whose subjectivity was being studied? (p. 250)

Maud's meditation on the word 'subject' overlooks one of its principal meanings: 'A person . . . that is in the control or under the

dominion of another.' It is hardly surprising that authors, accus-
tomed to having subjects, should not always relish being subject to
others.

A principal object of the quest of all the fictional biographers
I have been considering is The Truth About the sexuality of their
subjects. As Barnes puts it, 'all biographers secretly want to annex
and channel the sex-lives of their subjects'.[14] Speaking as a biographer, I have to say I think that is true. Of course, in *my*
literary biographies and those of my friends, the sexuality of the
subject is examined for its relevance to the subject's work. In *other*
literary biographies, sexuality is examined to promote publicity
and sales. That said, I have yet to meet a biographer whose urge
'to annex and channel' the sex life of their subject has taken them
as far as it takes Polly Alter—into making love to her subject's
lover.

In my own quest for The Truth About Wilfred Owen, I
examined all the evidence relating to his sexuality that I could find;
an understanding of his sexuality obviously being crucial to an
understanding of his poems. Because that evidence was as scanty as
my knowledge of homosexuality, I sent my typescript to a psychiatric specialist, asking for his comments. He said he agreed with my
conclusions (that Owen was a latent—but probably not an active
—homosexual), but added an important caveat to the effect that
literary biographers and critics use terms that psychiatrists use, and
make judgements that psychiatrists make, only after many hours of
consultation with their patients. Psycho-biography is not an accurate
science.

It is easy to see why writers might dread the approach of a
biographer. They foresee their dirty linen labelled and exhibited as
in police-court plastic bags; their lives travestied and cut down to
the size of a jealous gossip-columnist's; their writings ignored or
misread by bogus psychiatrists. The wonder is not that so many
make a bonfire of their papers, but that so few do. Millgate notes
the opposition between Browning's 'passionate desire for privacy
and his profound reluctance to destroy documents deemed precious
on literary as well as on purely personal grounds'.[15] This opposition,
a common phenomenon, would seem to have reached its ultimate

expression in Philip Larkin's will, with its instructions concerning the destruction of his papers and their publication. As Lenin famously asked in another context: What Is To Be Done?

The law does not prohibit biography. The families and friends of writers who have tried, by provisions in their wills, to prevent such post-mortem exploitation have all too often lived to see unauthorized biographies of the most inaccurate and scurrilous kind.

Spencer Curtis Brown, Somerset Maugham's literary executor, justified his contravention of Maugham's prohibition against giving assistance to biographers on the grounds that he believed Maugham's memory would be better served by the publication of a responsible biography than by the continuing proliferation of malicious gossip.[16]

I think Curtis Brown made the right decision. It raises, however, the question of what is a *responsible* literary biography.

Only the most rabid biographobe could deny that epithet to Richard Ellmann's *James Joyce*. His Introduction, you may remember, opens with a description of what an artist's biography should be:

We are still learning to be James Joyce's contemporaries, to understand our interpreter. This book enters Joyce's life to reflect his complex incessant joining of event and composition. The life of an artist, but particularly that of Joyce, differs from the lives of other persons in that its events are becoming artistic sources even as they command his present attention. Instead of allowing each day, pushed back by the next, to lapse into imprecise memory, he shapes again the experiences which have shaped him. He is at once the captive and the liberator. In turn the process of reshaping experience becomes a part of his life, another of its recurrent events like rising or sleeping. The biographer must measure in each moment this participation of the artist in two simultaneous processes.[17]

Ellmann's Introduction, with its masterly overview of Joyce's enterprise and his own, concludes:

Though Joyce, prophetically enough, called the biographer a 'biografiend', he also supplied the precedent for seeing his subject in all postures in order to know him. His passion for truth, however unpalatable, is a contagion which he would have his readers and his admirers share. (p. 7)

Ellmann's passion for truth, the depth and detail of his research, is revealed not with the audible flutter of index cards, but with brushstrokes worthy of Joyce himself. Consider the biographer's depiction of Mrs 'Dante' Hearn Conway who, on the verge of becoming a nun, had inherited a fortune and, says Ellmann, 'allowed herself to be won by an overdressed employee of the pillared Bank of Ireland' (p. 25). Those adjectives, 'overdressed' and 'pillared', bring the individual and the institution sharply into focus and help prepare us for what follows:

Soon after their marriage, to culminate a fine show of considerateness and good manners, Conway ran off to South America with her money tucked away in his pockets, and quickly ceased to write her promises to return. For the rest of her life Dante Conway remained the abandoned bride, and her burning memories of being deserted joined remorse at having left the convent to make her overzealous, in both religion and nationalism. (p. 25)

This, in turn, prepares us for the famous Christmas dinner scene of *A Portrait* in which Dante, provoked by praise of Parnell, explodes: 'A traitor, an adulterer! The priests were right to abandon him. The priests were always the true friends of Ireland.'[18]

Perhaps only Joyce himself, and Nora, can have had a more detailed knowledge than Ellmann of his life and work and of the 'complex incessant joining of event and composition'. The biographer's priorities are never in doubt. There is no needless detailing of events that have no bearing on composition; no straining of connections between them; no arguing that because something is said or done in the text it must have been said or done in the life; no long literary critical arias interrupting the narrative recitative. We are never in any doubt whose subjectivity is being studied. We do not see Joyce cut down to size or remade in the image of Richard Ellmann, but rendered as large as life: the author of books even more beautiful and complex than we had realized. No purely critical study has illuminated them more or won more readers and rereaders for *Dubliners*, *A Portrait*, *Ulysses*, and (even) *Finnegans Wake*.

This, of course, is not to say that Ellmann's biography is perfect, any more than Joyce or any of *his* books was perfect. It is a full-length Portrait of an Artist who lends himself to such a portrait, both because his life and work were so closely connected and because his writing life had such a satisfactory shape. These are factors of great importance to literary biographers, who obviously have less scope where there is little discernible connection between the life and the work, or where the writing life has a less satisfactory shape. Wilfred Owen's writing life has an almost ideal trajectory for a biography: it climbs fast and steeply from first to last, but think how it would have looked if he had lived for another fifty years writing advertising copy or sermons rather than poems. And how would a biographer handle such a life, other than by compressing those fifty years into an anti-climactic final chapter?

The trajectory of MacNeice's life is less satisfactory, for a biographer, than that of Owen's or Joyce's, but more satisfactory than Eliot's or Larkin's. It has two peaks—the late 1930s and the early 1960s—at which a rich seam of symbolism comes to the surface of his work. It has long been recognized that his poetry is dominated by images of fixity and flux, stone and water. These form the structural polarities of one of his earliest poems, written when he was 8:

> The water sound
> Gurgles and bubbles around
> In a wild country
> The cliffs are high
> Against the sky
> In a wild country
> The suns great ray
> Makes hot the traveller's way
> In a wild country.[19]

Cliff and water, fixity and flux: clear as a fingerprint in these lines of the child are the co-ordinates and configurations of the poems of the man. What I think has *not* been recognized is the way in which such images of stone and water become associated with the dominant presences of MacNeice's childhood, his mother and father. As his poem 'Autobiography' tells the story,

> In my childhood trees were green
> And there was plenty to be seen.
> *Come back early or never come.*

My father made the walls resound,
He wore his collar the wrong way round.

Come back early or never come.

My mother wore a yellow dress;
Gently, gently, gentleness.

Come back early or never come.

When I was five the black dreams came;
Nothing after was quite the same.

Come back early or never come.[20]

When MacNeice was 5, his mother, suffering from a deep depression, left home for a mental institution in which, two years later, she died. And when her husband, Rector of Carrickfergus, broke the news to his children, Louis dived down to the bottom of the bed, where (as he says in his autobiography) 'I hoped they would think I was crying. I felt very guilty at being so little moved but decided that when I grew up I would build my mother a monument. And everyone would know that I had built it.'[21] He was probably thinking of the large marble monument to members of the Chichester family—a father and mother and children—in his father's church. What is certain is that he came to associate his mother with the silent tombstones in the cemetery beyond the Rectory garden. By contrast, he came to associate his *father* (who 'made the walls resound') with the bells of his church and the ocean he so loved *beyond* the church. The interplay of silence and stone, sound and water, culminates in *Persons from Porlock*, a remarkable radio play broadcast four days before MacNeice's death. Auden called it

a magnificent example of . . . psychological drama. It covers more than twenty years of the life of Hank, a would-be painter. From the outside, these years are mostly a record of frustration and worldly failure. He starts out with the hope of becoming a 'pure' painter. He fails. He becomes a commercial artist but preserves too much artistic conscience to succeed as one. He takes to the bottle, and his girl friend leaves him. He starts painting again and is reduced to beggary. (There's a suggestion that these paintings of his last phase procured him posthumous fame.) In addition, however, to his interest in painting and women, and his alcoholism, he's enchanted by the idea of exploring caves: underground, and only underground, he feels happy and himself. And it's in a cave that he meets his death. . . . As he's dying, various characters who have played a part in his life appear to him and speak, helping him to arrive at a deeper self-knowledge.[22]

Entering MacNeice's life, to reflect what Ellmann calls the 'complex, incessant joining of event and composition', enables one to arrive at a deeper knowledge still. MacNeice's last hero is a bleak self-portrait of himself. Drawn, imaginatively, to the bottom of a cave, as almost fifty years earlier he had been drawn to the bottom of a bed, he returns to his parents in the underground stream that potholers call the Stygian Trap.

And what, you may ask, of MacNeice's Dark Lady? She never answered my letter and I shall not drag her into the light. And what did MacNeice think of biographers? In November 1940, about to cross the submarine-infested Atlantic, he wrote to his literary executor: 'In case any super-mug wants to do a life of me I would warn him against accepting, without careful scrutiny, any alleged information from my family.'[23]

Ah, well. Better a super-mug than a murderer.

Notes

1. A. S. Byatt, *Possession: A Romance* (London, 1990), 384.
2. Henry James, *The Aspern Papers and the Turn of the Screw* (Harmondsworth, 1984), 52, 129.
3. Quoted in Michael Millgate, *Testamentary Acts: Browning, Tennyson, James, Hardy* (Oxford, 1992), 101.
4. L. P. Hartley, *The Betrayal* (London, 1966), 5.
5. William Golding, *The Paper Men* (London, 1984), 46.
6. Byatt, *Possession*, 94.
7. Julian Barnes, *Flaubert's Parrot* (1984; repr. London, 1985), 40.
8. Julian Barnes, 'The Follies of Writer Worship', *New York Times Book Review*, 17 Feb. 1985, 16.
9. Audrey Tennyson, 'Talks & Walks' notebook, fo. 20 (Tennyson Research Centre, Lincoln).
10. Hallam Tennyson, *Alfred Lord Tennyson: A Memoir*, 2 vols. (London, 1897), i, p. xii.
11. Barnes, *Flaubert's Parrot*, 153–4.
12. Alison Lurie, *The Truth About Lorin Jones* (London, 1988), 1.
13. Byatt, *Possession*, 246.

14. Barnes, *Flaubert's Parrot*, 41.
15. Millgate, *Testamentary Acts*, 18.
16. Ibid. 193.
17. Richard Ellmann, *James Joyce* (1959; new edn., New York and Oxford, 1982), 3.
18. James Joyce, *A Portrait of the Artist as a Young Man* (rev. edn., Harmondsworth, 1976), 38.
19. Unpub. letter of 23 Oct. 1915 (Bodleian Library).
20. Louis MacNeice, *Collected Poems*, ed. E. R. Dodds (London, 1966), 183–4.
21. Louis MacNeice, *The Strings Are False*, ed. E. R. Dodds (London, 1965), 53.
22. Louis MacNeice, *Persons from Porlock and other plays for radio*, introd. W. H. Auden (London, 1969), 7–8.
23. Unpub. letter of 17 Nov. 1940 to E. R. Dodds (Bodleian Library).

❧ 3 ❧

Secondary Lives: Biography in Context

CATHERINE PETERS

Thinking about 'The Art of Literary Biography', I found myself suffering a severe attack of biographer's Angst. Is biography an art? There is nothing new, of course, about questioning its status. Virginia Woolf did so in the 1920s, in her acute essays, 'The Art of Biography' and 'The New Biography'.

Woolf was writing at a time when biographies had become witty, biased, and short.

But the diminution in size [she considered] was only the outward token of an inward change . . . the author's relation to his subject is different. He is no longer the serious and sympathetic companion, toiling even slavishly in the steps of his hero. Whether friend or enemy, admiring or critical, he is an equal . . . Raised upon a little eminence which his independence has made for him . . . he chooses; he synthesises; in short, he has ceased to be the chronicler; he has become an artist.[1]

Woolf saw the inescapable danger in this:

it would seem that the life which is increasingly real to us is the fictional life; it dwells in the personality rather than in the act. Each of us is more Hamlet, Prince of Denmark, than he is John Smith of the Corn Exchange. Thus, the biographer's imagination is always being stimulated to use the novelist's art of arrangement, suggestion, dramatic effect to expound the private life. Yet if he carries the use of fiction too far, so that he disregards the truth . . . he loses both worlds; he has neither the freedom of fiction nor the substance of fact.[2]

Her final conclusion was that biography was essentially different from poetry or fiction, 'lived at a lower degree of tension.'[3] The biographer, Woolf decided, is after all a craftsman, not an artist.

Two generations later, biography has put on weight again. Not only are biographies now often longer than *War and Peace*, they come trailing a security blanket of references and bibliography, and expressions of thanks to foundations, libraries, secretaries, friends, colleagues, spouses and the family cat. Whether or not it tries to be art, biography longs to be cosily enfolded by the academic industry. Biography is apparently prosperous; but it is also uneasy. Modern critical theory, we know, is scornful of the idea that the text can be related to its author's life in any useful or significant way. If we accept this, literary biography must either be demoted to a pretentious variant of tabloid muck-raking; or become a work of art in its own right, with the question of objective truth to the facts of the subject's life becoming secondary to the art of the biographer. Can biography keep faith with its subject and also keep up with changes in the perception of literature?

I think biography has to accept that it is a traditional, rather old-fashioned form, evolving slowly rather than by great imaginative leaps and profound intellectual discoveries. Attempts to cry it up on the whole do more harm than good. Biographers are the Prufrocks of the writing world, not Prince Hamlet, but an attendant lord, 'Almost, at times, the Fool.' The biographer's life is the first to be made 'secondary' to that of his or her subject.

Literary biography is still an extended act of attention to one person, a canonization of a life-and-works, a privileging of one existence over others, and an assumption that the life and the writing are intimately bound up together. Writing a biography is, at times, as obsessional an activity as being in love; and like obsessional love it can distort one's perceptions. The biographer, like any romantic novelist, believes in the importance of a central character and a strong and logically connected narrative which—give or take a modish disruption or two, usually to the opening scene—proceeds from cradle to grave in an unbroken arc. The biographer-as-artist is still living in the nineteenth century. It is hard to imagine a *nouvelle biographie*, analogous to the *nouveau roman*, in which anonymous characters moved through a neutral landscape, living out narrative-free existences. (It might, come to think of it, be an appropriate and challenging form for a biography of Samuel Beckett.)

44

But even if biography cannot be primarily innovative, it must evolve in ways that are bound to be connected with other forms of writing. Any literary form must change or die. Biographers—in particular literary biographers—are fully aware of what is going on in the literary world, and they too want to give new insights through new methods. But there are constraints that are not easy to overcome, and some biographic experiments strike me as courageous but misguided.

There is, to give one example, 'the ventriloquist biography'. By this I mean one in which the biographer seeks to annihilate the distance between self and his subject by taking on the subject's own voice. Identification is no longer seen as a danger, or at least a necessary but temporary stage in the biographer's relationship with his or her subject. Now it is deliberately cultivated to an extent where the two voices are merged. This is, perhaps, an over-literal development from Richard Holmes's contention that the biographer must create 'a continuous living dialogue' with his subject 'as they move over the same historical ground . . . It is fictional, imaginary, because of course the subject cannot really literally talk back; but the biographer must come to act and think of his subject as if he can.'[4] The continuous living dialogue certainly works well for Holmes—the first volume of his biography of Coleridge is a masterpiece which has brought that marvellous, infuriating genius closer to us than any other. But I think there is a danger that other biographers may forget Holmes's warning that 'all real biographical evidence is "third-party" evidence; evidence that is witnessed . . . the biographer . . . is continually being excluded from, or thrown out of, the fictional rapport he has established with his subject'.[5] Less scrupulous biographers attempt to go further, and take on the subject's persona, using disguised and adapted quotation for the biographical narrative, making the grammatical and stylistic quirks of the subject's writing self their own in a way that acts as a cover for inadequate or dubious evidence.

This way of cloaking biographers' personalities, a form, I suppose, of the 'death of the author', can result, paradoxically, in their becoming more, not less, visible, even intrusive. The deliberate theatricality of the enterprise distances us in the wrong way, rather than drawing us in. I feel that biographical ventriloquism belongs in fiction, where the novelist is not on oath. A number of recent novels have breached the barriers between historical fiction and biography, with varying success. But this is not strictly biography, for which truth to fact seems to me an inescapable precondition; whereas the novelist leaves the reader free to believe or disbelieve at will.

A more satisfying development has been the reintegration of biography with social history. Alethea Hayter's *A Sultry Month*[6] was the pioneering work here. It examines Benjamin Haydon's life through the public and private events of the last month of his life, leading up to his suicide: a technique which creates a multilayered and subtle portrait. Recently Tom Leonard has described his life of James Thomson, *Places of the Mind*, as 'a shape, containing a biography, made slowly in response to the shape of the Art of another'.[7] Leonard has interwoven Thomson's life and writings with other contemporary documents, historical as well as literary, in a way which attempts to overcome the problem of gaps in the evidence—Thomson destroyed many of his papers—and to attach the man to his times. Jenny Uglow's life of Elizabeth Gaskell, while using a traditional biographical framework, sets her subject firmly in the context of the intricate network of Unitarian family relationships in the North of England at the beginning of the nineteenth century, radically changing our perception of her.[8]

But in spite of a growing number of exceptions, writing a biography is still generally thought of as the art of skewing reality so that the light may fall more brightly on one figure. The idea that the subject is the hero or heroine of the biography is seldom challenged. Both writer and reader need to be aware that this concentration on one life, to which all others must become secondary, distorts both the historical record, and, perhaps even more importantly, the central figure itself. For there is no such thing as a 'secondary life' in the real world. Even the Agneses and Dorotheas who lead a pale, shadowy existence of support and self-sacrifice on the fringes of solid Victorian Lives of Great Men, and, more rarely, Women, had, one hopes, a firm sense of their own centrality, if only the centrality of their sacrifice. The biographer has to create something half-way between a vivid but distorted portrait of the subject and an integrated but indistinct figure in a landscape. Gaining distance—but not too much distance—can help to give a clearer perception of the central character itself.

The lives lived in the shadow of the main subject, often paralleling or contrasting with it, can be surprisingly illuminating. I would take issue here with Patricia Beer, who, in a recent review, deplored what she calls 'the current mania for writing about the sisters/wives/daughters/mistresses of famous men, regardless of how insignificant they, or indeed the famous men, might essentially be'.[9] How are we to judge significance? George Eliot had an answer, taking for the heroine of *Middlemarch* a woman who would not have rated a biography then or now, although

the effect of her being on those around her was incalculably diffusive: for the growing good of the world is partly dependent on unhistoric acts; and that things are not so ill with you and me as they might have been, is half owing to the number who lived faithfully a hidden life, and rest in unvisited tombs.[10]

In recent years some absorbing biographies have been written which have not only surprised us with the amount of intrinsic interest to be found in these peripheral lives, but also added to our understanding of the major figures who had obscured them. There is, for example, Robert Gittings and Jo Manton's *Claire Clairmont and the Shelleys*,[11] which brings its subject out into the light from the penumbra cast by the brilliance of Shelley and Mary Shelley; *Nora*,[12] Brenda Maddox's life of Joyce's wife Nora Barnacle; and *The Invisible Woman*,[13] Claire Tomalin's wonderful biography of Nelly Ternan. This might never have found a publisher if its subject had not been closely involved with Dickens. Though Nelly Ternan had a significant life of her own, her biography is shelved under 'Dickens' in my local bookshop, which seems to confirm Tomalin's title only too accurately. Yet the book is, if anything, more absorbing in its last third, which describes Nelly's life after Dickens's death. It would, all on its own, constitute a justification of a modern sub-genre: the biography of the forgotten servants and inspirers of literature.

However, these secondary lives can present almost insurmountable problems for the biographer. Too often the evidence is simply not there, as Margaret Forster found when she took up a challenge thrown down by Virginia Woolf. 'The life of Lily Wilson [Elizabeth Barrett Browning's maid] is extremely obscure, and thus cries aloud for the services of a biographer' Woolf wrote in the notes to *Flush*.[14] Forster has herself written a biography of Elizabeth Barrett Browning. But *Lady's Maid*,[15] her account of Lily Wilson's life, is written in the form of a novel, and concentrates on her years with Elizabeth Barrett and Robert and Pen Browning. Lily Wilson's childhood and youth, and her later experiences as housekeeper and minder to the impossibly difficult Walter Savage Landor, are entirely omitted. Wilson's hard-working and sacrificial life left too few traces to create an orthodox biography—no letters by or to her have survived, and most of the facts in Margaret Forster's book are taken from the letters of Elizabeth Barrett Browning. Large sections of the book, including all Wilson's letters to her mother, are invention, and Wilson, as she is called throughout, remains a secondary character even in her own life: well-behaved, knowing her place. The poignancy of her story is seen only indirectly.

The genre of the biography of a secondary life through which a more famous one is examined was parodied by *Flush* itself. It was dismissed by its author as 'a silly book . . . a waste of time'. *Flush* was written to make money, and it did: it was her only best-seller during her lifetime. Woolf's own verdict has, until recently, been generally accepted. But, as John Batchelor has pointed out, it is, more interestingly, a satirical work which subverts the form of Victorian biography.[16] Human characters, such as Mary Russell Mitford's drunken and feckless father, are tried by the tests of kennel-club genealogy and found wanting. Flush the spaniel and his human mistress, with their big brown eyes and droopy hairstyles, are revealed as physical mirror images, while their lives are lived on entirely different premisses. Flush learns the English class system as it operates among dogs in a London park, and then, in Italy, discovers a liberating democracy. The clichés of biography are examined and exposed by applying them to a non-human sensibility. *Flush* in a light-hearted way followed up Woolf's earlier essays on biography, and suggested ways of reinventing the genre which are only now being taken seriously.

Full-scale biographies of these 'secondary lives' are becoming more common. But publishers, however desperate for a new subject, are still keener on the umpteenth biography of a celebrity than on one of a fascinating but previously unknown minor figure. More frequently the modern biographer adopts the strategy of paying more attention to such secondary lives, particularly those related by blood or marriage, within the structure of the 'major' life. It is one reason for the increased length of biographies.

The biographer has, of course, traditionally been concerned with genealogy and family history, perhaps too much so. When I worked in a publisher's office I tried to persuade the author of an excellent but lengthy biography that going back two generations was enough. Without success: his account of two brothers born in the late nineteenth century begins somewhere in the Middle Ages. It is still a problem to determine how much weight and space to give to family history. How much, for example, do the early lives of the subject's parents and grandparents really add to our understanding of the central figure? This must vary from life to life, and the temptation to delve into the family history may have to be resisted. The early chapters of my biography of Wilkie Collins, concerning life before Wilkie, were cut back several times, and are probably still too full of details that fascinate me, but don't necessarily interest the reader. But I had a particular purpose: I wanted to redress the usual patriarchal distortions by paying as much attention to his maternal ancestors. His grandfathers, both failures in a worldly sense, had, in spite of differences in their backgrounds, a considerable number of similarities. These had never been noted, partly because of the traditional emphasis on the male line of descent, encouraged in this instance by Wilkie Collins himself, who wrote a life of his father in which he included a good many anecdotes about his paternal grandfather, while ignoring his mother's family entirely. Even his mother's sister, a famous portrait painter, is dismissed in half a sentence. This told one something, if only in a negative way, about Wilkie Collins's feelings towards strong and successful women, but I felt there was more to discover about his mother's family.

I found I was right when I discovered an unknown manuscript autobiography written by Wilkie's mother. This radically changed my perception of her background. It gave weight to his friends' perception of her as a considerable personality and influence on her sons, and added to my understanding of Wilkie Collins's view of women. It also shifted the balance of power between his parents, going a long way to contradict the view of his father as a gloomy domestic tyrant, extracted by some, with little external evidence, from Wilkie Collins's early novels, *Basil* and *Hide and Seek*. Harriet Collins's account of her husband as a young man portrayed him as an ardent lover and an amusing and easy-going companion, given to practical joking in the rather heavy-handed way current in the early years of the nineteenth century. Her autobiography also revealed for the first time that, following the loss of the little money her father had inherited, her family's fortunes changed from precarious to disastrous, and she had to earn her own living. The story of her sister Margaret, who became a successful painter, had always been known in outline, though Harriet's manuscript added a good many details, and also provided a financial, as well as an artistic, reason for her calling. What was not known was that Harriet herself in youth had experiences that might have come straight from a Victorian novel. She very nearly became an actress, at a time when that was, in most people's eyes, equivalent to being a prostitute. She got as far as being accepted by the Theatre Royal in Bath before being firmly rescued by an Evangelical parson and encouraged to become a governess instead. She taught first in a school in London, where, by her own account, she only managed to keep her job because the proprietress was French and didn't realize how ignorant she was. Later she taught in a number of private families, travelling as far as Scotland, where she discovered the depths of meanness to be found in aristocratic families. Sometimes she was happy, and sometimes not; but she always retained a lively sense of her own individual worth, reflected in the far from down-trodden governesses in her son's fiction. It was a tough but not disastrous initiation into the world which she recounts with a good deal of humour and insight. Harriet ended her story with her marriage to the painter William Collins, and a suggestion, more or less fulfilled, of a life happy ever after.

Her story, much condensed here, finally had to be shortened almost as much in my biography of her son. But it was, as she knew, worth telling, and I would have liked to have given it at far greater length than proved practicable. Knowing much that did not surface in my biography did, however, give me a confidence in handling her character and her relationship to her sons. It would be good to see her manuscript published at last, as an addition to the growing amount of testimony to indomitable nineteenth-century women. It gave substance to Wilkie Collins's love and admiration for her, and also confirmed my suspicion that his attitude to women was deeply ambivalent. It went some way to explain his reluctance to being tied down to one in marriage.

The lives of the two women with whom Wilkie Collins lived proved more difficult to uncover. He destroyed many of his personal papers, and more disappeared after his death. I did discover some of the bare facts of their lives before they knew him, which confirmed their poverty-stricken backgrounds—Caroline Graves's father was not, as she pretended, a gentleman but a carpenter; Martha Rudd was a servant in Great Yarmouth before she came to London. But their personalities, interests, and habits could only be deduced from indirect evidence. However, as Wilkie Collins was often described as a man who really enjoyed the company of women, and who had a capacity for intimate friendship with them, the lives of his women friends seemed worth investigation. As might be expected, they tended to be independent-minded and unconventional. One formidable woman, who was his friend for most of his adult life and seemed a likely influence on the direction of his writing, was a journalist, Frances Dickinson, later Elliott. They were friends by 1854, at a time when she was living under a cloud of social disapproval, and probably met some years earlier; they were both contributors to *Bentley's Miscellany* from 1852. Totally forgotten now, she was an immensely popular author in her day, writing gossipy and occasionally scandalous articles under the pseudonym 'Florentia', mostly about the English expatriate society of Italy, which prompted the outraged reactions earned nowadays by *Private Eye*. She also wrote novels, popular history, and travel books, much reprinted, while leading a private life more suited to the heroine of a sensation novel.

I became so intrigued by Frances Dickinson's rackety and inconsistent life—quite as odd as that 'of the better-known Caroline Norton—that I spent far too long researching it. Here was a woman who disrupted all the stereotypes, using the disguised facts of her private life for the material of her journalism, whilst managing to keep the more scandalous aspects hidden in a way that would be quite impossible nowadays. As an 18-year-old heiress she made a disastrous marriage. She left her husband after seven years, alleging his adultery with two of her maids, as well as violence and cruelty to her. He refused her access to her four daughters, but by the fortunate accident that he was a Scotsman, and their residence was in Scotland, she was finally able to obtain a Scottish divorce in 1855, two years before the passing of the first English Divorce Act, and reclaim her children. But the process was protracted and complex, and the question of whether it was legal in England, or legal at all, given that the marriage ceremony took place in England, was fought all the way to the House of Lords, which accounted for a ten-year gap between the date when she left her husband, and the time when she was finally free. Being a woman, though the innocent party, she was to some extent ostracized by the upperclass society in which she had moved, and went to Italy where she spent much of her later life. Here, already, was material to feed Wilkie Collins's fascination with the legal tangles of the marriage laws and their unfairness to women. But there was more to come.

Frances Dickinson's life continued its complicated and unconventional trajectory throughout Collins's life, and beyond. In 1857 he introduced her to Dickens, when she played the part of the Scotch nurse in some of the London performances by Dickens's amateur Company of Collins's play *The Frozen Deep*. No biographer of Dickens has noticed the curious fact that if Frances Dickinson had, as Dickens wished, agreed to perform when he took the play to Manchester, her part would not have been played by the professional actress Mrs Ternan, and Dickens might never have met her daughter Nelly. In another strange twist, Frances Dickinson later became friends with Frances Ternan, Nelly's sister, who became the second wife of Tom Trollope, Anthony Trollope's brother. Through her friendship with Dickens on the one hand and the Trollopes on the other, Frances Dickinson became one of the few people to know a good deal about Dickens's relationship with Nelly Ternan.

Her acquaintance with Dickens soon ripened into an intimate friendship, and he, as well as Collins, found himself drawn into advising her on her tangled private affairs. In 1860 he wrote to her, discussing her unsatisfactory relationship with an elderly admirer, who was evidently not coming up to scratch.

are you quite sure that what you are disposed to resent as indifference, is not the stealing apathy of advanced age? Under other circumstances, say in your humble servant for example—it would be affronting or idiotic; but not in these, I think? . . . There is no doubt that your position is a trying one . . . But would it not be more trying still, if you were more pursued, sought out, and hovered about?[17]

In December 1863 Frances Dickinson married the eminently respectable Dean of Bristol, the Very Reverend Gilbert Elliott, a widower of 63, who is almost certainly the person referred to in Dickens's letter. But certain facts seem to have been kept from the Dean. Dickens wrote to Wilkie Collins, three months before the wedding, that Frances Dickinson was

extremely anxious you should know that profound confidence as to that adventure with the Doctor has become more than ever necessary, by reason of her having established the fact that the marriage (as no doubt he very well knew at the time) is no marriage and is utterly void. My own impression is that she contemplates a real marriage with somebody else, at no distant time.[18]

This non-marriage, the 'adventure with the Doctor' which might have come straight from the pages of a Collins novel, has baffled enquiry: I have not been able to find any trace of it in the public records, nor has Graham Storey, the editor-in-chief of Dickens's letters. Perhaps its invalidity was due to the conflict of Scottish and

English law. However, there is a hint in one of Frances Dickinson's gossipy articles from Bagni di Lucca that she was involved in an intimate friendship with the local doctor, with whom she took long, unchaperoned walks in the countryside, so it may have taken place in Italy.[19] When she married the Dean she firmly cut through the tangles of her past life, describing herself on the marriage certificate as single, rather than divorced, which might have been embarrassing, to say the least, for a pillar of the Church. This marriage was also soon in trouble, and less than three years later Dickens was asked to mediate between the Elliotts, a task he eventually gave up in despair. Frances Elliott wanted a *de facto* separation from the Dean, while keeping the semblance of a marriage. She also wanted to hang on to what was left of her fortune, no easy matter before the passing of the Married Woman's Property Acts. When the Dean proved resistant, she attempted to blackmail him by threatening to reveal the earlier secret marriage, now claiming it was valid. Some kind of settlement was finally agreed, and Frances Elliott triumphantly retired to Italy and continued to write, using her latest married name as a cloak of respectability. In 1872 Wilkie Collins dedicated his novel *Poor Miss Finch* to 'Mrs Elliott, of the Deanery, Bristol'—not an address where she was often to be found, as he was well aware. In his dedication Wilkie wrote:

Perhaps, one of these days, I may be able to make use of some of the many interesting stories of events that have really happened, which have been placed in my hands by persons who could speak as witnesses to the truth of the narratives. Thus far I have not ventured to disturb the repose of these manuscripts ... The true incidents are so 'far-fetched;' and the conduct of the real people is so 'grossly improbable!'[20]

Frances Elliott would have known what he meant.

I have given you some account of two women whose lives helped to illuminate that of my subject, but I might also have cited men as secondary characters: Dickens, for example. Dickens makes an appearance in the lives of both Thackeray and Wilkie Collins, and it amuses me to think how surprised he would have been to know that anyone considered *him* secondary. Yet for Thackeray

Dickens functioned mainly as an irritant, and, however much he denied it, a yardstick of popular acclaim and financial success. They were friends, but never close friends, and only in one chapter of my book, when they became sworn enemies over the Garrick Club affair, was there any danger of Dickens getting out of hand. For the biographer of Wilkie Collins—whom Dickens considered, reasonably enough, to be definitely secondary to him —the Inimitable too often threatened to take over the book, as he took over his friends' lives. Rather than being brought out from the shadows, Dickens had to be confined (at times with the greatest possible difficulty) to his secondary role. The chapters which covered the early years of the Dickens/Collins friendship and their amateur theatrical days were rewritten more often than any other section of the book, because Wilkie kept on disappearing from sight, as he must often have done (being a small man and at best only an adequate actor) whenever Dickens was around.

Then there was the painter Augustus Egg, who introduced Collins to Dickens. He was a more docile character, and one about whom surprisingly little was known. When Egg died his friends agreed in saying nothing about his private life. The secret they were so determined to keep turned out to be a marriage, unknown to the *DNB* and not mentioned in any obituaries or memoirs. Egg, who had been in love with Georgina Hogarth, who rejected him, was married to an Esther Brown at St Anne's Limehouse in 1860, three years before he died at Algiers. There were no children. Egg left a will, made a year after the marriage, which tied his money up tightly in a trust for his wife, who was on no account to be allowed to anticipate her yearly allowance of £200. Why was this marriage kept so secret that it was forgotten by posterity? Here were hints of another of the many Victorian sexual dramas that seemed to surround Wilkie Collins. They varied from the well-known near-marriage arrangement of George Eliot and George Lewes, to the secret double lives—wife in one house, mistress in another—of the artists Frith and Cruikshank. Cumulatively they created a very different picture of contemporary attitudes to Wilkie Collins. He differed from his friends not in what he did, but in his refusal to hide it: these 'secondary lives' had shifted my perception not only of my subject, but also of his times.

Notes

1. Virginia Woolf, 'The New Biography', *Collected Essays*, ed. Leonard Woolf, 4 vols. (London, 1966–7), iv. 231.
2. Ibid. 234.
3. Virginia Woolf, 'The Art of Biography', *Collected Essays*, iv. 227.
4. Richard Holmes, *Footsteps: Adventures of a Romantic Biographer* (1985; repr. Harmondsworth, 1986), 66.
5. Ibid. 68–9.
6. Alethea Hayter, *A Sultry Month: Scenes of London Literary Life in 1846* (London, 1965).
7. Tom Leonard, *Places of the Mind: The Life and Work of James Thomson ('B.V.')* (London, 1993), p. xiii.
8. Jenny Uglow, *Elizabeth Gaskell: A Habit of Stories* (London, 1993).
9. Patricia Beer, review of *Lawrence's Women: The Intimate Life of D. H. Lawrence*, by Elaine Feinstein, *London Review of Books*, 25 Mar. 1993, 11.
10. George Eliot, *Middlemarch* (1872), closing sentence.
11. Robert Gittings and Jo Manton, *Claire Clairmont and the Shelleys* (Oxford, 1992).
12. Brenda Maddox, *Nora: A Biography of Nora Joyce* (London, 1988).
13. Claire Tomalin, *The Invisible Woman: The Story of Nelly Ternan and Charles Dickens* (London, 1990).
14. Virginia Woolf, *Flush* (1933; repr. London, 1991), 160.
15. Margaret Forster, *Lady's Maid* (London, 1990).
16. John Batchelor, *Virginia Woolf: The major novels* (Cambridge, 1991), 63.
17. *The Letters of Charles Dickens*, ed. Walter Dexter, 3 vols. (London, 1938), III 173.
18. Ibid. 359.
19. Frances Dickinson, 'The Baths of Lucca', *New Monthly Magazine*, 109 (Feb. 1857).
20. Wilkie Collins, *Poor Miss Finch*, 3 vols. (London, 1872), i, p. v.

4

Biography: Cult as Culture

JÜRGEN SCHLAEGER

In a paper recently given at a seminar on 'British Biographical Writing: Truth, Subversion, Gender, Ethics', a young colleague of mine from our German department recounted an experience she had when she first came to England.[1] One day she visited the Dickens House Museum and paused for a moment in front of an exhibit that was presented as 'Dickens's chair'. Whilst she was standing there, probably wondering whether to muster the appropriate feelings of awe or to laugh at such celebrity fetishism, a little schoolboy came in, carefully spelt out the words on the information sheet and then, having realized the magnitude of his discovery, shouted: 'Dickens's chair! Dickens's chair!' Immediately his classmates rushed in, placed themselves in a semicircle around the relic, and started to take down on their notepads everything the information sheet told them; some of them even added a sketch of the chair.

My colleague used this incident to illustrate what seemed to her the striking difference between the reverential attitude of the English to their national heroes and the complete absence of a desire for ancestor worship in Germans. And for her, the clearest instance of this is the difference in status of biographical writing in the two countries: all-important, culturally central in England, marginal in Germany. She then went on to discuss the historical reasons for the obvious neglect of biography in Germany: the 'belated nation'-syndrome, the rigour of historical scholarship, the philosophical tradition, and the misappropriation of hero-worship by the Nazis. Although everything she said about the differences in the two traditions made perfect sense in terms of the larger historical perspective, it did not give an answer, not even implicitly, to the question why biography should have become a major cultural concern in England in recent years and why this 'fashion' has not yet caught on in Germany.[2] I would therefore like to look at this cultural difference from another angle. I think there must be specific reasons for the rise of biography to power in England, reasons which do not invalidate the explanatory power of her general argument, but which show up cultural forces that have changed the intellectual climate in England and have given biography the status it now enjoys. Assuming that these cultural forces are similarly strong in Germany the analysis will have to give reasons why they have not provoked the same reaction.

I thought it an appropriate hors-d'oeuvre to begin my discussion on a biographical note, not as an offering to the gallery but in recognition of the spirit of a genre in which it would be absurd to separate the thinking from the person. With biography the warning of an 'intentional fallacy' is grossly misplaced. As a craft as well as a topic for analysis it demands a radically hermeneutical and person-centred approach. Everything in biography and about biography is interpretation of individuals. There is no meaningful talk about a 'life' beyond interpretation. For biographers and their subjects 'life' *is* interpretation, not interpretation of a reality beyond. Beyond interpretation there is only a mass of unrelated details and facts, brute matter, biographical ur-slime. The accusation that this is exactly what places biography outside the pale of serious intellectual endeavour, that this is a recipe for a subjectivist free-for-all, is beside the point. In terms of a 'Life', subjectivism—both in the writer and in his/her subject—is a *conditio sine qua non*.

But if biography is about individuals and if individuals are what an ever-growing readership is interested in, why not go to the source? Why not concentrate on autobiography as the genre which presents a 'Life' most directly and authentically? For a very long time, autobiography enjoyed a much greater reputation than biography; its primariness was considered superior to the secondariness of a 'Life' written by somebody else. But now, the former has clearly lost out to the latter, if not in numbers then in status. For every review of an autobiography one can find a host of reviews on biography. So a short comparison between these two related ways of writing a 'Life' may bring us a step closer to an understanding of the present reversal. It may also help us to understand certain conditions that separate the two cultures under consideration.

Biography and autobiography share a number of fundamental conditions and strategies but they also differ in some very interesting aspects. Both are about individuals, both assert the priority of individualism. But whereas autobiography is about the self, biography is about the other. It may be objected that in writing a diary or an autobiography a self experiences himself/herself as the other, or that biographers can get so deeply involved in their subject that they experience the other as self. But if we have doubts about the fundamental difference between biography and autobiography, we should ask ourselves if we talk about ourselves in the same way as we talk about others. Both kinds of writing, of course, share the characteristics of deliberate constructions, but their legitimizing strategies, their authority, and their points of view are entirely different. Ultimately the autobiographical discourse is a discourse of anxiety. Autobiographers have to be true to themselves and true to the image they would like to present to the public or to posterity. Very often these two obligations are extremely difficult to reconcile. The persuasiveness of the result almost wholly depends on the authenticity and authority of the self that speaks. Biography, on the other hand, is a discourse of usurpation. The truth-criterion does not consist in the authenticity of an inside view but in the consistency of the narrative and the explanatory power of the arguments. As long as a culture believes in the superiority of authentic self-expression, autobiography will be valued by it as the best way to get access to an individual life. If, however, this conviction is eroded, if there are serious doubts about the reliability of an individual's self-expression, the biographer's position will be strengthened, because he/she may have analytical instruments at his/her disposal, that allow a much more penetrating assessment of what shaped a particular life.

In recent decades psychoanalysis, structuralism, and other modern or post-modern interpretative paradigms have asserted or implicitly assumed that there is no authenticity, or rather that authenticity is a culturally determined myth. For these approaches, men/women as they appear in autobiography are always self-made, self-fashioned, the result of interpretative efforts, not real selves that have managed to appear on paper by some strange kind of magic. Moreover, they have radically de-privileged self-awareness as a reliable basis for analysis. For them, self-awareness is fundamentally flawed, either because it presents only the distorted outside of processes whose real centre lies in the unconscious, or because it fosters the illusion of self-determination, while in reality it is completely subjected to social pressures and influences.

They argue that in our own culture as well as in comparison with other cultures the autobiographical act represents a strange anomaly. Individualism of the Western kind, which is, after all, the basis of any kind of autobiographical endeavour, is, in their view, not the natural result of the logic of progress, a result which will appear in other cultures automatically once they have been Western-ized, but it is unique, and even in our culture a late arrival. If it is not something that was attained once and for all, but arose in very special historical circumstances, then there is no guarantee that it may not disappear when these circumstances change radically. And this is exactly what post-modernists claim to be the case now. Some of them say that individualism's heyday is already over and that its demise is imminent. They say that the marriage between language and experience, which it fostered, is about to break up. 'Plain style', they argue, which was a time-honoured concept of language that had endowed it with the power of reference and had carried with it the myth of authenticity, has been replaced by a rhetorical concept of language, and in a rhetorical concept of language 'reality' and 'reference' are modes of expression, not pleas for real presences. The dichotomy of fact and fiction is said to be in a state of dissolution—it no longer seems to make sense. They also say that the opposition between individualism and collectivism has disap-peared and that it is no historical accident that, precisely at this very moment, the political system that had come down heavily on the side of collectivism has given up its ghost.

If we are willing to concede what cultural historians and sociolo-gists have claimed, that in a curious way individualism throve on the emergence of clearly structured political systems, on the institutionalization of the nation state and of public opinion, then the conclusion is inescapable that it will come under pressure when these institutions lose their power to stabilize by providing a backdrop for individual self-projection. Individualism lived on its significant other. With the difference vanishing, there is only an amorphous mass of fragmented models for life, all of which are more or less equally important. In such a cultural scenario, life becomes a multiple-choice game, a pluralistic project; every life can consequently be turned into a colourful mosaic, full of sound and fury signifying nothing definite. It can also be reinvented again and again to serve very restricted personal life-projects, and the number of such projects has become all but infinite: feminist, royalist, class, and race; literary, political, military; the possibilities for the selection of a subject and the number of possible candidates for a perspective on his/her life have multiplied tremendously in the last decade. It is quite obvious that in such circumstances, autobiography is bound to lose authority. But why not biography too?

Is there anything in this new situation which is detrimental to the autobiographer's effort, but beneficial to the biographer? If we take for granted for a moment that there still is a strong interest in the lives of individuals in English culture, biography stands a much better chance to resist the anti-individualistic pressures of postmodern society. Psychology, psychoanalysis, and a number of other theories that provide an argumentative framework for combining the general with the particular allow biographers to carry on, while they are serious obstacles to autobiographical self-analysis. It is quite acceptable for a biographer to psychologize his/her subject, but it is inconceivable for an autobiographer to speculate on his/her own subconscious motivations and present them as an explanation. The difference between writing a Life and writing about a life is crucial here. Moreover, the authenticity of self-expression has, to a large extent, lost its truth-value. The self is no longer accepted as the most reliable source for the truth of its life. Nowadays it takes the thoroughness of a historian and the penetration of a psychologist to construct a plausible account of or perspective on a subject's life. And these are the talents of the successful biographer, not of the autobiographer.

There are early signs for the shift in perspective from autobiography to biography in Edmund Gosse's deservedly famous *Father and Son* (first published in 1907). Formally, *Father and Son* is a biography, but it is also the story of the author's own life. One masquerades as the other.[3] Gosse obviously realized that the biographical approach would give his book greater authority and would be more acceptable to his readers than a very personal story of his sufferings. Gosse also foreshadows the 'intertextual' nature of modern biography. He wrote *Father and Son* after he had written a Life of his father and a number of other Lives. In the process he fell back on these efforts as well as on an autobiography of his grandfather, on personal papers, diaries, and letters left by his father, and on his own earlier construction of his father's life. With him the writing of a biography had become a rewriting rather than a transformation of a real life into a book. If one of the tenets of post-modernism is that selves are texts, and texts are not about reality but about other texts, that they are 'intertextually constituted', then such a biography foreshadows the post-modern condition.

In the post-modern condition the position that personal experience has an authority of its own has become untenable. No modern biographer can repeat Boswell's claim to have Johnsonized the land for the treatment of his own subject. It would be absurd to state that Glendinning has Trollopized, or Holroyd has Shavianized English culture. But, somehow, this loss in the general significance of a particular life has not impaired the popularity of the genre. On the contrary, it has gained significantly in status and readership.

The solution to this contradiction does not lie, as one might suppose, in the dexterity with which biography has adapted to the post-modern mainstream. Even if it is true to say that, as the secondary discourse of life *par excellence*, it seems to have come into its own in an age when 'secondariness' is supposed to be everything we can ever hope to achieve in this matter, the rise of biography to power has nothing to do with its putative post-modernism. Quite the contrary.

I should like to put to the test a thesis which demolishes the assertion that the post-modern condition is congenial to biography.

In England 'the rise to power of a new literary genre [biography]' (Richard Holmes)[4] is, if anything, a reaction to cultural forces and pressures that post-modernists have dramatized into a universal condition of post-industrial Western society, but which is merely just another attempt to stay in control via theory. Compared with the images of our culture which post-modernism projects, biography is, in spite of its intertextual construction, fundamentally reactionary, conservative, perpetually accommodating new models of man, new theories of the inner self, into a personality-oriented cultural mainstream, thus always helping to defuse their subversive potential. By implication this is tantamount to saying that the absence of biography as a focus of cultural activity in Germany points to either the absence of such a conservative mainstream or a cultural situation in which the real pressures of post-modernism are dealt with in a different way. I'll come back to this point later.

The contrast between biography's status in England and its position in Germany is striking. Whereas in England the publication of a life-story is often celebrated as a major cultural event, biography in Germany has barely eked out a meagre existence. If you ask a German academic or writer how many biographies he thinks have been published during the last five years or so, he will, maybe, remember about two dozen. In England you had better ask who has not been done recently. This, I think, is symptomatic of a much broader cultural phenomenon.

If you will allow me to make one more personal observation I should like to describe an impression which I always have when I am in England. Wherever you go, wherever you are, faces stare up or down at you as if crying: 'Look at me! Look at what I have done! And what have *you* done?' Of course, I don't mean the faces of real people. Living specimens of the breed are much too modest and too well-behaved to ask such impertinent questions. The faces are in pictures and in portraits and on the covers of biographies. In common-rooms and banqueting halls, in stately homes, libraries, and bookshops, from monuments and in churches, literally thousands of faces seem to confront the visitor with the same everlasting questions. For me the country oozes biography from every pore. You will now understand why for a person with my non-English sensibilities a visit to the National Portrait Gallery is traumatic. The existence of such an institution is in itself a strong indicator of a personality-centred culture. The Dickens's chair syndrome is, indeed, ubiquitous. Even if this impression of mine is the over-reaction of a Teutonic mind, the cultural pressure to define oneself against such a phalanx of national celebrities must be tremendous for the intellectually ambitious in England. What aggravates this situation is the centrality of London, with Oxford and Cambridge as literary suburbias, where they are all in a position to watch each other's activities at close range and where mimetic envy, that ever fertile source of productivity and creativity, is rife.

At home, I never feel the same. Of course we have our national heroes—people we admire secretly or openly for what they have done or achieved, or, at considerable risk, have refused to do—but whenever I see a portrait of one of them I have to smile inwardly at the obvious difference between the pictorial or sculptural pose and the man's or woman's place in my view of history. These are not faces that ask me what I have done with my life or tell me what I have to do. I admire them as people from another world, people who did admirable things at quite another time and in quite another place. Basically, there is no sense of continuity between them and me. Serious and thoroughgoing identification of any sort is out of the question.

Now, such an attitude may be too personal to bear generalization. But if, for a moment, we assume that my reactions are due to the fact that I am German by birth and education, and not to the fact that I am a second son, or grew up without my father, was spoilt by my grandmother, or am obsessed with any number of personal fixations and complexes, my experience of the National Portrait Gallery may be indicative of significant differences between the two cultures under consideration.

It would be much too simple to explain the cultural divide between England and Germany in this respect by symmetrically opposed traditions:

English empiricism vs. German idealism;
English national identity vs. German lack of national identity;

English historical continuity vs. German discontinuity;
Cultural centralism vs. cultural regionalism.

All these symmetrical oppositions must, of course, play an important part in any attempt to explain the differences. What they do not explain, however, is how biography came to be a major industry in England while it remained marginal in Germany. English empiricism and the sense of national continuity both go a long way towards explaining why there has been a strong biographical tradition in England ever since the eighteenth century. What they fail to account for, though, is that in recent years it seems to have lost the stigma of being inescapably second-rate and culturally marginal with the cultural élite. It is no longer second to any other genre or discipline, not even to the novel or to history proper. What used to be the troubled face of biography has now become the self-assured, sometimes even complacent smile of a widely recognized and highly successful kind of writing.

So, where do we have to look for answers? If you remember what I said about post-modernism and the 'reactionary' character of biography, we may be able to pin down some of the answers to cultural pressures particular to our time and age. If biography thrives on an unshaken belief in individualism, if it is, as one critic put it, 'commonsensical, empirical, humane', if it is indeed 'the discourse of a surviving common culture', then its rise to power is intimately bound up with a serious threat to these beliefs.[5] This threat is forcefully acted out by post-modernist theory and its favourite game: deconstruction. Biographers seem to agree that their craft is immune to, resistant to deconstruction.[6] Biographers are 'in the business of ancestor-worship',[7] that is to say, they believe in identity, however complex it may turn out to be under intense scrutiny. 'Biographies . . . are works of reference.'[8] They take for granted that Lives have beginnings and ends, that they can be, have to be situated on a time-scale and in the history of the nation. Biographers still have 'a truth-telling programme'.[9] In short: they insist on all those aspects of human life and endeavour which postmodernists have radically called in question.

If it is true that, according to the American sociologist Christopher

Lasch, the self is 'under siege' because 'commodity production and consumerism have created a world of mirrors, insubstantial images, illusions increasingly indistinguishable from reality', then biography fulfils the function of an antidote.[10] Selfhood implies a personal history, friends, family, a sense of place and time, a public or common world to which one can relate oneself and against which one can define oneself. If these certainties recede into the shadows there is bound to be the need for resistance, and biography serves such a need—even in its more salacious, unashamedly voyeuristic forms.

In biography, one could say, an individualistic tradition reasserts itself. Whereas post-modernist theory produces aggravating symptoms of disintegration, biography tries to provide a cure or compensation. It is still a kind of post-mortem exploitation (Henry James), but it is none the worse for that. Quite the contrary; what used to be its flaws now turn out to be its assets. Its very weaknesses have become its strengths. It used to be despised because of its hybrid position between fact and fiction. It was considered to be neither fish nor fowl nor good red herring—although red herrings there were aplenty in many biographies. It was neither serious history nor aesthetically pleasing fiction. It often wavered between psychological particulars and sociological generalities. It frequently levelled the crucial distinction between inside and outside, private and public, thoughts and deeds. Now, with the pressing need for a reassertion of individualism, it seems to have come into its own. Life as lived and experienced is complex, is a mixture of fact and fiction, of 'Sein' and 'Bewusstsein'—and biography, this bastard genre, is 'wonderfully suited to represent these complexities' (Richard Holmes).[11] It tells *and* shows them.

The very fact that it seems to have drawn equal in popularity with the novel is also remarkable. It may be true that this is due to its fictional character, that 'a good biography is itself a kind of novel', that 'the contemporary biographer [comfortably] works within the narrative structure of traditional fiction' as the editors of *The Troubled Face of Biography* put it, but this does not turn a biography into a novel proper. On the contrary. The novel has long left behind the close partnership with truth and experience which it forged in the eighteenth century. Lifelikeness is no longer a criterion for quality. Under the influence of a kind of pan-fictionalization the novel can no longer claim and, indeed, does no longer claim legitimacy through its closeness to experience and truth.

A biographer on the other hand—whatever the extent to which he or she makes use of narrative, of fictional strategies—is inescapably wedded to a truth-telling programme. Even if nothing of what is told is truth in the narrower sense of being open to factual proof, it is still read as a text about a subject that really existed. In a world which is increasingly made up of 'mirrors, insubstantial images and illusions', which is dominated by a plurality of viewpoints and choices, facts, particular unmistakable individualities, or even mere referential gestures seem to have become a precious commodity. These are, to be sure, aspects of our lives which we no longer naïvely accept as the basis for universal truths about the self, life, and society, but for which we do still have an insatiable appetite. And biography is the craft that exploits this appetite. In a salad-bar and self-service buffet culture the need for a proper dinner, served in style, becomes irresistible—and a 'Life' is such a feast with all the customary ritual trappings and pleasant surprises.

Biography is a matter of life *and* death. Victoria Glendinning once demanded an answer to the question 'why, especially as people get older, they tell you they would rather read biography, for what it gives them, than fiction that is acknowledged as fiction'. I think that the thirst for facts, experience, and identity in an age when they are threatened by a loss of authority may be one of the answers sought. She herself, however, hinted at a deeper, more existential reason: 'I think myself it may have something to do with the lies and silences at the heart not only of life-stories, but of life itself; something to do with the fact of life, by which I mean of course the fact of death.'[12] But death, the treatment of death, has its own history. It is as much a fact of life as it is culturally and ideologically determined. From this point of view biography may be seen not only as part of the perennial effort of man to escape the inescapable, but also as an attempt to reverse a process in which death has become a merely biological event. 'After all, what *is* death? Just nature's way of telling us to slow down.' Such a statement sums it up neatly. In the face of a meaningless death, biography gives life an extension. It is, as such, one of the most successful efforts at secular resurrection. Most modern biographies are reticent about the details of their subjects' death. That they are dead is taken for granted; that their death was preceded by a life worth living and, even more to the point, worth writing about underlies the task to which the genre is devoted. Biography pits the abundance of past life against the present monotony of death. Life in biography is luxuriant, death is sterile.

It may even be that the salacious interest in the sex life of their subject, which so many biographers show these days and which the more ambitious try to hide behind psychoanalytical jargon, owes more to a subconscious awareness of it as the basic life-force than to our fascination with slippery details. Sex, in whatever form and however monotonous at times, is still so much more exciting— even on the written page—than the monotonous presence of death in our post-modern world.

We started out by discussing cultural difference, and wondering why, in view of the services biography seems to perform for English society, the Germans have not availed themselves of them. If the rise of biography to power in England has anything to do with the pressures of the post-modern condition, its failure to do so in Germany must in some way be related to the way in which this post-modern condition is experienced in my country. In a sense we Germans don't have the same problem with the post-modern condition and consequently have to forego the pleasures of a craft or an art that reacts to its threats. Individualism and experience never counted for much in German intellectual life. The 'I', the self, remained imprisoned in the concept of subjectivity propagated by idealist philosophy. And ancestor-worship has become problematic after Hitler just as national identity has become a difficult proposition after Auschwitz. So it is not at all surprising that post-modernism and deconstruction fail to arouse strong resistance in our culture. The general, educated public obviously does not feel the need to defend positions it has hardly ever thought crucial. Thus, post-modernism is taken rather as one intellectual fashion among others than as a threat to ingrained traditions. Of course, we are as interested in life and as afraid of death as anybody else, but we have other well-established strategies to deal with the problem of keeping up our interest in life and fending off our apprehensions of death.

Germans generally expect redress not from ancestor-worship or from a biographical restaging of other people's lives but from hard work, from devotion to a cause, from systematic thinking, from the philosophical tradition, in short, from practices that are as far removed from what biography does as can be. If, as one colleague, who ought to know, told me recently, there are signs that the interest in biography is growing even here, it could only be taken as an indication that German culture is slowly coming round to a more empiricist attitude to life.

One last word about the biographers. Michael Holroyd once wrote that a biographer 'must continually lead two separate but overlapping lives—his own and that of the person about whom he is currently writing'.[13] And he goes on to say that 'the more he finds out about his subject, the more he finds out about himself'. Andrew Sinclair chimes in with the statement that 'The writing of biography is more than a discovery of another person. It is a matter of self-discovery.'[14] Victoria Glendinning professed that 'it may be a vain hope to think that I am able or willing to keep the personalities apart'.[15]

If these statements imply more than the old hermeneutical truism that all writing is more or less coloured by the personality of the writer, biographers are a strange breed of people indeed. They are writers who seem to show a preference for living by proxy to living their own lives. Somehow they seem to have succeeded in breaking down the distance between the writer and his/her subject. As one of the consequences, our age and English culture in particular should have managed to produce Boswells and Eckermanns by the score. But has it? Isn't there a definite lack of authoritative figures such as Dr Johnson or Goethe for this kind of symbiotic relationship to prosper? And is the narrowing of the distance between author and subject really desirable or even a fact? I tend to take the aforementioned statements as made with tongue in cheek. Distance òr its absence is employed as a presentational strategy. It does not really imply that Holmes has become Stevenson or Glendinning Trollope. The self-discovery they talk about is a discovery of self as other if anything. The other life has taken over functions that used to be fulfilled by institutions of collective significance—value systems, codes of conduct, social virtues, etc. Moreover, a blurring of the line that separates self from other would mean a definite loss of power over the subject. It would mean exchanging the advantages of a basically voyeuristic situation for the limitations of a face-to-face situation.

The illusion of complete identification is only the result of a literary strategy. In a way the relation of the successful biographer to his or her subject is no longer that of the devoted observer of a great man's portrait hanging high above him or her on the wall; nor is it that of a symbiotic Boswell, but rather that of a person shown to be sitting in front of a TV-set watching a programme with him- or herself sitting in front of the set watching . . . and so on. Or think of a Camp-Coffee label showing a camp-site with a man sitting at a table on which there is a Camp-Coffee bottle with a label showing . . . The biographers of our time no longer sit in front of the set or at a real table in their camp looking at ready-made stories or real objects, but they can only place themselves somewhere on the tangled receding line of traces and images their subjects have left. To stay in the game of individualism depends more than ever on the biographer's talent to be player and referee at the same time.

Notes

1. Martina Wagner-Egelhaaf, 'Biography in Germany: The State of the Art.' Paper given at the conference 'British Biographical Writing: Truth, Subversion, Gender, Ethics', held at Schloss Hofen, Austria, in April 1993.
2. Cf. Helmut Scheuer, *Biographie: Studien zur Funktion und zum Wandel einer literarischen Gattung vom 18. Jahrhundert bis zur Gegenwart* (Stuttgart, 1979). Also Michael Holroyd, 'How I Fell into Biography', in Eric Homberger and John Charmley (eds.), *The Troubled Face of Biography* (henceforth *TFB*) (London, 1988), 99: 'Biography has risen in the English speaking world but not elsewhere.'
3. Cf. Gertrude Stein, *The Autobiography of Alice B. Toklas* (1933) as another interesting example for an undercover presentation of one's own life.

4. Quoted by Michael Holroyd, 'How I Fell into Biography', *TFB* 99.
5. *TFB*, Introduction, p. viii.
6. Ann Thwaite, 'Writing Lives', *TFB* 32; Holroyd, 'How I fell into Biography', ibid.
7. Victoria Glendinning, 'Lies and Silences', ibid. 61.
8. Robert Blake, 'The Art of Biography', ibid. 76.
9. Robert Skidelsky, 'Only Connect: Biography and Truth', ibid. 12.
10. Christopher Lasch, *The Minimal Self: Psychic Survival in Troubled Times* (New York, 1984), 30.
11. A statement made at the Schloss Hofen conference.
12. Glendinning, 'Lies and Silences', *TFB* 62.
13. Holroyd, 'How I Fell into Biography', *TFB* 94.
14. Andrew Sinclair, 'Vivat Alius Ergo Sum', ibid. 123.
15. Glendinning, 'Lies and Silences', ibid. 53.

5

Psychiatry and Literary Biography

ANTHONY STORR

This paper is based on three premisses. The first is that detailed causal psychoanalytic interpretations of the character and behaviour of deceased persons in terms of what may have happened to them in early childhood are intrinsically unreliable. The second premiss is that, in contrast, ideas and concepts originally derived from psychoanalysis have become so incorporated into intellectual discourse that biographers automatically employ them without always realizing whence they came. The third premiss is that, although psychoanalytic causal interpretation has not been as useful a tool for the biographer as the early Freudian disciples hoped, clinical psychiatry —based on the diagnosis and description of various forms of psychiatric illness such as obsessional neurosis and manic-depressive disorder—has provided biographical insights into literary figures which are invaluable and often unappreciated.

On Christmas Day, 1928 Sigmund Freud wrote a letter to Lytton Strachey who had sent him a copy of his recently published *Elizabeth and Essex*. Freud wrote:

I am acquainted with all your earlier publications, and have read them with great enjoyment. But the enjoyment was essentially an aesthetic one. This time you have moved me deeply, for you yourself have reached greater depths. You are aware of what other historians so easily overlook —that it is impossible to understand the past with certainty, because we cannot divine men's motives and the essence of their minds and so cannot interpret their actions. Our psychological analysis does not suffice even with those who are near us in space and time, unless we can make them the object of years of the closest investigation, and even then it breaks down before the incompleteness of our knowledge and the clumsiness of our synthesis. So that with regard to the people of past times we are in the same position as with dreams to which we have been given no associations—and only a layman could expect us to interpret such dreams as those. As a historian, then, you show that you are steeped in the spirit of psycho-analysis. And, with reservations such as these, you have approached one of the most remarkable figures in your country's history, you have known how to trace back her character to the impressions of her childhood, you have touched upon her most hidden motives with equal boldness and discretion, and it is very possible that you have succeeded in making a correct reconstruction of what actually occurred.[1]

Eminent Victorians and *Queen Victoria* owed nothing to psycho-analytic theory. *Elizabeth and Essex* reflects Lytton Strachey's increasing interest in psychoanalysis, gleaned from talks with his brother James, who was by then embarked on his huge enterprise of translating Freud's Collected Works into English. Freud's polite endorsement of Lytton Strachey's psychoanalytic interpretation of Elizabeth's character is so cautious, so hedged about with reservations, that it throws doubt upon whether such an enterprise is possible; a doubt shared by historians at the time of publication, who poured scorn on Strachey's guesswork. *Elizabeth and Essex*, engaging though it is, has never established itself as a serious biographical study comparable with *Queen Victoria*. What can we know of the inner emotional life of public figures who do not leave us intimate diaries or other records of their thoughts and feelings? Freud's reservations about the possibility of understanding such people from a psychoanalytic viewpoint are surely right.

Yet Freud himself, as is often apparent in his writings, could not refrain from indulging in psychoanalytic speculations about historical figures who particularly interested him, including Leonardo da Vinci and Dostoevsky. Many of these speculations have turned out to be plainly wrong. Joseph Frank's massive, scholarly biography of Dostoevsky clearly demonstrates that Freud's interpretation of the novelist's psychopathology in his paper *Dostoevsky and Parricide* is based on a misconception of the character of Dostoevsky's father. From a hazy and inaccurate memory of something he had read in a biography of the novelist, Freud concluded that Dr Dostoevsky was a particularly severe, punitive parent, and that Dostoevsky's epilepsy was not true epilepsy, but an emotional reaction to hearing of his father's death. In a letter to Stefan Zweig, Freud wrote:

Somewhere in a biography of D. I was shown a passage which traced back the later affliction of the man to the boy's having been punished by the father under very serious circumstances—I vaguely remember the word 'tragic', am I right? Out of 'discretion' of course, the author didn't say what it was all about.[2]

Freud assumed that the punishment was for masturbation, and therefore amounted to a threat of castration. He concluded that Dostoevsky, as a consequence, alternated throughout his life between outraged rebellion against his father and masochistic submission to him. In fact, Dr Dostoevsky was a particularly conscientious parent who partly taught his children himself, never used physical punishment, and who, at expense which he could ill afford, sent his children to private schools in order that they should not be beaten. Moreover, Dostoevsky's epilepsy did not manifest itself until ten years after his father's death. When it did, it fulfilled all the clinical criteria for true epilepsy caused by organic damage to the brain. It could not have been the result of psychological trauma alone.

Let us take another example. Freud's famous analysis of the paranoid psychotic Judge Schreber was based on his subject's memoirs rather than on any personal encounter. Freud's assumptions about Judge Schreber's presumed homosexual ambivalence towards his father were based on the notion that Schreber's father, a well-known physician and pedagogue, deserved respect. Freud refers to his 'great reputation' and to his promotion of what he calls 'the harmonious upbringing of the young'. In fact, Dr Daniel Schreber was an authoritarian monster who subjected his sons to all kinds of restrictive devices designed to prevent nocturnal emissions, and many other horrors. Judge Schreber's elder brother shot himself at the age of 38, whilst the Judge himself went mad. Freud apparently made no attempt to discover what Judge Schreber's childhood was actually like, or what manner of man his father really was.

Freud also collaborated with the American diplomat, William C. Bullitt, in a psychological study of the American President, Woodrow Wilson. Since both authors were heavily prejudiced against their subject, this biography has been universally rejected as a tendentious example of using psychoanalysis for what is now called 'character assassination'. As a biography, it is virtually worthless.

There are many examples of biography based upon psychoanalytic interpretation which are equally suspect. I admire Frank E. Manuel's *A Portrait of Isaac Newton* and concur with him in thinking that Newton's suspiciousness, readiness to take offence, and tendency towards depression may well have originated from his abandonment by his mother, who remarried when Newton was 3 years old and who left him in the care of others. But some of Manuel's psychoanalytic speculations are so wild as to detract from the value of his otherwise excellent biography.

Another example is provided by Richard Ellmann who criticizes Leon Edel for assuming that Henry James's homosexuality could be attributed to the smothering love of his mother, when the facts do not support such an interpretation. Ellmann also rightly observes that the psychoanalytic tracing of supposed ultimate causes reduces differentiation. He points out that the biographies of Woodrow Wilson by Freud and Bullitt, of Martin Luther by Erik Erikson, and of Flaubert by Jean-Paul Sartre, are all so closely concerned with their Oedipus complexes that 'the President, the religious reformer, and the writer might almost be confused with one another'.[3] I can recall a learned book on Leonardo by K. R. Eissler, a distinguished psychoanalyst and guardian of the Freud archives, which alleged that Leonardo's interest in drawing swirling water must have originated from bed-wetting. I say 'must have' advisedly. The early Freudians were so utterly convinced that their picture of infancy was correct that they had no hesitation in making such interpretations. In his biography of Freud, Ernest Jones wrote:

When one considers the material used in the five arts—paint, clay, stone, words, and sounds—any psychologist must conclude that the passionate interest in bringing an orderliness out of chaos must signify at the same time an extraordinary sublimation of the most primitive infantile enjoyments and the most extreme denial of them.[4]

My impression is that, thankfully, such biographies belong to the past. Their heyday was forty or more years ago, when Freudian psychoanalysis, on both sides of the Atlantic, was regarded by its adherents as indisputable truth. Many fundamentalist Freudians, like Freud himself, preferred speculation to scholarship, making confident assertions about the traumas suffered by their subjects in early childhood without sufficient evidence to support their theories.

On the other hand, ideas derived from psychoanalysis have provided a new and inescapable dimension to biography. Ernest Gellner writes that, in our day, psychoanalysis has become the dominant idiom for the discussion of the human personality and human relations. Peter Gay, the historian and biographer of Freud, has written a book called *Freud for Historians*, in which he points out that many psychoanalytic ideas, like *conflict, repression, projection,* and *ambivalence,* have become so much part of ordinary discourse that they can be described as platitudes.[5] Ellmann adds *aggression, anxiety, compulsion, the unconscious, defense mechanism, narcissism, death wish, erogenous zones, fixation, guilt feeling, sublimation,* and *wish fulfillment,* as words used by Freud which we cannot do without.[6] Although the kind of psychoanalytic interpretation which causally attributes adult character to real or hypothetical incidents in infancy can be disregarded, what might be called a psychoanalytic point of view or attitude has inescapably influenced the biographer's study of character.

Since Freud, the central place of sexuality in human life has been fully recognized, and no modern biographers can afford to disregard this aspect of their subjects' nature in the way that their predecessors usually did. Sir Roy Harrod's biography of Maynard Keynes, published as recently as 1951, made no mention of his subject's homosexuality. Although Keynes's sexual orientation may have been irrelevant to his economics, it was an important aspect of his personality. But it was left to Michael Holroyd to reveal it in his biography of Lytton Strachey.

On balance, I think that we should acknowledge and cautiously welcome the influence which psychoanalysis, in the wide sense of creating a climate of opinion, has had on biography, whilst still rejecting detailed psychoanalytic reconstructions of a subject's infancy which can never be proven. But even this modest appreciation of psychoanalysis as contributing in a general way to our biographical understanding requires some reservations. Although Freud's insistence upon the importance of sex in determining character has obliged biographers to be more outspoken, I am not sure that it has always made them more tolerant of sexual diversity. Because Freud's portrayal of the journey through infancy to adulthood insisted that heterosexual genitality ought to be the mature end-point of the normal individual's emotional development, those who fail to reach this goal are more penalized as immature than they were in days before Freud's theories were widely known or accepted. Celibacy used to be admired as displaying self-control and a preference for the spiritual rather than the physical. Now it is usually interpreted as an ignominious flight from sex or as concealing some form of perversion. It is arguable that the Victorians were more tolerant of homosexual feelings, if not of homosexual practices, than we are. Robert Bernard Martin, in his biography of Gerard Manley Hopkins, points out that, although the death penalty for sodomy was on the statute-books until 1861, the idea of homosexuality as a condition or form of sensibility in the absence of physical expression was not generally accepted.[7] Today, Tennyson's *In Memoriam* could not be published except by a poet who was openly and avowedly homosexual. Those who, like Tennyson, are predominantly heterosexual, or at least bisexual, seem to be allowed less latitude in expressing passionate feelings towards their own sex because, since Freud, the persistence of such feelings is regarded as evidence of abnormality or immaturity.

Although liberating in some ways, psychoanalysis has made us suspicious of virtue. There is little room for altruism, for self-sacrifice, for unselfishness, or for generosity in the Freudian scheme. Such impulses are usually interpreted by psychoanalysts as overdetermined defences against drives which are entirely selfish. Perhaps I am naïve in believing that men and women can sometimes behave nobly, without ulterior motives; but I think that Freudian ruthlessness has sometimes been overdone.

Moreover, Freud is sometimes credited with changes in attitude towards biography which may not originate with him. Modern biographers are less inclined to take the statements of their subjects about their own motives at face value than were their Victorian predecessors. We realize that we all deceive ourselves, and that public figures are even more liable to self-deception than are private individuals. But how far is this change in attitude really due to Freud, the great unmasker?

If we return to Lytton Strachey, we find that his portraits of Cardinal Manning and Florence Nightingale display his conviction that dominance, ambition, and disregard for others underlay their achievements. But Strachey's iconoclasm in these examples owed nothing to Freud. It was part of a wider, general discontent with Victorian values, in which Freud also participated. Both Darwin and Marx, as well as Freud, were concerned with cutting human beings down to size; with demonstrating that man's higher, spiritual impulses had primitive origins in biological drives or economic motives. The reductive, analytic approach to problems, whether biological, sociological, or psychological, was characteristic of the era. Scientific understanding was equated with reducing structures to their elementary constituents. The comprehension of synthesis, of how discrete entities come to be welded into a larger whole, was far less emphasized. Yet, what is interesting about particular human beings is not only what traumatic events may or may not have disrupted their smooth passage from infancy to adulthood. We should also be concerned with how successfully a person has succeeded in making a coherent whole, a personality, out of the character traits, temperamental qualities, intellectual abilities and deficiencies, with which he or she has been endowed by nature. In the case of the creatively gifted, style is a manifestation of this synthesis. As Jerrold Northrop Moore puts it in his biography of Elgar, 'The sign of a successful synthesis is a unified and unique style plain for all to recognize. . . . The process by which a man has forged such a unity is the most profound and most exalted of human stories.'[28] Freud has nothing to say about such a process, but it is a central feature of Jung's psychology.

At this point I want to examine how far descriptive, clinical psychiatry rather than psychoanalysis can be of service to the biographer. I have never written a full-scale biography, but I have written several character sketches or biographical essays in which psychiatric concepts have proved invaluable. For example, although psychoanalytic interpretation throws little light on Kafka's personality, I do not think it possible to understand him without recourse to psychiatry. Kafka's infancy and early childhood were certainly not ideal; but not so desperately traumatic that one could assume childhood experience to be solely responsible for all his adult peculiarities. What people say about their early childhood and how they perceive it may be governed as much by innate, genetically determined traits of personality as by what actually happened. Within the same family, siblings perceive their parents very differently. However, some knowledge and experience of the people whom psychiatrists label 'schizoid' certainly help me, and I hope also help my readers, to understand Kafka without indulging in vain speculation about his infancy.

How can a single descriptive adjective further our understanding of so complex and unusual a character? By definition, every individual is different from every other individual. Yet, if we are to understand one another at all, we are compelled to categorize our fellows, although, eventually, we may describe particular people chiefly in terms of the ways in which they differ from the category assigned. For example, X is a WASP, but not a typical WASP in all respects because though white, Anglo-Saxon, and Protestant, his closest friends are black.

As I see it, the essential dilemma of the schizoid personality is a desperate need for intimacy combined with an intense fear of close involvement with other people. The schizoid person withdraws into him- or herself and attempts to do without human relationships as far as possible. But since it is emotional involvement which gives meaning to life, at any rate in youth, the schizoid person is at constant risk of finding life meaningless and futile. Anyone working in a university will be familiar with the undergraduate who, though often intellectually gifted, is unable to make friends or enjoy a normal social life, and who adopts a spurious air of superiority designed to show that he or she is above such mundane needs as love or even approval. It requires tolerance and patience to get behind this mask and discover that it conceals a frightened child who desperately needs human contact and understanding but who is terrified of receiving it. Schizoid people, because of their fear of physical intimacy, often exalt the intellect at the expense of the body, and by disowning their physical being become alienated and unsure of their own identity.

There seem to be three main reasons for this fear of intimacy, all of which may be present together, but one of which usually predominates.

First, some people may avoid intimacy because they fear that they will be so dominated or overborne that they will lose their identity as separate individuals. Schizoid people think of others as being powerful, ruthless, and immune to influence, whilst thinking of themselves as disregarded and ineffectual. Because they feel that their own needs and wishes are ignored, they come to believe that their very being is threatened; that they might as well not exist. Parents sometimes treat their offspring as appendages of themselves rather than as individuals in their own right. The schizoid fear that close involvement leads to subjective feelings of being a nonentity may partly originate from such early experience.

Second, some people may be reluctant to embark upon close relationships because they fear that it will end and that they will be worse off than if they had never risked involvement. Such a fear may be based upon an actual experience of loss in early childhood by bereavement or desertion. This is what happened in the case of Newton.

A third reason for avoiding intimacy seems paradoxical. Some schizoid individuals fear that they will harm or destroy anyone with whom they become closely involved. This appears to contradict the idea that schizoid subjects feel weak and helpless. But the power to exhaust or empty the parent is shared by every small child, especially if the parent is elderly or ailing. The emotional demands made by schizoid people are in reality so overwhelming that their fears are partly justified. If they allow themselves to become involved with another person at all they tend to make demands which are in reality exhausting. Often, they seem to clamour for the unequivocal, total devotion which mothers properly give their new-born babies but which no adult has any right to claim from another.

Kafka, both in his behaviour and in his writings, demonstrates his passionate wish for intimacy combined with a fear of close involvement which owes something to each of the three factors which I have just described.

Kafka's description of his relationship with his father illustrates the fear of being overborne, treated as non-existent, or even annihilated. In his *Letter to His Father*, Kafka writes of this 'sense of nothingness that often dominates me.'[9] The particular example which he chooses to illustrate this feeling and the part in causing it played by his father is as significant to Kafka as was his mother's failure to kiss him good-night to the 7-year-old Proust. In both cases, a single incident has become a symbol, epitomizing an attitude to life. Kafka remembered whimpering for water at night. After various threats had proved ineffective, his father took the child out of bed and left him alone on the balcony outside the shut door. Kafka writes:

Even years afterwards I suffered from the tormenting fancy that the huge man, my father, the ultimate authority, would come almost for no reason at all and take me out of bed in the night and carry me out on to the *pavlatche*, and that therefore I was a mere nothing for him.[10]

Kafka's father was undoubtedly an insensitive bully; but Kafka, who had a great deal more sense than many psychoanalysts, is careful to point out that his father is not wholly to blame; that it was the relation between them which was at fault, and that his own hypersensitive nature was as much responsible for his fear of annihilation as was his father's lack of sensitivity.

Kafka's relationship with his fiancée, Felice Bauer, further illustrates his fear of being overwhelmed by the proximity of others, and also demonstrates the fear of being abandoned and, to a lesser extent, the fear of damaging any person with whom he might become intimate to which I referred earlier.

Kafka was involved emotionally with Felice Bauer for five years. Yet, during all this time, the couple actually met no more than nine or ten times, often for only an hour or so. Kafka contrived that the relationship should remain almost entirely epistolary. This was a temporary solution to the schizoid dilemma of a desperate need for intimacy combined with a desperate fear of actual proximity.

The fear of being overwhelmed is illustrated in a letter replying to Felice's wish to be with him when he was writing.

You once said that you would like to sit beside me while I write. Listen, in that case I could not write (I can't do much anyway), but in that case, I could not write at all. For writing means revealing oneself in excess; that utmost of self-revelation and surrender, in which a human being, when involved with others, would feel he was losing himself, and from which, therefore, he will always shrink as long as he is in his right mind—for everyone wants to live as long as he is alive . . .[11]

Kafka used to carry Felice's letters around with him, claiming that they gave him continuous support and made him feel more competent. His underlying fear of abandonment is demonstrated by his dreadful anxiety if she fails to reply to his letters immediately.

Has there ever been, Felice, in the last three months, a single day on which you have not had news from me? You see, there hasn't been such a day. But today, Tuesday, you leave me entirely without news; since four o'clock on Sunday I know nothing about you; until tomorrow's delivery that will be no less than sixty-six hours, filled in my mind with every alternating good and bad contingency.[12]

Other letters demand that Felice tell him every detail of her life: what she is wearing, what she eats, what her room is like, whom she sees. Although Felice is far away in another city, Kafka is reproducing the anxious enquiries which insecure children address to their mothers when they leave the house. 'But where are you going? How long will you be? When will you be back?' His need for her is desperate, his fear that she may abandon him is evident. By knowing exactly where she is and what she is doing at every minute of the day, Kafka is reassuring himself that Felice is potentially accessible even when she is not actually with him.

In Kafka's case, the fear that he might destroy Felice by his demands is less obvious, but can also be detected in his letters. Kafka constantly reiterates that he is unable to manage life, that he is a hopeless person, and that he would be impossible to live with. I think it is clear that he fears, with good reason, that his demands are so extreme that he would drain any woman who attempted to meet them.

Psychiatric knowledge and experience have made it possible for me to understand Kafka better than I could have without such knowledge. Reciprocally, Kafka's letters and other writings have enriched my understanding of certain psychiatric cases. Kafka, tormented as he was, retained astonishing insight; and, because he was scrupulously honest as well as being a great writer, he provides authentic illumination of one kind of human tragedy.

I want to conclude with a brief consideration of an entirely different psychiatric disorder. Writers are so notoriously prone to recurrent depression and to manic-depressive illness that every aspiring literary biographer ought to know something about these conditions. A variety of studies have confirmed the frequency of these disorders in writers; and, in a lecture which I gave to the Royal Society of Literature, I attempted to explain why writing is particularly likely to appeal to sufferers who are gifted enough to make it an important part of life. It is also established that genetic inheritance is more important than infantile experience in determining susceptibility both to recurrent depression alone and also to bipolar illness.

Poets are particularly likely to suffer from recurrent episodes of depression which are severe enough to rate as mental illness. Among them are William Collins, John Donne, William Cowper, Thomas Chatterton, John Clare, Christopher Smart, Samuel Taylor Coleridge, Edgar Allan Poe, Gerard Manley Hopkins, Alfred Tennyson, Edward Lear, Edward Thomas, Sylvia Plath, John Berryman, Anne Sexton, Hart Crane, Theodore Roethke, Delmore Schwartz, Randall Jarrell, and Robert Lowell. Clare, Collins, and Smart were all admitted to 'madhouses'. Donne, who wrote the first English defence of suicide, *Biathanatos*, was recurrently tempted by suicide himself. Lowell was in and out of hospital with attacks of mania as well as of depression. Five of the poets just listed committed suicide. If you are inclined to question the genetic factor, please study the Tennyson family as described in Robert Bernard Martin's excellent biography of the poet.

Some knowledge of how severe depression can distort the individual's perception of life and of him or herself can help us to understand the terrible despair and self-hatred which Cowper expressed in some poems. It is surely essential to bring psychiatry to bear on any study of Dr Johnson, as Jackson Bate has done in his marvellous biography. How else can one appreciate that a man who achieved so much and who still gives us so much pleasure could say, 'I have lived totally useless'?

It is equally important for the biographer to have some appreciation of the state which psychiatrists label 'hypomania.' Although recurrent depression without alternating periods of being 'high' is more common, there are also a number of writers who show extreme mood-swings in both directions. More particularly, there are some writers who, at first sight, simply appear to be gifted with more energy than the average person. Closer examination reveals that they are prone to depression, but strive to prevent this descending upon them by feverish overactivity. In psychiatric jargon, this is known as employing a 'manic defence'. Dickens is a good example. We know that he was prone to moods of depression, both from his own account of himself and from his biographers. Sometimes these periods of depression were provoked by life events like his rejection by Maria Beadnell or the death of his sister Fanny; but sometimes the black mood descended after a period of intense effort. Dickens dealt with his liability to become depressed by keeping himself ceaselessly busy. You will remember that he was not only a novelist who worked on more than one novel at once: he was also a journalist and editor, an actor and a producer, a social reformer, and a tireless walker in the countryside. Like many people prone to depression, Dickens needed constant public recognition if he was not to fall into despair. This is why he continued with his dramatic public readings in spite of their proving so exhausting that they were followed by symptoms of partial paralysis which presaged his final stroke. I do not think it is possible for the biographer to understand either Dickens or Balzac unless he or she has some knowledge of manic-depressive disorders.

In short, the literary biographer is entitled to reject psychoanalytic interpretations of character based upon suppositions about infantile experience and misperception which cannot be authenticated. But some knowledge of psychiatry, more particularly of manic-depressive disorders, of schizophrenia, and of the types of personality who are susceptible to these illnesses, is indispensable.

Notes

1. Quoted in Michael Holroyd, *Lytton Strachey*, 2 vols. (London, 1967–8), ii. 615–16.
2. Quoted in Joseph Frank, *Dostoevsky*, i, *The Seeds of Revolt, 1821–1849* (London, 1977), 382.
3. Richard Ellmann, 'Freud and Literary Biography', *The American Scholar* (Autumn 1984), 465–78.
4. Ernest Jones, *Sigmund Freud: Life and Work*, 3 vols. (London, 1953–7), iii. 445.
5. Peter Gay, *Freud for Historians* (New York, 1985), 17.
6. Ellmann, 'Freud and Literary Biography', 465.
7. Robert Bernard Martin, *Gerard Manley Hopkins* (London, 1991), 50.
8. Jerrold Northrop Moore, *Edward Elgar: A Creative Life* (Oxford, 1984), p. viii.
9. Franz Kafka, *Letter to His Father*, trans. Ernst Kaiser and Eithne Wilkins, in *Wedding Preparations in the Country and Other Stories* (Harmondsworth, 1978), 34.
10. Ibid.
11. Franz Kafka, *Letters to Felice*, trans. James Stern and Elizabeth Duckworth, ed. Erich Heller and Jurgen Born (London, 1974), 155–6.
12. Ibid. 23.

❧ 6 ❧

Women's Lives: The Unmapped Country

LYNDALL GORDON

'What is a woman?' Virginia Woolf asked in a speech to professional women in 1931. 'I assure you, I don't know. I do not believe that you know.'[1]

Back in the nineteenth century, Charlotte Brontë, Emily Dickinson, Henry James, and Olive Schreiner had all pointed to the undefined nature of women. 'What is now called the nature of women is an eminently artificial thing', wrote John Stuart Mill in 1869, '— the result of forced repression in some directions, unnatural stimulation in others.'[2] If women were social constructs, what was their nature? And where were they to seek it if not in the unexplored reaches of their own lives? These lives which spanned the period of 'the Woman Question', from the 1840s to the first generation to gain the vote, show how the largest imaginations drew on their own experience in order to propose a new model of womanhood.

'I am a rising character', is the answer of Charlotte Brontë's most autobiographical heroine, Lucy Snowe, when she is asked, '*are* you anybody?'[3] There is a rising character in Charlotte's own remote life in the Yorkshire parsonage, in the trials of love and solitude which test her strength, and in the new, vehement voice which sweeps through Victorian society from the publication of *Jane Eyre* in 1847 to *Villette* in 1853. The rising character took shape through encounters with two men of the world who were in positions to estimate its calibre: M. Heger, her teacher in Brussels, re-created as the tigerish but stimulating M. Paul Emanuel in *Villette*; and George Smith, her admiring publisher who, at the time she was writing this novel, withdrew, under pressure from his mother, in order to marry someone richer, younger, healthier. Charlotte

Brontë re-created him as the physically irresistible Graham Bretton, responsible, intelligent, but locked in the norms of his time. This perception was part of a covert dialogue with Smith: his obedience to worldly custom transformed the later plot of the novel where it came to be the more graceless and unconventional Paul Emanuel who proves the more appropriate mate for the 'rising' woman. Smith's reply was to pay her an unexpectedly low sum for this her greatest work.

In 1852, the same year that Charlotte Brontë completed *Villette*, Florence Nightingale noted that middle-class women were told that they had no passions.[4] What does Charlotte Brontë tell us about passion from a woman's point of view? What can we learn about a woman whose passions were denied yet who remained emotionally partnered between the daylight life of stagnant duty and the hidden dark of anarchic attachment? There was psychic danger in this divide, but there was also a strategy for survival: to be quiet on the surface where the public gaze falls, yet to hold within reach an area of existence which had opened as 'a new region'.[5]

Charlotte Brontë's feminist friend, Mary Taylor, told her: 'You are very different from me in having no doctrine to preach.' It is true she was no polemical feminist, but she did not abrogate the Woman Question; she broadened it from the arena of public rights to the more hidden arena of private feeling, those spaces in the mind where, as Mill observed, women were more insidiously and deeply enslaved than through more obvious restrictions to do with work, property, and the vote. This form of emancipation is yet to come: Jane Eyre's repeated refusal to violate her nature portends a future we might realize.

Charlotte Brontë's first biographer, Mrs Gaskell, spoke to mid-Victorians about the selfless, dutiful, refined, and above all, pathetic aspect of her subject, while our age feels the tug of the unknown in the woman surfacing through contemporary artifice: we see a stronger, more fiery, more resourceful Charlotte behind the legend of a doomed family in Romantic solitude, behind the frail trembler in the shadow of tombstones. To find the woman who chose 'to walk invisible',[6] it is necessary to open up the gaps in her life. The sheer abundance of fact tempts the biographer to stitch together a seamless story which elides these unseen gaps. Many of her letters, as well as large batches from her closest correspondents vanished: whatever conflicted with the growth of Brontë legend. The gaps invite some play of imaginative truth, and clues to such truth may be derived from careful reading of her autobiographical works. A poem she wrote in Brussels, 'Frances' (1843), suggests that her love for her teacher was rooted as much in ambition as in physical passion. Her pleas for letters, after her return to Haworth, express an unusual form of desire that blends with desire for a voice in the presence of which her own might rise. Though publicly she presented herself as 'the weakest, puniest'[7] of Papa's children, a passage she wrote on the subject of secret strength gives her rationale for survival. However meek and quiet a writer may appear, there is 'a truculent spirit' that scorns pathos. 'While strangers, perhaps, deem his existence a Polar winter never gladdened by a sun', the writer maintains his creative fire 'and is apt to laugh in his sleeve, when any misguided sympathizer whines over his wrongs'. He is able to cultivate 'merciless contempt'[8] for reviews. This passage confirms what Charlotte called her 'home' character: honest, outspoken, sarcastic, formidable in the act of judgement. Her power amused her, invisible as it was. For her, the true writer pre-empts the world's displeasure, turning from the world before the world can turn from her. She affirmed, 'It would take a great deal to crush me'.[9]

Here is a glimpse of the woman who walked invisible. Her life was shaped by ties with those to whom she revealed her nature, her sisters and schoolfriends; and shaped too by men who could not sustain her emergence. The distress caused by M. Heger and George Smith was not because they could not know her, but because of their promise: they invited her to a tantalizing partial emergence and then withdrew when she voiced notes alien to their sense of fitness. Only in novels did she emerge fully; there, alone, did she call up men adventurous enough to give assent to the woman to be.

What such a woman was to be remained in the making, as her energy and passion surged forward, inexorably, through Charlotte Brontë's works. What then is the nature of women? This is the overwhelming question she left behind, and any answer remains, as yet, uncertain: to some a shadow of obscurity, to others a shadow of promise. Pause, she said at the end of *Villette*, pause again. This indeterminate shadow is the vital centre of women's lives.

The life of Emily Dickinson also turns on the dichotomy of public and private, the tension between the coyness of her dated little 'Daisy' persona and her hidden power. In a room of her own, in a small New England town, she conferred on herself the 'delirious charter' to explore the eruptive ground of her interior life. In her domestic seclusion, white dress, and daisy manner, it is a womanish life — but one that secretes another. In 1862 she takes us through the homey duties of her regulated day — putting new flowers in the glass and throwing the old away with the accepted little air of having so much to do; yet mild domesticity guards the 'Bomb' in her 'Bosom' for which no words exist but which she demonstrates with an explosion of dashes that break up the given language as she recounts that, some time back, 'Existence — stopped — struck — my ticking through — '.[10] This may have been the transforming experience in the letters of 1859–61, addressed to an unidentified 'Master', which suggest an impossible but strangely empowering form of love. To what extent can we understand this 'still — Volcano — Life — ' that flickers in the night when it is 'dark enough to do'?[11] The coral lips open and close on deeps still uncharted by readers from whom she demands some reciprocal venture. Can we advance into the inviting silence of what remains unstated in the dashes that push the language apart? Can we fathom the intransigence of a commitment to immortality that made only the most superficial concession to her own time and seems still to speak past us to the understanding of an age yet to come? Where the interest of Charlotte Brontë's life lies in the lone daring, the exposure to misunderstanding, and the honesty with which she opened up the nature of her sex, twenty years before Mill's treatise on *The Subjection of Women*, the interest of Emily Dickinson — a keen reader of the Brontës[12] — lies in her readiness to take the unseen space for granted in the great body of poetry which she termed her 'letter to the World'.[13]

Minny Temple left only a batch of letters and an ineradicable impression on a group of young men who summered at North

Conway, New Hampshire, just after the American Civil War. Amongst them was her cousin, the sole non-combatant, Henry James. He hovered, shy and silent, on the edge of that circle about a young woman who was 'ever the heroine of the scene'.[14] He spoke of 'noble flights' when, in after years, he recalled Minny's elevation of spirit in the face of her death at the age of 24, her longing to live and know, as well as her sifting of character in the Newport circle of their youth — an approach to character that was to shape his art.

He was not able to love her in the ordinary way, he told his brother William. To the end he had continued to hope to take the lead in a 'masculine' way but allowed himself to be prevented by recurrent 'invalidism'.[15] But when the woman of flesh passed away, James could possess her in a strange posthumous relationship: 'Twenty years hence we shall be living with your love and longing with your eagerness and suffering with your patience.' He told William: 'I could shed tears of joy far more copious than any tears of sorrow when I think of her feverish earthly lot exchanged for this serene promotion into pure fellowship with our memories, thoughts and fancies.'[16]

Decades later, the ageing Henry and William James would agree that in the course of their lives they never again met anyone like her. In her time, she was uncategorizable; like Charlotte Brontë and Dickinson, a portent of women yet to be. A tide of recollections would rise and return in James's mind: her swift, sliding gondola step; her wide laugh; her instinct for truth of character; her care for the play of life in others; her leading him on to understanding — her nuance of suggestion; above all, her appetite for life, even as she was forced to withdraw from it. Unchanged in the crystal walls of memory, Minny could take up a suitably distant and undemanding role as secret sharer of several of James's works.

In contrast with women who used their own experience to define their nature, here is the view of a man who withdrew from life to make the most of an objective, even spectatorial stance. To what extent was this a valid, even necessary perspective? To what extent was there something questionable in the posthumous 'fellowship' to which James promotes Minny Temple — that returning ghost who feeds his imagination, and, at the same time, haunts him with regret for an unlived life? Yet this curious relationship did promote Minny as co-author of a new exemplar from the New World, a source for Bessie Alden in 'An International Episode' (1878), for Isabel Archer in *The Portrait of a Lady* (1881), and two decades later, for the dying Milly Theale, with her longing for life and extraordinary elevation, exercising her generous spirit from beyond the grave, in *The Wings of the Dove* (1902).

In the second volume of his autobiography (1914), James gives us his final image of Minny, this time unmediated by fiction: she had been, in short, the real-life 'heroine' whose rare sensibility had made her unlike anyone else. It is perhaps the most sensitive portrait any man has done of a woman, as the old James, forty-five years after Minny's death, takes us through his deeply studied analysis of her last, dauntless letters.

In contrast with Minny's literally buried life (rising only in James's imagination), Olive Schreiner exemplified a fully risen and wholly visible woman: a speaker on platforms, defending the underdog, be it the Boers during the Anglo-Boer War, Blacks when they were denied the vote in the newly united South Africa in 1910, or her own struggling sex. One of her attractions is the startling directness of a voice that seems to come straight from her soul in *The Story of an African Farm* (1883) and in *Woman and Labour* (1911). She was born on a remote mission station on what was then the Cape border, and hers is a missionary voice turned to prophecies of women to be. Her forward-looking *Dreams* (1890), written in England, is located in the African landscape of her past: flat brown earth stretching to far horizons; fierce heat that throbs slowly against the skin; dust drying the nostrils. '. . . The effect of this scenery is to make me so silent and strong and self-contained,' she wrote, 'and it is all so bare, the rocks and the bushes, each bush standing separate from the others, alone by itself.'[17] She would be renewed 'with a sense of wild exhilaration and freedom.'

So, for long periods, Schreiner had to return to the wide, empty veld, broken only by the *koppie* [hillock] where the heroine of the *African Farm* goes to read, think, and question the position of women in society. Schreiner herself remains in some ways more interesting than her platform positions which take us back to the past: back to Rhodes against whom she shut her door when he visited her outpost on the veld at Matjiesfontein, back farther to feminist, socialist, and free-thinking circles in late-Victorian London. But the woman herself speaks to the future, most clearly through her letters. For during the productive periods of her life she lived in lone places and depended on letters to explain herself and her setting to a large number of friends. She had, too, the gift of intimacy and spoke with unafraid candour, a woman without a mask.

As Schreiner used her native veld as the ground for self-discovery, so Virginia Woolf saw the lower waters as a challenge to exploration. In the talk she gave in 1931, she described the writer as a fisherwoman, unreeling her rod into the pool of consciousness. The line darts to the depths, but the rod of reason hauls her back, and she comes to the surface panting with rage and disappointment. 'How dare you', she says. 'Calm youself', admonishes the fisherwoman, for the time had not yet come when she could use the strange knowledge, about women's bodies, for instance, from the lower waters.

Between 1908 and 1912, as she composed her first novel, Virginia Woolf projects herself, through Rachel Vinrace, on a voyage of discovery. Looking down into the sea, Rachel imagines 'the great white monsters of the lower waters'[18] who would explode if brought to the surface. She herself is surfacing all through the novel, then dies before her shape is clear. Yet there is some promise in her brief existence for, though it cannot come to fullness of being, it suggests that whatever is latent in the species might emerge in some other, more viable specimen — like Virginia Woolf herself.

Madness marked this author's own point of contact with the buried self, when her imagination took to the lower waters and when, sometimes, it went too far for reason to haul it back. She was tempted to these risks because, as she put it, 'in the lava of madness I find my subjects'.[19] It was during the twenty dark years of Virginia Woolf's youth, the precarious period of recurrent breakdown, that she first ventured into the unknown region of a woman's life that lies between established forms of life. Psychologically, Virginia Woolf went further than her predecessors, and to venture into this territory of the mind took enormous daring, and exacted an enormous price. Her findings were tentative, as they must be for some time to come. *The Voyage Out* suggests it will take six generations for women to come into their own.[20]

Back in 1871, when George Eliot had looked at the blundering lives of women, she had concluded that, as long as their potentialities could not be determined with any accuracy, their social lot must remain in question. 'Meanwhile', she said, 'the indefiniteness remains'.[21] If biography is to face this indefiniteness, it means that the surface, collectable facts of women's lives — their social lot, their occupations, the platitudes in many of their letters, and even their set dramas of feeling and fantasy — will not suffice. Half a century later, in the course of Virginia Woolf's 'voyage out', she referred repeatedly to a glimpse of the fin of a submerged form in the waves. 'Why is there not a discovery in life?' she asked. 'Something one can lay hands on & say "This is it?" . . . I have a great & astonishing sense of something there.'[22]

Here is the biographical challenge we face when we embark on women's lives. Revising *Virginia Woolf: A Writer's Life* in 1991 confirmed my sense at the outset that there was no end to understanding her life. My solution was to see the renewed search as the central event, and that this search had its elusive source in what she called the 'night' as opposed to the 'day' of a visible life. Her search was conducted from the start through the perspective of a woman, and this aspect, too, I wished to elicit. One difficulty was to do justice to a feminism that was subtler and more complex than the feminism of the 1970s and 1980s which locked Virginia Woolf to a simplistic ideology of women's anger versus male power. Anger was strongly present in her life, but to give it undue prominence would have distorted her career in which a far-sighted and constructive ideology prevailed: a refusal of power itself, and a need to discover a nature that lies deeper than androgyny, showing only the fin of a submerged form. Future biographers will have to lend themselves to what is indefinable — the imaginative reach of this woman — rather than fall back on the well-known catalogue of abuses (sex abuse, obtuse doctors) which keeps readers to the straight highway of routine idea. Early in her career, Virginia Woolf devised a biographical parable called 'Memoirs of a Novelist' (1909) in which a well-meaning but misguided biographer buries her subject irretrievably beneath layers of extraneous fact which reveal only the biographer's set image of women's lives.[23] In another biographical parable, 'The Mysterious Case of Miss V.' (1906), the absence of Miss V. behind the frailest of habitual façades blurs into death.[24] In short, we must cast ourselves into the mystery of existence as alert women experience it; we must undertake the gaps, uncertainties, and so-called 'madness', inconclusive as they are, for there is no other route to full biographical truth.

On 23 November 1926 Virginia Woolf wrote in her diary: 'I am now & then haunted by some . . . very profound life of a woman, . . . & time shall be utterly obliterated; future shall somehow blossom out of the past.'[25] She would obliterate chronology by relating the lifespan within a single moment. If we could only seize that moment, biography might be transformed from a plodding genre into art — imaginative truth would inform the inevitable selection of factual truth with a profounder insight deriving from Wordsworth's conviction that 'One moment now may give us more / Than years of toiling reason'.[26] Virginia Woolf pushes this even further when she says, 'the actual event practically does not exist', and subversive as this may be of our craft, I fear it is, in a sense, so: we can have no access to an event which is not mediated by our consciousness. Unless we fall back on mere compendia of barren fact, biography will be subjective — even if it contrives to conceal that subjectivity.

Henry James, taking a detached position (subtle enough to question the validity of detachment), demonstrates how we might observe and reconstruct others' lives. He shows us how to make of the act of attention a complementary act of exploration: for him, perception of truth was as much an adventure as the spring of a beast in the jungle. The Jamesian observer, like the biographer, is not passive: what we come to know demands some sharing that is, in its own way, transforming. As James became the secret sharer in Minny's character and experience and, most important, in her sense for the possibilities of life, so we, too, might be sharers in the unknown aspect of others' lives — not sensation-seekers or higher gossips, but entering into these lives to the point where our own lives cannot remain entirely unchanged. As we plunge into the spaces that push the language apart in Dickinson's poems, we enter this indeterminate ground, emulating an act of introspection that will 'distill' for us, as for Dickinson, 'amazing sense'[27] from the life — *any* life. For all these women, professional artists as well as artists in life, imply that no life is too meagre, too bound by domestic limits, to be grounds for search. More explicitly than any previous writer, Virginia Woolf offered the reader this experience: 'In your modesty you seem to consider that writers are of different blood and bone from yourselves. . . . Never was there a more fatal mistake.'[28] Our insignificant lives are as much the material of biography, fiction, and poetry as those of writers; and as much in need of an act of understanding.

The hidden aspect of women's lives — in fact, all lives of the obscure — may require, then, more transgressive experiment if we are to answer a question I posed in *Shared Lives*, a memoir of three obscure women: what unrealized possibilities lie unnoticed behind the silence of women's lives in the outback of history, biography, and memoir, the standard records of the past? I had to transgress the established form of biography to devise an eclectic form which fused genres of letter, diary, oral history, public history, and dream, in order to give expression to the limited lives of women coming of age in the 1950s and 1960s within a South African society of maximum constraint and artifice. One way to register and erode the artifical structures of these three lives was to ask what women share in the interstices of the plots laid down for them by their society.

Women's lives deviate from the set stories of traditional biography. We are adept at stories, the approved stories our culture has produced: the romantic doomed-genius story (for the Brontës); the quaint-spinster story (for Emily Dickinson); the child-abuse/frigidity story (for Virginia Woolf). But what story will elicit the uncategorized ferment of hidden possibilities? What form do we give to the potent shadow in which women of the past lived? I have proposed, here, that what is most distinctive in women's lives is precisely what is most hidden — not only from the glare of fame, but hidden from the daylight aspect which women present for their protection or (as Dickinson suggested) for the protection of those who could not face the 'Bomb' in her breast.[29]

We must swerve, then, from the public highway to track through what George Eliot called 'the unmapped country within us'. Biography is a searching genre; it strives for infinite complexity, hesitant before obscurity of motive where the subject stands in shadow. We doubt and pause, confronted with the mystery of another's life. 'I'm Nobody!' said Emily Dickinson. 'Who are you?'[30] Poet and biographer meet on this indeterminate ground. What we hold to are their works. 'Art *makes* life', said Henry James, and through art (including the arts of living), Charlotte Brontë, Emily Dickinson, Minny Temple, Olive Schreiner, and Virginia Woolf come forward as practitioners and seers of a nature yet to be. If women's biography is a form in the making, it is dependent on these pioneers and others like them, who had the pluck to forge a route with their own lives.

These lives differ from those of the exemplars of the past: they swerved from the unnatural and, for the most part, unattainable perfections of the Virgin, the saint, the nun, or the perfect secular virtues of the Angel in the House. The emergent women were not flawless, but all the more interesting for the extent to which, like most of us, they struggled and failed and yet, unlike us, contrived to hold to some shape that lurks half-elusive, half-articulated, in the recess of our lives. Their self-discoveries and deviant aims led them to project a rising character, a still unrecognized creature who appeared to be crawling out from under the stone of history.

Notes

1. *The Pargiters* (London, 1977), p. xxxiii.
2. J. S. Mill, *The Subjection of Women* (1862; rev. 1869), repr. in John Stuart Mill and Harriet Taylor Mill, *Essays on Sex Equality*, ed. Alice S. Rossi (Chicago, 1970), ch. 1, 148.
3. *Villette*, ed. Herbert Rosengarten and Margaret Smith (1853; repr. Oxford, 1984), ii, ch. 27.
4. *Cassandra*, written in 1852, revised and printed privately 1859, Appendix to Ray Strachey, *The Cause: A Short History of the Women's Movement in Great Britain* (1928; repr. London, 1979), 407–8.

5. *Villette*, ii, ch. 17.
6. To William Smith Williams (4 Jan. 1848), *The Brontës: Their Lives, Friendships and Correspondence*, ed. Thomas J. Wise and J. Alexander Symington (Oxford, 1933; repr. 1980), ii. 174.
7. To William Smith Williams (4 June 1849), ibid. ii. 338.
8. *Shirley*, ed. Herbert Rosengarten and Margaret Smith (1849; repr. Oxford, 1979), i, ch. 4.
9. To William Smith Williams (4 Jan. 1848).
10. 'I tie my Hat', no. 443 in *The Complete Poems of Emily Dickinson*, ed. Thomas H. Johnson (London, 1970; repr. 1975), 212.
11. No. 601, ibid., 295.
12. Her books in the Houghton Library, Harvard, show that she was reading everything the Brontës published.
13. No. 441, *Complete Poems*, 211.
14. Henry James, *Autobiography*, ed. Frederick W. Dupee (Princeton, NJ, 1983), ii. 509.
15. *Letters of Henry James*, ed. Leon Edel, i, *1843–1875* (London, 1974), 224 (29 Mar. 1870).
16. Ibid. 228, 226.
17. To Havelock Ellis (5 Apr. 1890), *The Letters of Olive Schreiner*, ed. Richard Rive, i, *1871–1899* (Oxford, 1988), 168.
18. *The Voyage Out* (1915; repr. London, 1992), ch. 1.
19. To Ethel Smyth (22 June 1930), *The Letters of Virginia Woolf*, ed. Nigel Nicolson and Joanne Trautmann, 6 vols. (London, 1975–80), iv. 180.
20. *The Voyage Out*, ch. 16.
21. 'Prelude' to *Middlemarch*.
22. *The Diary of Virginia Woolf*, ed. Anne Olivier Bell and Andrew McNeillie, 5 vols. (London, 1977–84), iii. 62 (27 Feb. 1926).
23. *The Complete Shorter Fiction of Virginia Woolf*, ed. Susan Dick, 2nd edn. (New York, 1989), 69–79.
24. Ibid. 30–2.
25. *The Diary of Virginia Woolf*, iii. 118.
26. 'To My Sister', *Wordsworth's Poems*, ed. Philip Wayne (London and New York, 1955), i. 39.
27. No. 448, *Complete Poems*, 215.
28. 'Mr Bennett and Mrs Brown' retitled 'Character in Fiction', *The Essays of Virginia Woolf*, iii, *1912–24*, 436, ed. Andrew McNeillie (London, 1988).
29. 'I tie my Hat', *Complete Poems*, no. 443.
30. No. 288, *Complete Poems*, 133.

PART II

Some Individual Studies

John Wilmot, Earl of Rochester: An Author in Search of a Character

KEN ROBINSON

It would be odd if any biographer in the 1990s believed that biography is 'life without theory', that it is possible to see the subject's life as in itself it really was. From the philosophy of science through the social sciences to critical theory, the naïve conception of objectivity no longer has intellectual credibility. Biographers, of course, strive for the degree of accuracy that their art will allow, but what they write is in an important sense invention. If they are to do their job well they cannot avoid the drudgery of the Record Office and the Archives, but their real work starts when all the data is assembled: it is the work of giving a subjective or felt dimension to the material. Biographers are not biographers but chroniclers if they merely offer us the facts. What we look for from them is an understanding of what it felt like to be this person living through these events at this time. If they are lucky, biographers will have at their disposal autobiographical material in the form perhaps of letters or journals, which might give a flavour of the subject's life as experienced. Literary biographers will have in addition novels, plays, poems, or essays within which the author's personality and self are in some way inscribed. But such documents can pose as many problems as they might offer to resolve. It is the biographers' task to see beyond even this autobiographical evidence to find their own impression points and their own truths. Frank Kermode has written of the ways in which 'the pleasures of interpretation are . . . linked to loss and disappointment, so that most of us will find the task too hard or simply repugnant, and then, abandoning meaning . . . slip back into the old comfortable fictions of transparency and single sense, the truth'.[1] The biographer is no less prone to such disappointment than the exegete or literary critic but there is in the end no such thing as the definitive biography. Biography is a form of story-telling, like that special form of autobiography, psychoanalytic therapy, in which historical truth is established by what is narrated not by what actually happened. Schafer suggests that therapeutic narratives do not simply relate or elucidate what may actually have happened in the past; they also create the real experience of living by locating what is to be attended to and what is most signal. Real-life-as-experienced is a precipitate of the narrative rather than the other way round. Biographical truth we might equally say is established by what is narrated not by what actually happened. We expect it to be based on reliable evidence but its validity, like the validity of the psychoanalytic narrative as Schafer sees it, is finally an internal matter.[2] And, like the psychoanalytic narrative, it will be theory-laden. Different biographers, like psychoanalysts working from different theoretical foundations, will each offer a different felt life-history.

I have felt it particularly necessary to stress at the outset that biographies cannot be definitive because John Wilmot, Earl of Rochester (1647–80) throws up particular problems which face biographers at every turn with their prejudices. The chronicle of Rochester's life is relatively sparse and his *œuvre* is relatively small. Much of both is sensational, but both also present remarkable uncertainties. Such sparseness and uncertainty highlight the degree to which the biographer must take responsibility for creating a life; but they also offer a possible impression point. The uncertainties of the life and the canon are not mere accidents of history: they are evoked by, constitute a response to, and mirror something of Rochester the man, something which we can find reflected too in the difficulties critics have experienced with his poetry. In this paper I shall attend to this rather unconventional evidence for the light that it casts on the poet.

The uncertainties surrounding Rochester's life start literally *ab ovo*. He became the Earl of· Rochester as the son of the royalist General, Henry Wilmot, who had been instrumental in Charles II's escape from Worcester in 1651 and active in his service until his death in 1658. But it was said in some quarters that his father was not Henry Wilmot but his mother's cousin by marriage, Sir Allen Apsley, who became one of Rochester's legal guardians after Wilmot's death.[3] Given that his mother Anne had little opportunity to be with her exiled husband, it is neither surprising that rumours about his paternity should have circulated nor impossible that they were true. There can be no resort to DNA testing, no certain solution. But for my present purposes, who his father was is less important than the fact that Rochester's contemporary biographers saw fit to register doubt, though, as we shall see, it is important that he was raised as Wilmot's son. His contemporaries were equally confused about the date of his birth. Gilbert Burnet, his first biographer, gives it as April 1648. Burnet would almost certainly have shown his biography to Rochester's mother for her approval between writing it shortly after the poet's death and its publication in the same year.[4] We might, therefore, expect its date to be accurate; all the more so since it is repeated in Anthony à Wood's *Athenae Oxonienses*.[5] But the date that is normally accepted is that given by the astrologer Gadbury who claims to have got it from Rochester himself. According to Gadbury, Rochester was born at seven minutes past eleven on 1 April 1647 (though even Gadbury's evidence is not free from confusion).[6] It is oddly appropriate (and not only for the date of the start of the Newcastle conference, 1 April 1993) that Rochester should have been born on April Fool's Day on the eve of Charles II's succession. He would after all play the unofficial court jester so often, indulging and indulged by his monarch even when he was officially banished. It is in part because of his often spectacular career as court fool that some of his contemporaries as well as later biographers have found it difficult to believe that his death-bed repentance as a reformed rake and sinner could have been heartfelt and sincere. Here we meet the final uncertainty of his life. The fool they supposed had lost his senses. His friend William Fanshaw who visited him in his sickness certainly thought so, and he was not alone.[7] In his funeral sermon Robert Parsons felt it necessary to deny that the poet's 'Piety was the effect of madness or vapours'.[8] Amongst the modern biographers Pinto is more in line with Parsons, seeing the conversion as the end of a

long conflict, whilst Treglown emphasizes both 'his almost unendur-
able last illness [which] drove him out of his mind for considerable
periods of time' and the intense pressure he was under 'to repent
and to be seen to do so',[9] pressure not only from his mother but
from Burnet for whom Rochester's death had a potential political
dimension, as it did too for Halifax.[10] From conception to grave
Rochester's life is a puzzle. Larger than life as a courtier who in
Samuel Johnson's words 'blazed out his youth and his health in
lavish voluptuousness',[11] his escapades attracted to them a plethora
of apocryphal stories and gossip which are on the one hand difficult
for the biographer to sift but on the other, as we shall see,
symptomatic of the poet's characterology.

The problems facing those who have worked on the Rochester
canon are no less difficult. Famous for his obscene verses and satires,
his name was a magnet for a mass of often doubtfully and sometimes
erroneously attributed poems in both manuscript and print. The
title-page of the 1680 edition of his poetry, *Poems on Several
Occasions by the Right Honourable the Earl of Rochester* (Antwerp,
1680), symbolizes the difficulties which await the textual scholar
and the biographer. Despite its title-page the collection includes a
large number of poems which are not by Rochester, it was published in London not Antwerp, and it continued to appear in
different editions for some ten years under the same title-page. It
was not until David Vieth's magisterial *Attribution in Restoration
Poetry* appeared in 1963 that there was a large-scale systematic
attempt to sort out the canon. Vieth approached his task with a
rigour designed to exclude all poems from the canon about whose
authenticity there was reasonable doubt (though it is now recognized that some of his exclusions were made more on the basis of
his ear for Rochester's poetry than on the basis of hard scholarship).
Later editors like Keith Walker and most recently Paddy Lyons
have enlarged the canon,[12] restoring to it poems which Vieth would
not admit. The textual scholar of Rochester's work can easily find
himself drowning in 'doubt's boundless sea'. Vieth attempted
to set clear boundaries, Walker and Lyons render them less clear
but in so doing they offer a picture of the canon which better
represents the dubieties that accompany the man. One example

of the texts in question is the verse play *The Farce of Sodom, or The Quintessence of Debauchery* for which Lyons offers the first reliable text since the inception of modern Rochester scholarship. The history of its vicissitudes catches the flavour of Rochester's text in general as it comes down to us through the filter of his period. *Sodom* exists in several manuscript versions, none of which is authoritative but three of which ascribe it to Rochester. It is reputed to have been printed in 1684 and again in 1689. The 1684 publication — if it ever existed — appeared under a title-page bearing the date 1680 and proclaiming it to have been published in Antwerp, like the *Poems*. The publisher of the 1689 edition, Benjamin Crayle, was fined a massive £20 for libellously attributing it to Rochester.[13] It may be, as Lyons argues, that the prosecution was undertaken as part of 'the first effort to sanitise the canon of his works' which culminated in Tonson's relatively polite publication of the *Poems* in 1691,[14] but we cannot be sure, just as we cannot be certain about the authorship despite modern claims that it is indeed by Rochester. Probably written in 1672 and addressed to the Declaration of Indulgence *Sodom* is a political satire which uses obscene fantasy to attack the English court.[15] Charles, for example, becomes King Bolloximion and Buckingham becomes the Buggermaster-general Borastus. It satirizes those 'who declare their sin as Sodom, and hide it not, that take it upon their shoulders, and bind it to them as a Crown'. These are the words of Isaiah 3: 9 as quoted by Parsons in his funeral sermon to picture Rochester's brazen recommendations of sin. If *Sodom* is his, it is as much one of his 'Panegyricks upon Vice' as a satire.[16] It fits with poetry known to be by Rochester which offers pyrotechnic displays of obscene wit, which turn in upon themselves with a disgust that sits in uneasy tension with this bravura quality. *Sodom* might seem to show Rochester's hand but it might be another case of his notoriety attracting attributions which lack decisive authority even if they are in their own way informed about his style.

Rochester created himself as an icon, a myth, in his own lifetime: the icon of the libertine courtier and wit, man of fashion and womanizer which looks out from the Huysmans portrait. This self-fashioned myth lies behind all the uncertainties that I have been outlining, behind the apocryphal and behind dubious attributions. It is this mythic character which attracts conjecture and gossip and which fuels the problems of ascription. It invites the accretion of dubiety. Amidst this myth and all the uncertainties it gives rise to, it is difficult to locate the real Rochester. And the same is the case with his poetry. Whether we are looking at a poem like the 'Satyr' that is riven through with purposeful inconsistencies which militate against a settled solution to the debate it stages between traditional and new thinkers, or whether we are reading a lyric like 'All my past life is mine no more' which offers itself as both a lament for man's estate in a hard determinist universe and an excuse for inconstancy in such a way that it cannot be said to be either one or the other or both, it is impossible to find a single voice, set of opinions or values which we might regard as characterizing Rochester. The effect of the poetry is to play one voice off against another, doing society in different voices but never revealing Rochester's own. It engages the reader in what I have elsewhere called a kaleidoscopic series of reversals in which no sooner does the poem settle on a dominant note than it undermines it in an endless and recursive movement.[17] We might be tempted to think of this endless deferral from one position to another as an expression of Rochester's scepticism, as a way of embodying the classical idea that given any proposition, it is possible to take a variety of viewpoints on it, no one of which can be said to have priority over the others; but this would be to miss the point. It would be to reduce the dynamics of the experience of reading the poems to a consistent intellectual stance. Rochester's poems will not even allow us to rest in scepticism. They offer the illusion of possible certainty only to disillusion. In some of the satires and lampoons the poetry has its being not in its attack on particular historical figures but in the delicate balance between violence and art, a violence which threatens to become gratuitous, to break out of the poem's controlling art and to destroy it. The iconoclast who in 1675 could smash the glass phallic sundial which stood in Charles II's privy garden is also an iconoclast in poetry. This is evident in, for example, the obvious destruction of pastoral idealism in 'Fair *Cloris* in a Piggsty lay' in which the pastoral shepherdess becomes a masturbating pig-girl, 'huddled in dirt' like the morally idealistic scholiast of his 'Satyr'. But it is also manifest at the level of form, in the ways Rochester's poetry breaks the icons of stable poetic form, consistency, and linear resolution, whether that resolution be provided through logic or lyric. The anti-idealism of 'Fair Cloris' is disturbed by the notion that 'by her own Thumb between her leggs, / She's innocent and pleas'd' to set up a dialectic that is never resolved. And how thoughtful is this dialectic? Would it be appropriate to hear in the word 'innocence' a reference to the debate close to the hearts of the Church Fathers about which is preferable: fornication or masturbation? If we do hear an echo, does the poem engage seriously with questions of sexual morality or is it merely part of the wit of an educated *jeu d'esprit*? Rochester's poetry, like earlier Cavalier poetry, continually teases us with its possible depths. We cannot enter into them because to do so would be to lose touch with the witty surface, but nor can we deny them. It may be that the poetry is all surface, that it is like 'Upon Nothing' a paradox offered by an April Fool full of sense and nonsense signifying nothing. Critics, like April Fools, can easily get caught out by the bluff and double bluff of Rochester's work. And so can biographers.

The vicissitudes of the biography and canon, centring as they do on incertitude about the site of the man and his works, mirror something about Rochester, something endemic to his mythic self-presentation which is also there behind the complex refractions of his poetry. That something is his false-self personality. If critics and scholars have difficulty in tuning in to the Rochester beneath the myth, their difficulty reflects Rochester's own problems in tuning into himself or, to put it another way, his problems in living with a false self. The psychoanalyst D. W. Winnicott has written at length of the false-self system in which the false self is created to deal with a world which in some way represents a threat to the true self. The true self is associated with spontaneity, the false self with compliance. The false self is a way of presenting a face to the world but a face which is not integrated with the true self as a living reality. Such is Rochester's presentation of himself as a myth. Winnicott offers an aetiology which is based on the earliest infant–mother relationship in which, unlike the good-enough mother who 'meets the omnipotence of the infant and to some extent makes sense of it' time and again so that 'a True Self begins to have life',

> The mother who is not good enough is not able to implement the infant's omnipotence, and so she repeatedly fails to meet the infant gesture; instead she substitutes her own gesture which is to be given sense by the compliance of the infant. This compliance on the part of the infant is the earliest stage of the False Self, and belongs to the mother's inability to sense her infant's needs.[18]

Winnicott's true self cannot be easily pointed to as the persona of the false self can be; rather it is something felt at the core of the person, a sense of being alive and creative which is felt in relations with others in the world. Those who have developed a false self can easily feel a sense of futility, their life can feel imitative rather than spontaneous. It can feel phoney. It is open to us to hypothesize about the earliest stages of Rochester's false self but I prefer to start from one particular aspect of his false self which is clear for all to see, and that is his living through an identification with his father. The degree of identification is very marked. It points to Rochester as it were acting out a script written and already acted by his father (or at least by Henry Wilmot).

Briefly, Henry Wilmot was also something of a myth in his own time, not least because of his part in the escape from Worcester. He was the type of the Cavalier good-fellow. In Clarendon's words, he 'loved debauchery' and 'excessive good fellowship, (in every part whereof he excelled and was grateful to all the company'.[19] Indeed, according to a contemporary poem he was one of the leading 'gallants of the times' and a member of a poetry club. It is worth quoting lines from the poem because like Clarendon's description of Wilmot they might easily have been written of his son:

> Tis pleasure to drink among these men
>   For they have witt and valour good store,
> They all can handle a sword and a pen
>   Can court a lady and tickle a whore,
> And in the middle of their wine,

Discourse of *Plato* and *Arretine*.
And when the health comes fall-down on their knees,
And hee that wants, cry, *to me boys to mee*.[20]

There is no need, I think, to expatiate on the point-by-point similarity between father and son suggested by these lines, but it is perhaps worth noting that Rochester also discourses of 'Arretine' in 'A Ramble in Saint James's Park' and in *Doctor Bendo's Bill*. First, in the service of the Queen and then as one of Charles II's closest advisers, Wilmot drank hard, ran up debts, and was not slow to draw his sword in a dispute. When his son was six months old he was, for example, embroiled in a duel with Lord Digby in which he was wounded. In 1649 he was created Gentleman of the Bedchamber to Charles II as his son would be sixteen years later. And in 1652 he was elevated to Earl of Rochester. His son saw very little, if anything, of him, but Hyde, who clearly felt that Wilmot did not take enough interest in his family, wrote to him in Germany in 1653 mentioning that his son now in Paris with his mother was anxious for letters from him. John was, he told Wilmot, an excellent boy who deserved his father's fondness for him.[21] Anne had travelled to Paris in what seems to have been an abortive attempt to see her husband, but absent though his father was, Rochester was raised as Wilmot's son, the son of the legendary figure of Worcester, of a man used to danger, to donning disguises (though sometimes he scorned them) and used to moving under false names. He appears to have complied with the role set him by his father and perhaps required by a mother who, because she had to make do with her husband's son whilst her husband was away, replaced his needs with hers. He would drink heavily — he told Burnet that 'for five years together he was continually Drunk';[22] he would tickle whores, duel, run up debts, show courage in the face of danger in action at sea in 1665 and 1666, and serve his King. And he would revel in disguise, as a porter, or as a beggar, or 'in odd shapes',[23] most notably as an Italian mountebank, practising under the name of Alexander Bendo for several weeks. According to Burnet he delighted in disguise. Perhaps it gave him a curious freedom to own the phoniness that was latent in his false self.

Something of this freedom finds expression in the paradoxical wit of *Doctor Bendo's Bill*:

if I appear to anyone like a counterfeit, even for the sake of that, chiefly, ought I to be construed a true man? Who is the counterfeit's example? His original; and that which he employs, he employs his industry and pains to imitate and copy. Is it therefore my fault if the cheat, by his wits and endeavours, makes himself so like me, that consequently I cannot avoid resembling him?[24]

The myth that Rochester created for himself, based on his father, trapped him. Once it was established he had to keep up to it. His life and poetry show him forever within it but registering its futility and pushing it and himself to the point of extinction. There is the ironic acting out of a role in 'To the Post Boy', which Treglown has described as 'a real-life adoption of the role of a villainous Renaissance stage malcontent',[25] as well as the life it alludes to which brought him disease, considerable pain, and an early death. Or there is the iconoclasm turned upon himself as an icon, the reduction of rakish potency to premature emission in 'The Imperfect Enjoyment' or to slavery 'to such a bitch as Willis' in 'On Mistress Willis'. And there is the abject disillusionment at human reason in the 'Satyr'. Winnicott warns that there is a 'not infrequent tie-up between the intellectual approach and the False Self. When a False Self becomes organized in an individual who has a high intellectual potential there is a strong tendency for the mind to become the location of the False Self.' Rochester's biographers do not doubt his intellectual potential. In his 'Satyr' he employs that intellect to attack itself, registering the futility of reason as the locus of the false self. Individuals like Rochester who in Winnicott's terms 'destroy themselves one way or another, instead of fulfilling promise . . . invariably produce a sense of shock in those who have developed high hopes' of them.[26] Even allowing for the rhetoric of the funeral sermon, Parsons's is shot through with precisely this sort of dismay and it surfaces occasionally in the critics. This sense of shock is all the more likely because Rochester could stand at such ironic distance from his false-self persona but was unable to escape it, though he did search for a site for a true-self experience, for a character with which he felt internally integrated at the core, recognizing in animals the possibility of spontaneity he could not find in himself. Perhaps too he hoped to find something of it away from the court in the country, but all too often he found himself as encarcerated by his myth in Oxfordshire as he did at Whitehall. The emphasis is upon experiencing the brittleness of the façade of the false self rather than on self-discovery just as the emphasis of the poetry is upon the shattering of certainties. He told Parsons of how once having been 'the principal Disputant against God and Piety' at an 'Atheistical Meeting', and having 'received the applause of the whole company', he 'was terribly struck' by the insincerity of his pose.[27] Parsons presents the experience as the first stage of his recantation, but what are we to understand by his death-bed conversion? Did he at last manage to drop something of the myth and feel in touch with a true self? Both Parsons and Burnet report on the effect that Isaiah 53 had on him when Parsons read it to him. It was so great in fact that he committed the whole chapter to memory. It affected him not just rationally but by 'an inward force upon him'. Commenting on the second verse he said, according to Burnet, that 'the meanness of [Christ's] appearance and Person has made vain and foolish people disparage Him, because he came not in such a Fools-Coat as they delight in'.[28] We might understand him to be referring to experiencing a true self free from acting the court fool on its 'gawdy guilded Stage', but the constraints that both clergymen might have put on him in their desire to convert him, not to mention the pressure from his mother, should make us cautious about assuming too much. It is just as possible that he substituted one form of compliance, to the icon he had created himself as, for another.

There is no better illustration of the false-self system that Rochester found himself imprisoned in than the Huysmans portrait. Rochester looks out from the canvas dressed in all the finery that befits him as an icon of the rakish courtier and wit. His eyes fix the observer with a look that seems a mixture of defiance and sadness. In his right hand he holds a crown of bays which he is about to place upon the head of his monkey and the monkey in its turn is handing back the products of reason in the form of, we may suppose, some of Rochester's verse torn from the volume it holds. It sits upon books on a table. Also on the table are further scraps of torn manuscript. Between them, poet and monkey present and render futile the icon in a canvas which takes the eye from the poet's face, along his right arm to the crown, down through the line of the monkey and its tail, around to Rochester's left hand holding yet more manuscript and up to his face in a circular movement that emphasizes the emptiness of the icon.[29] If we compare it with Max Pollack's 1914 etching of Freud at his desk this emptiness will become all the more apparent. In Pollack's etching the onlooker's eyes, arrested by Freud's gaze which penetrates out beyond his desk and the frame of the portrait, move back to some of Freud's 'valuable treasures'. Shadowy and powerful in silhouette, like the deeper levels of the unconscious, they look in upon him and inform his gaze. Like the Huysmans portrait the etching sets up a circular movement, looking out and looking in, but here the movement shows not the outer persona as an empty shell but the inner and outer as integrated. It embodies the complex dynamics of inner in relation to outer in Freud as man and analyst, binding together personal and professional. Freud's idea that 'everyone possesses in his own unconscious an instrument with which he can interpret the utterances of the unconscious in other people'[30] might stand as its epigraph. If we were to put an epigraph to the Huysmans it might be the opening lines of the 'Satyr', remembering that reason is here the location of the false self:

> Were I (who to my cost already am
> One of those strange prodigious Creatures *Man*)
> A Spirit free, to choose for my own share,
> What Case of Flesh, and Blood, I pleas'd to weare,
> I'd be a *Dog*, a *Monkey*, or a *Bear*,
> Or any thing but that vain *Animal*,
> Who is so proud of being rational.

Notes

1. Frank Kermode, *The Genesis of Secrecy: On the Interpretation of Narrative* (Cambridge, Mass. and London, 1979), 123.
2. Roy Schafer, 'Narration in the Psychoanalytic Dialogue', in W. J. T.

Mitchell (ed.), *On Narrative* (Chicago, 1981). Cf. Paul Ricoeur, 'The Question of Proof in Freud's Psychoanalytic Writings', *Journal of the American Psychoanalytic Association*, 25 (1977), 835–71.

3. See *The Life and Times of Anthony à Wood*, ed. A. Clark, 5 vols. (Oxford, 1891), iv. 476, and *Parochial Collections [First Part] made by Anthony à Wood and Richard Rawlinson*, ed. F. N. Davis (Oxford, 1920), 277.

4. Gilbert Burnet, *Some Passages of the Life and Death of the Right Honourable John Earl of Rochester* (London, 1680).

5. Anthony à Wood, *Athenae Oxonienses*, ed. P. Bliss, 3 vols. (London, 1813–20), iii. 1231.

6. John Gadbury, *Ephemeris or a Diary* (London, 1695), p. xxiii. For the confusion see, for example, Johannes Prinz, *John Wilmot Earl of Rochester: His Life and Writings* (Leipzig, 1927), 22 and n., and *The Letters of John Wilmot Earl of Rochester*, ed. Jeremy Treglown (Oxford, 1980), 5 n.

7. See Johannes Prinz, *Rochesteriana: Being Some Anecdotes Concerning John Wilmot, Earl of Rochester* (Leipzig, 1926), 57–8.

8. Robert Parsons, *A Sermon Preached at the Funeral of the Rt Honourable John Earl of Rochester* (Oxford, 1680), 33.

9. Vivian de Sola Pinto, *Enthusiast in Wit: A Portrait of John Wilmot, Earl of Rochester, 1647–1680* (London, 1962); *Letters*, ed. Treglown, 36.

10. See H. C. Foxcroft, 'Some Unpublished Letters of Gilbert Burnet', *Camden Miscellany*, xi (1907), and D. L. Poole, 'Some Unpublished Letters of George Savile, Lord Halifax, to Gilbert Burnet', *English Historical Review*, 26 (1911), 535–42.

11. Samuel Johnson, *Lives of the English Poets*, ed. G. Birkbeck Hill, 3 vols. (London, 1905), i. 221.

12. *The Poems of John Wilmot, Earl of Rochester*, ed. Keith Walker (Oxford, 1984), and *Rochester: Complete Poems and Plays*, ed. Paddy Lyons (London, 1993).

13. See Larry Carver, 'The Texts and the Text of *Sodom*', *Papers of the Bibliographical Society of America*, 73 (1979), 19–40, and D. S. Thomas, 'Prosecutions of *Sodom*: Or, the Quintessence of Debauchery . . .', *Library*, 5th ser. 24 (1969), 51–5.

14. *Complete Poems and Plays*, ed. Lyons, 314.

15. See Richard Elias, 'Political Satire in *Sodom*', *Studies in English Literature*, 18 (1978), 423–38.

16. Parsons, *A Sermon*, 9.

17. Ken Robinson, 'The Art of Violence in Rochester's Satire', in Claude Rawson (ed.), *English Satire and the Satiric Tradition* (Oxford, 1984).

18. D. W. Winnicott, 'Ego Distortions in Terms of True and False Self', *The Maturational Processes and the Facilitating Environment* (London, 1965), 145.

19. Edward Hyde, 1st Earl of Clarendon, *The History of the Great Rebellion and Civil Wars in England*, ed. W. D. Macray, 6 vols. (Oxford, 1888), iii. 203.

20. *Wit Restor'd in Severall Select Poems Not formerly publish't* (London, 1658), 16–17.

21. *Calendar of the Clarendon State Papers*, ed. W. D. Macray *et al.* (Oxford, 1886–1932), 15 Aug. 1653.
22. Burnet, *Life and Death of Rochester*, 12.
23. Ibid. 27–8.
24. *Complete Poems and Plays*, ed. Lyons, 119.
25. *Letters*, ed. Treglown, p. 2.
26. Winnicott, 'Ego Distortions', 144.
27. Parsons, *A Sermon*, 23.
28. Burnet, *Life and Death of Rochester*, 142.
29. For a fine discussion of this portrait see Anne Righter, 'John Wilmot, Earl of Rochester', *Proceedings of the British Academy*, 53 (1967), 47–69.
30. *The Standard Edition of the Complete Psychological Works of Sigmund Freud*, trans. James Strachey, 24 vols. (London, 1953–74), xii. 320.

🐾 8 🐾

Conrad's Truancy

JOHN BATCHELOR

Literary criticism within the academy, since (at least) the American
New Criticism of the 1940s and 1950s, has regarded biography as at
best a humble adjunct and at worst an intrusive enemy of its
activity. I take it that the patristic texts which supported the New
Critics and which still underlie literary theory's desire to disengage
the author from the text are the famous essays by Wimsatt and
Beardsley, 'The Intentional Fallacy' and 'The Affective Fallacy'.[1]
These critics sought to belittle 'biographical or genetic inquiry' by
saying that it was undertaken 'in the spirit of a man who would
settle a bet' and that its tendency was to 'confuse' the distinction
between 'the poem and its origins' and to cause the poem or work
of art 'as an object of specifically critical judgement' to 'disappear'.
As I say in the Introduction to this volume, I believe that the
reading of literary biography gives us a process different from that
indicated by the New Critics, one in which literary understanding
is progressive. We read the work. Then we read the biography.
Then we read the work again and we see more.

The leading academic literary biographer of the century has been
Richard Ellmann, whose lives of Joyce and Wilde achieved both a
wide audience and high intellectual repute. What were all his
readers looking for? Hostile reviewers of Ellmann's books have
suggested that his readers were attracted by 'the higher prurience',
and there can be no doubt that Ellmann was interested in his
subjects' sexual behaviour. Ellmann wanted us to know, for example, that Joyce was in a way a sexual masochist who was tormented
by the notion that Nora might cuckold him and who also desired
the humiliation that cuckoldry would involve.[2] Ellmann also
wanted us to know that Wilde's preference with his male partners

was for oral and intercrural rather than anal sex, and that Wilde's affairs with Robbie Ross, John Gray, and Lord Alfred Douglas ran in parallel with his taste for the dangerous pleasures of rough trade. Do we need to know these things? On one level we do not. But, as John Sutherland has said, 'it is not entirely prurience that drives one's curiosity about James Joyce's fascination with the turd'.[3] While the works of art obviously exist independently of biography, literary understanding of those works can be seen as progressive: the works are illuminated by the lives. For example, in the 'Sirens' episode of Joyce's *Ulysses*, at 4.00 o'clock in the afternoon of 16 June 1904, Leopold Bloom is having a late meal in the Ormond Hotel, knowing that his wife Molly is keeping her tryst with Blazes Boylan. In this scene Bloom responds to songs of lost love and treachery — a tenor aria from an opera, *M'Appari* from Flotow's *Martha*, sung by Simon Dedalus, and a popular patriotic ballad sung by a bass, Ben Dollard — with a mix of pain and pleasure which is exquisite but puzzling. It is puzzling in that it prompts the following question: if Bloom is in some sense everyman, does the novel really do here what it seems to do, that is, dramatize sexual masochism as part of the nature of everyman? Knowledge of Joyce's personal ambivalence about his own putative cuckoldry allows us to say that the answer to that question is 'yes' and does, therefore, enrich our understanding of this scene. The biographical information cannot alter the text but it can lend additional depth, resonance, and colour to what is visible on the written surface at this point.

Ellmann's kind of minute enquiry into such things as sexual deviation and psychological disturbance has probably become the norm rather than the exception now among biographers, but with many subjects it is hard to reconstruct the fine grain of the life in terms that make sense. John Ruskin, for example, may have been inverted as well as paedophile. He was obsessed with little girls and with food and power but he also seems to have been greatly attracted to other men, especially Millais and Rossetti — and for many of the last thirty years of his life he was mad. That is an unacceptably broad statement, but it is hard to express the matter more precisely: the subject is dead and not available for interview,

1. Louis MacNeice.

2. William Wilkie Collins, by Sir John Everett Millais, 1850

3. Lord Rochester, attributed to J. Huysmans.

4. Sigmund Freud at his desk. Etching by Max Pollak, 1914.

5. Joseph Conrad.

6. Virginia Woolf, London 1939. Photo Gisèle Freund

7. Aldous Huxley.

8. Matthew Arnold. Photograph by Camille Silvy, 1861.

9. Emily Tennyson, by G. F. Watts.

10. D. H. Lawrence, *c.* December, 1908.

and the terms of late twentieth-century discourse are unsatisfactory. 'Inverted' and 'paedophile' are too clinical, and 'mad' is too general, and none of Ruskin's biographers — John Rosenberg, John Dixon Hunt, and Tim Hilton[4] — has yet constructed a coherent portrait of Ruskin's temperament.

A similar difficulty is presented by Joseph Conrad. When he was 20, in 1878, Conrad shot himself through the chest in Marseilles; later he represented this injury as the result of a duel and his earlier biographers took him at his word and reiterated the duel story. He lied about the duel for what can be seen as compelling reasons for a young man coming from Polish aristocratic and Catholic culture, where to be known to have attempted suicide would have involved a catastrophic loss of honour. The duel story retained its currency in Conrad biographies until the discovery of a letter (in the 1950s) from Conrad's uncle, Tadeusz Bobrowski, which gives a circumstantial account of the suicide attempt. Subsequent biographers, notably Jocelyn Baines, Frederick Karl, and the Polish scholar Zdzisław Najder,[5] have revised the story. Najder succeeds in doing for Conrad what the other scholars whom I have named have failed to do for Ruskin: he uses late twentieth-century discourse to explore the psychology of a writer who is dead and cannot be interviewed, and he comes up with a reading which seems to fit all the facts. Najder shows that Conrad suffered from clinical depression throughout his life; that his suicide attempt is part of the same condition that caused the agonizing writing blocks which delayed his productivity as a novelist and underlay the full nervous breakdown that he suffered when he had finished writing *Under Western Eyes* — this was an episode in 1910 in which Conrad became very disengaged from reality and lay in bed conversing in Polish with the characters of his novel while his English wife Jessie tried in vain to persuade him that the people to whom he thought he was talking were products of his own mind.

Najder's book is a narrative or 'chronicle', not a critical biography. My own task, in my book *The Life of Joseph Conrad*,[6] has been to describe as accurately as I can the relationship between the life, in all its anguish, and the works of art. This activity is a variant of the higher prurience in that it is driven in a way by the same need, the need to possess oneself of the fine grain of the writer's nature. This kind of prurience has hazards. One of the problems of reading extensively in the letters and manuscripts as well as in the published work of a depressive personality is that one becomes infected to some extent by the subject's characteristics: in the case of Conrad, by his agonizing reluctance to write, to get on, and also by his tendency to set up impossibly high objectives for himself and then castigate himself for the inevitable failure which follows.

Conrad — Józef Teodor Konrad Nałezc Korzeniowski — was born of Polish gentry in the Ukraine in 1857 at a time when Poland, as a country, did not exist. He was orphaned at the age of 11 because his parents died as a direct result of punishment that they had received for their part in a Polish insurrection against Russian rule in 1863. He became the ward of his uncle, Tadeusz Bobrowski. These facts contain a psychodrama: Apollo Korzeniowski, Conrad's father, survived in his imagination as a role model whose leading characteristics were honour, courage, romanticism, and patriotism, and, also, high literary endeavour — Apollo Korzeniowski was a poet and playwright and had translated Shakespeare and Dickens into Polish. Uncle Tadeusz was by contrast perceived as a pragmatist and an appeaser, a man who was seen by his enemies as having collaborated with the Russians and thus hung on to his fortune. To the young Conrad he offered an entirely different role model; a figure who had perhaps compromised his honour but had worked out a strategy for survival in almost impossible circumstances.

Conrad as a child and early teenager suffered from an illness which was thought until he was 14 to be epilepsy, and was clearly a nervous disorder — it is hard to be more specific than that. At the age of 16 he left Poland to join the French merchant marine — the background to this is obscure, and Uncle Tadeusz clearly had mixed feelings about it, but it's likely that one reason why his family acquiesced in this is that it was felt to be good for Conrad's health. When he was in France Conrad enjoyed himself and got heavily into debt which got him into trouble with Uncle Tadeusz (Uncle Tadeusz gave him a handsome allowance, and there was never any question of Conrad being expected to live on a sailor's wages: he was to live as a gentleman). At the age of 20, as we have seen, Conrad shot himself. An immediate effect of this suicide attempt was that Uncle Tadeusz came to Conrad's rescue and paid off all his debts. Depressives do engage in manipulative behaviour, and obviously a suicide attempt which forces an authority figure to bail one out is a successful piece of manipulative behaviour. It is also, I think, an early mark of collision between Conrad's two role models: a willingness to resort to extremes rather than take temperate measures, Korzeniowski behaviour as against Bobrowski behaviour.

Shortly after this Conrad took the step which brought him into English culture and made him — in due course — into an English, as against a French or Polish, novelist: he joined the British merchant marine. His immediate reason for doing this was reactive: France signed a treaty with Russia under which Conrad would become subject to Russian military service and since his father had been a Russian political prisoner the terms of that service would have been long and harsh. He was a British sailor for sixteen years, more or less, and the popular view of his life's shape is that he was a career sailor who became a writer more or less by accident. My own view is that he was always a writer by vocation but that the seemingly undirected years in the merchant marine were beneficial to a man of depressive temperament. The merchant marine conferred status on him by the fact of being an officer (and thus a 'gentleman') and it enabled him to put off taking decisions about the direction of his own life, and to cherish a self-image independent of the facts. This self-image was always based on the circumstances of his Polish childhood and of those early role models, the flamboyant, risk-taking, literary, romantic father and the rich, temporizing, prudent, and pragmatic uncle. He was predisposed by these models to see himself both as a visionary and as a man of letters and also as a nobleman with a hereditary entitlement to wealth and status. Until 1914, when *Chance* became a commercial success, wealth and status — status in the sense both of social acceptance as a gentleman among English people and of literary recognition — eluded him, and this reinforced his low self-esteem. As an officer of the merchant marine he could dream of these things. During his sea years he read a great deal, in French[7] and English, and for the last five of those years — from 1889 to 1894 — he was writing *Almayer's Folly*. There are reflections of the depressive Conrad in the anti-heroes who appear in the novels of his first five years of writing life: the split between self-image and reality, the impossibly high objectives and the corresponding escapism and self-delusion, are characteristic of Almayer in *Almayer's Folly*, of Willems in *An Outcast of the Islands* and, especially, of Jim in *Lord Jim*. (In the cases of Almayer and Willems one can add from the list of depressive characteristics mendacity and manipulative behaviour, and in the case of Jim one can add suicide. Other more or less depressive Conrad figures who commit suicide include Decoud in *Nostromo* and Heyst in *Victory*.) But the link between the depression and the art is not only, and indeed not primarily, a matter of reflection or mimesis. It is also a matter of what I call an adversarial split between the neurotic who acts out his suffering and the artist who has — in the end — won for himself the confidence and strength to write the novels.

Conrad was an obsessional and spell-binding letter-writer, and the letters are in many cases lacerating displays of a suffering personality. He wrote to Edward Garnett on 31 March 1899; this was at a time when *Heart of Darkness* (or 'The Heart of Darkness' as it was then called) was appearing in serial form in *Blackwood's Magazine* and Conrad was well into the writing of *Lord Jim* (which had been interrupted for the writing of *Heart of Darkness*). In other words, with hindsight we can see that at this date the novelist was at the height of his powers.[8] He wrote to Garnett now, partly seeking reassurance about the quality of *Heart of Darkness* (he wanted to know whether Garnett had seen Part III of the serialization in *Blackwood's Magazine*), and partly to apologize for apparently establishing a distance from Garnett. Like all his letters, this letter is part of an elaborately tessellated self-portrait — he is out to create an image of himself in the mind of the friend:

31st March, 1899.
in Sorrow and Tribulation
Dearest Garnett,
What do You think of me? Think I love you though I am a dumb dog or no better than a whining dog. There's not a bark left in me. . . . Have you seen p III [part three] of *H. of D.* [*Heart of Darkness*]? My dear fellow I

daren't send you my *M S*. I feel it would worry you. I feel my existence alone worries you enough. . . . Fact is I am not worthy to take up your thought. The more I write the less substance do I see in my work. The scales are falling off my eyes. It is tolerably awful. And I face it, I face it but the fright is growing on me. My fortitude is shaken by the view of the monster. It does not move; its eyes are baleful; it is as still as death itself — and it will devour me. Its stare has eaten into my soul already deep, deep. I am alone with it in a chasm with perpendicular sides of black basalt. Never were sides so perpendicular and smooth, and high. Above, your anxious head against a bit of sky peers down — in vain — in vain. There's not rope long enough for that rescue.[9]

The self who writes this letter is depressive in two distinct ways. He is suffering from depression. Also, he *knows* that he is suffering from depression and uses that knowledge to characterize himself and thus to manipulate his friend into a relationship which I would call ambivalent: he wants both intimacy and distance, he feels the relationship with Garnett as a kind of power-struggle in which he seeks to extricate himself from a subordinate role. The monster and the deep pit are projections, I take it, of the terrible split between perceived ambition and perceived achievement. The monster is a mutation of the heroic self-image built on the paternal role model; when you sense that you are failing, this is what self-hatred can do to your self-image. And sufferers from depression do, typically, experience their suffering as being at the bottom of a shaft and cut off from human contact.

The remarkable thing is that Conrad can write all this down. And indeed many of his friendships look like psychotherapeutic relationships in which Conrad is more or less consciously seeking therapy, affirmation of his own identity and worth through inter-action with the friend. The letters become a kind of channel or conduit through which the novelist pours out his agony and seeks help, thus splitting off the mind which suffers from the mind which creates; the acting out of anguish protected a large part of his being which was thus cordoned off and liberated to write the novels.

Heart of Darkness can be seen as an important stage in a healing process, the work in which Conrad became strong enough to confront his own psychological illness. This reading is reinforced both by the circumstances of publication — it was a prestigious commission, for the thousandth number of *Blackwood's Magazine*, and that fact flattered Conrad and lifted his spirits — and by the appearance of the manuscript of *Heart of Darkness*. This manuscript, now in the Beinecke Library at Yale, is written in pencil, clearly at great speed, and with a flow which argues confidence and buoyancy in the writer; and I think that this momentarily lifted writer finds the will to confront a symptom of depression. Depression leads to disengagement from reality, and *Heart of Darkness* explores this disengagement and displays one well-known way of dealing with it. As Freud wrote in *Civilization and its Discontents*: 'No other technique for the conduct of life attaches the individual so firmly to reality as laying emphasis on work; for his work at least gives him a secure place in a portion of reality, in the human community.'[10]

Freud's observation seems to be anticipated by Marlow's perception of work as therapy in *Heart of Darkness*: 'I don't like work — no man does — but I like what is in the work, — the chance to find yourself. Your own reality — for yourself, not for others — what no other man can ever know.'[11] For much of the text of *Heart of Darkness* 'reality' is that which *contrasts* with the experience encountered by Marlow. Mismatches between language and reality are noted by Marlow as he makes his journey: a code rooted in European law attaches to the Africans descriptive terms — 'enemies', 'criminals' — which are (to the Africans' perception) absurd. Kurtz's young Russian disciple adds to this list the word 'rebels' to describe Kurtz's victims, and there the mismatch for Marlow between language and reality becomes so intense that it detonates in mirth: 'I shocked him excessively by laughing. Rebels! What would be the next definition I was to hear? There had been enemies, criminals, workers — and these were rebels. Those rebellious heads looked very subdued to me' (p. 132). I think it is because his sense of himself is grounded in 'reality', thus (in the examples hitherto given) confidently known, that Marlow equates lying with death: 'You know I hate, detest, and can't bear a lie, not because I am straighter than the rest of us, but simply because it appals me. There is a taint of death, a flavour of mortality in lies'

(p. 82). To disengage language from reality — to tell lies — is to undo the self and court disintegration.

But Marlow does lie, of course, both by letting the mephistoph-elean brick-maker believe that he, Marlow, has influence at the Company's head office in Brussels and by assuring Kurtz's 'Intended' that her name comprised Kurtz's dying utterance. And his description of the first of these lies causes a kind of disturbance in the text as though that memory (of having lied) causes Marlow in the act of narrating to lose, momentarily, both his control of his narrative enterprise and his sense of self:

Do you see him [Kurtz]? Do you see the story? Do you see anything? It seems to me I am trying to tell you a dream. . . . It is impossible to convey the life-sensation of any given epoch of one's existence — that which makes its truth, its meaning — its subtle and penetrating essence. . . . We live, as we dream — alone . . . (p. 82)

This knowledge — that the apparently secure and confident self can be experienced as isolated and unstable — presses upon the reader as he or she moves through the text of *Heart of Darkness* until it becomes what I would refer to as the novella's alternative reality, the reality experienced by Marlow when, in the course of his great dialogue with Kurtz, he finds himself plunged into a condition of moral relativity. This I see as the point at which Conrad confronts his own psychological illness most courageously. Marlow recognizes that he, Marlow, resembles Kurtz more closely than anyone else. Marlow's word for this moral and epistemological ordeal is 'terror':

I had to deal with a being to whom I could not appeal in the name of anything high or low. . . . There was nothing either above or below him. . . . Confound the man! he had kicked the very earth to pieces. He was alone, and I before him did not know whether I stood on the ground or floated in the air. (p. 144)

As earlier, the act of narrating this past crisis precipitates in Marlow anxiety about his present authority as narrator: 'I've been telling you what we said . . . but what's the good? They were common everyday words . . . But what of that?' (p. 144). In his isolation Kurtz's soul (as distinct from his intelligence) has 'gone mad' and part of the terror for Marlow consists in having to understand that condition, 'to go through the ordeal of looking into [Kurtz's soul] myself' (p. 145). We may note the distance we have come from the earlier Marlow who was consoled by the therapy of work and the tangibility of facts. That earlier Marlow had taken comfort from *An Enquiry into some Points of Seamanship* (the dog-eared book belonging to Kurtz's Russian disciple) because its simple diction contrasted sharply with the complexity of his present experience: it gave him 'a delicious sensation of having come upon something unmistakably real' (p. 99). The ordeal of looking into Kurtz's soul has altered Marlow's perception of the 'real', an uncomfortable awareness of the slipperiness of language. Kurtz is a voice discoursing self-importantly ('My Intended, my ivory, my station, my river' (p. 116)) and Marlow moves seamlessly, as though propelled by his recollection of Kurtz's voice, from his description of Kurtz's spoken eloquence to an account of the split in 'reality' opening up in Kurtz's written eloquence, his report for 'the International Society for the Suppression of Savage Customs' which after seventeen pages of high liberal rhetoric deconstructs itself with its 'postscriptum': 'Exterminate all the brutes!' (p. 118). This exposure of a glaring contradiction within a single body of discourse has been part of Marlow's education. The encounter with Kurtz has forced him into a condition of moral relativity.

Kurtz dies with a phrase which is commonly taken to be a judgement on his own misdeeds:

Did he live his life again in every detail of desire, temptation, and surrender during that supreme moment of complete knowledge? He cried in a whisper at some image, at some vision — he cried out twice, a cry that was no more than a breath — 'The horror! The horror!' (p. 149)

My own view of this is that Marlow misreads Kurtz's last words. The answer to Marlow's question ('Did he live his life again', etc.) is, conceivably, 'No'. Later Marlow asserts that Kurtz 'had summed up — he had judged' and that his final cry is 'an affirmation, a moral victory' (p. 151). But how can Marlow be in a position to know this? Kurtz is, after all, a 'devil' who has 'taken a high seat among the devils of the land' (p. 116) and he may be inverting his moral vocabulary (like Milton's Satan, who says 'Evil be thou my good' (*Paradise Lost*, iv. 110)), and using the word 'horror' to describe that which he admires, enjoys, and hopes to have more of. Marlow has reached the limit of his new-found sophistication here: his moral and epistemological horizons have been extended but he is still the same old Marlow underneath and his moral conservatism and good nature (and British sense of decency) prevail. This makes him a limited narrator, like Emily Brontë's Nelly Dean or Henry James's Maisie. All that we as readers, looking over this limited narrator's shoulder at the dying Kurtz, can say confidently about 'The horror! The horror!' is that we don't know what is going on in Kurtz's mind and therefore we cannot say what his dying words mean.

When Marlow tells the 'Intended' that Kurtz's last words were her name he believes that he is telling her a lie, but in a sense he is telling her something close to his own perception of the truth, since he is convinced that Kurtz experienced a change of heart at the moment of his death: such a change might reasonably have included a revulsion from his African mistress and regretful recollection of the girl back home. Marlow has become a novelist: since there is no 'truth', no agreed interpretation of Kurtz's last words, the supposed 'lie' is not distortion but creation.

Heart of Darkness is a work in which Conrad confronts his own sense of the split between language and reality — which in him is a state of disengagement symptomatic of depression — and uses that split for artistic purposes. In doing so he secures command of his own anguished temperament and is thus able to create the great difficult novels of his major phase. Knowledge of his depressive illness can help us to account for the extraordinary shape of that major phase. Typically Conrad would set up impossible goals for himself and then punish himself for failing to meet them, and his reaction to self-imposed responsibility was to retreat, escape, lie, prevaricate, and procrastinate. We all do these things, but Conrad did them self-destructively and pathologically. The relationships between *Heart of Darkness* and *Lord Jim* and between *Lord Jim* and

The Rescue are emblematic of his career. He had received an advance to write *The Rescue* which it was his clear duty to get on with. He found himself blocked with *The Rescue* and wrote *Lord Jim* which began as a short story and developed into a novel. The writing of *Lord Jim*, in turn, was interrupted by the writing of *Heart of Darkness*, which also grew from its initially planned pattern. Typically, Conrad's greatest novels were the products of truancy from the novels that he was supposed to be writing. This became the pattern: Conrad would tell himself that he was writing a short story, and that short story would then grow into a substantial novel: *Lord Jim, The Secret Agent, Under Western Eyes, Chance, Victory*, and *The Rover* were all written this way. Conrad needed to disobey the secure, responsible people in his life who believed in obligation, contracts, and money in the bank, and to strike defiant, heroic, and romantic attitudes. In short, if we recall his childhood, he needed to reject Bobrowski behaviour in favour of Korzeniowski behaviour. Depression was his lifelong companion, and I believe that the route that he found from depression to achievement was delinquency. But a biographer of the dead cannot verify his or her diagnosis: Conrad is not available to be asked — even in the spirit of one who wishes to settle a bet — whether this reading is right. And, if Conrad were available for questioning, is it likely that he would tell the truth?

Notes

1. W. K. Wimsatt and Monroe C. Beardsley, 'The Intentional Fallacy' (1946) and 'The Affective Fallacy' (1949), repr. in David Lodge (ed.), *Twentieth Century Literary Criticism* (London, 1972), 334–58.

2. Frank Budgen quotes Nora Barnacle as saying: 'Jim wants me to go with other men so that he will have something to write about.' Ellmann adds: 'She seemed to have failed him in this wifely duty' (Richard Ellmann, *James Joyce* (1959; new edn., New York and Oxford, 1982), 445). In Joyce's play *Exiles*, Richard Rowan (who is partly a self-portrait of Joyce) remarks to his friend: 'In the very core of my ignoble heart I longed to be betrayed by you and by her.' Ellmann asserts that Joyce shared Richard's secret longing (p. 279).

3. John Sutherland, 'After Lives', *London Review of Books*, Nov. 1992, 8.

4. John Rosenberg, *The Darkening Glass* (London, 1963); John Dixon Hunt, *The Wider Sea* (London, 1982); Tim Hilton, *John Ruskin: The Early Years* (New Haven, Conn., 1985).

5. Jocelyn Baines, *Joseph Conrad* (1960; repr. Harmondsworth, 1971); Frederick Karl, *Joseph Conrad: The Three Lives* (London, 1979); Zdzisław Najder, *Joseph Conrad: A Chronicle* (Cambridge, 1983).

6. John Batchelor, *The Life of Joseph Conrad: A Critical Biography* (Oxford, 1994).

7. Just how much he read in French has recently been studied in detail by Yves Hervouet in *The French Face of Joseph Conrad* (Cambridge, 1990).

8. Garnett had helped Conrad to get going as a novelist and Conrad had been in the habit of submitting all his work for Garnett's scrutiny before publishing it — he had recently stopped this practice partly, I suspect, because he found Garnett's comments on the MS of *The Nigger of the 'Narcissus'* (published in 1897) unhelpful. Garnett made a large number of pencilled comments on this MS, often objecting to Conrad's dialogue as uncharacteristic of sailors, but Conrad adopted very few of the changes that Garnett recommended.

9. *Collected Letters of Joseph Conrad*, ed. Frederick Karl and Lawrence Davies (Cambridge, 1986), ii. 176–7.

10. Sigmund Freud, *Civilization and its Discontents* (London, 1930), 17.

11. *Youth, Heart of Darkness, The End of the Tether* (Dent Library edn., 1946), 85. All page references to *Heart of Darkness* in this essay are to this edition.

Virginia Woolf and Offence

HERMIONE LEE

The fact is the lower classes *are* detestable.[1]

On the tow path we met & had to pass a long line of imbeciles. . . . — It was perfectly horrible. They should certainly be killed.[2]

> 'The Jew having a bath,' she said.
> 'The Jew having a bath?' he repeated.
> 'And tomorrow there'll be a line of grease round the bath,' she said.
> 'Damn the Jew!' he exclaimed. . . .
> 'Do you share a bath with him?' he asked.
> She nodded.
> He made a noise like 'Pah!'[3]

Our verdict was that the crowd at close quarters is detestable; it smells; it sticks; it has neither vitality nor colour; it is a tepid mass of flesh scarcely organized into human life. How slow they walk! How passively & brutishly they lie on the grass! How little of pleasure or pain is in them! But they look well dressed & well fed; & at a distance . . . they had the look of a picture.[4]

One has to be so cheerful with the lower classes, or they think one diseased.[5]

The mothers of Pimlico gave suck to their young.[6]

[At the Parthenon] 'The Germans come out like things hidden in a pocket', I said.[7]

Went to Peace Conference, by way of a joke, yesterday, & saw several baboon faced intellectuals; also some yearning, sad, green dressed negroes & negresses, looking like chimpanzees brought out of their cocoanut groves to try to make sense of our pale white platitudes.[8]

I have just travelled Kensington High Street — which almost made me vomit with hatred of the human race. Innumerable women of incredible mediocrity, drab as ditchwater, wash up and down like dirty papers against Barkers and Derry and Toms. One was actually being sick or fainting in the middle of the street.[9]

Are you offended? I am. I feel, reading these extracts from Virginia Woolf's writings, a twinge of the nausea which affects both the observed and the observer in that last extract. These quotations illustrate feelings and attitudes which are given free play in her diaries and letters and which make themselves felt, less directly but discernibly, in her published work. Today they would certainly qualify as 'hate speech' or 'fighting words', terms used in the debate on political correctness to refer to offensive racist and sexist language in need of monitoring. It may well be that on the same campuses where censorious codes of permissible speech have been instituted, *A Room of One's Own* or *Three Guineas* are being taught as pioneering texts in women's studies programmes.

It is a transatlantic cultural peculiarity, though, that while political correctness is still perceived as a predominantly American phenomenon, it is in Britain, and not in America, that an old attack on Virginia Woolf as an unacceptable purveyor of hate speech has surfaced again. She is being represented as a writer who perpetrates offences — racism, anti-Semitism, malice, snobbery, and elitism — offences which, according to this line of attack, produce an enervated, precious, class-bound set of texts full of snobbish housewives picking at their *bœuf en daube* and being condescending to the lower classes.

The current attack on Virginia Woolf's incorrectness was ignited in January 1991 by Tom Paulin, on a Channel 4 series called *J'accuse*. Tom Paulin snarled through gritted teeth about Virginia Woolf's breathtaking bigotry, repellent prejudices, 'preening self-regard', and deeply conventional imagination. Woolf's anti-Semitism and misanthropy were illustrated by some of the examples I gave above; her imperialism, less convincingly, was attested to by Clarissa Dalloway's gushing enthusiasm for the British Empire in *The Voyage Out*, Lady Bruton's capacity for governing 'rude barbarian hordes' in *Mrs Dalloway*, and the Irish servant in that novel who whistles all day. An actress behind him read these illustrations, wrenched from their context, in as vitriolic tones as she could muster. 'Meet Virginia Woolf', Tom Paulin concluded, 'and you'll understand why England can never be a classless society.'

Tom Paulin's attack was echoed more recently by John Carey, who accounts for 'modernism' as a concerted movement by the literary intelligentsia in the early part of this century in this country to exclude the newly educated 'masses'. Virginia Woolf features as a detestable snob, identified as 'Clive Bell's sister-in-law' and thereby with his prescription for *Civilization* (about which she had great reservations) as 'conditions favourable to the preservation of the gifted few'.[10] In her argument with Arnold Bennett, John Carey's hero, she 'breathtakingly' appropriates to herself the knowledge of ordinary people in which he, Bennett, in fact, surpasses, and she is entirely deficient. Her 'self-deluding' 'loathing and fear' of the masses confirms her in her sense of difference and superiority.[11] Woolf's attitudes are identified with those of Wyndham Lewis, Wells, Lawrence, Eliot, and Pound. For instance, her attempt to imagine 'that anonymous monster The Man in the Street' is placed next to Pound's vision of the multitudes as 'a torrent of human excrement', what he calls 'Democracies electing their sewage'.[12] The politics of all these writers, grouped together (particularly their taste for eugenics) is found to be strikingly close to 'Hitler's most dearly held beliefs'.[13]

Reviews of John Carey's book were often critical, in some cases appalled, but I noted that whether or not the book was attacked, its views of Virginia Woolf — her 'cold snobbery',[14] her 'sick hatred',[15] — were mostly endorsed. Paulin's programme, too, met with some amused sympathy. In the last book published on Leonard and Virginia Woolf, by Peter Alexander, the index for Virginia Woolf's 'Character and Opinions' includes: anti-Semitism; chauvenism [*sic*]; cruelty, apparent; failure to understand people; homosexuals, scorn of; ignorance of working class; ignorance; patriotism, hatred of; racism; snobbery; social incompetence; strange appearance; weakness as novelist.[16]

Why has Virginia Woolf's offensiveness become an issue again, in this country? Possibly the continuing domination of masculine critics wielding literary axes (the sort of people Virginia Woolf most despised) in the universities and on the arts pages has something to do with it. Possibly the recent debates about high art versus popular culture have affected our readings of the influential modernists (as exemplified in the Arts Council's 1990s attempt to devise a strategy for the arts, the stand-off between Radio 3 and Classic FM, the arguments over the future of the BBC, and a spate of superficial discussions about the relative merits of Keats and Bob Dylan on *The Late Show*). Certainly this phase of cultural self-consciousness coincided with the coming out of copyright of Joyce and Virginia Woolf in 1991, which allowed for them to be polarized as representatives of democratic versus highbrow art. (The demotic figure of Leopold Bloom seems to outweigh, in this kind of discussion, the relative textual difficulties of, say, *Finnegans Wake* and *The Waves*.) And the valuable aspect of political correctness, increased sensitivities to minority rights, is infiltrating current literary judgements, most of all in the new and not-so-valuable wave of squeamishly puritan attitudes towards biography. Not many critics of Andrew Motion's scrupulously revealing life of the deeply incorrect Philip Larkin could allow themselves to say, like Anthony Burgess, 'There is something vaguely charming about the Larkin extremism. Of course, it is only words.'[17] *It is only words* is no excuse for a life, these days.

What is striking, though, about the current attack on Virginia Woolf for offensiveness, is that there is nothing new in it. There are famous examples of 'hate speech' against her and her elitist group from the 1920s onwards. Lawrence's 'black beetles',[18] Wyndham Lewis's 'select and snobbish club',[19] Lewis's vision of a 'very dim Venusberg indeed',[20] and Q. D. Leavis's 1938 class attack on *Three Guineas* in *Scrutiny*[21] are well known. This line of attack, though of course most prevalent in the 1930s, persisted throughout the 1950s. Two less well-known remarks on Virginia Woolf, both from 1955, provide examples. One is by John Berger, attacking both highbrow and lowbrow art in Britain as different forms of escapism from contemporary problems, and identifying Virginia Woolf with a new BBC radio soap-opera of female domestic life: 'There is the tittle-tattle of Mrs Dale's Diary and the tittle-tattle of the followers of Virginia Woolf.' Both, says Berger, are as sterile as each other.[22] The other is in a book on the English class system by T. H. Pear, a professor of psychology, defining intellectual snobbery: 'The names of writers believed to have derived inspiration from psychological sources — Pirandello, Joyce, Kafka, Virginia Woolf, Koestler, are freely used, together with those of "difficult" novelists, by an intellectual snob.'[23] The class attack on Virginia Woolf, or the enlisting of her name to make a point about British social divisions, has persisted in this country for half a century.

Since the 1960s, particularly in the States, feminist scholars have been rescuing Virginia Woolf from a minoritizing identification with an elite group and replacing her as a heroine of revolutionary socialist feminism. The gigantic programme for the Third Annual Virginia Woolf Conference, held in June 1993 in Missouri, listed numerous papers on topics such as 'The Radical Politics of Virginia Woolf's *To the Lighthouse*', 'Decolonizing Discourse in *The Voyage Out*', 'The Revolution Continues: Learning from Woolf how to Tell the Table of Patriarchy's Secret Traitors', and '*Three Guineas* as a Primer of Resistance'. Nothing could be more different from the current British attack on Woolf, which entirely ignores the political re-evaluations made of her work and life over the last thirty years. Not all of us would feel able to endorse Jane Marcus's reading of the charwomen in *To the Lighthouse* as speakers of 'the female logos at the meeting place of art and labour', 'translations of a temporary antiphallogocentric discourse, awaiting the time when the charwoman herself will write fiction',[24] rather than class-bound caricatures. Not everyone could imagine, with her, Virginia Woolf 'inciting her fellows to rebellion, the working-class writers, the exiles, the Jews, the Africans, the eccentrics',[25] or describe her, as Madeline Moore does, above all 'as a feminist, as a revolutionary, as a lover of women'.[26] But probably more of us would describe her like that than as the next best thing to Hitler.

Most readers, however, feel the need to take a political *side* on Woolf. She has always been appropriated for a wide and conflicting variety of feminist positions, which have included Elaine Showalter's critique of *A Room of One's Own* as a 'kind of Amazonian Utopia, population 1',[27] and Andrea Dworkin's disappointment with her for her suicide and her politeness: 'She was less than she could have been.'[28] More recent work on Woolf in this country has tried to move on from what Rachel Bowlby describes as criticism which 'frequently takes the form of violent attack or defense . . . Bloomsbury snob versus socialist feminist', and to examine instead Virginia Woolf's 'continual refusal to come to a conclusion'.[29] Even within such work, though, there is still a discernible embarrassment about the unacceptable face of Virginia Woolf: Bowlby has to footnote 'the awkwardness of Virginia Woolf's occasional refusal of a relationship between literature and politics, giving support to the myth of Bloomsbury elitism'.[30] John Mepham's intelligent reading of Woolf has recourse — with reference to the negroes at the Peace Conference — to talking about 'Virginia Woolf's less attractive attitudes', which he says she 'tidies away out of sight in the fiction', as opposed to the diaries.[31] Gillian Beer, in a brilliant essay on Virginia Woolf's powerful reading of England and empire,[32] has to allow for the occasional lapse into 'social condescension', where the figure of the aeroplane turns into an excuse for 'a dangerous narrative position . . . gazing *de haut en bas*'. Two American writers who have confronted the issue head on, Alex Zwerdling[33] and Lorrie Goldensohn,[34] account for Woolf's 'offensiveness' in terms of her pathology, her 'middle-class guilt', and her 'failures of imaginative empathy'.

Perhaps there is really not much else to be done about the offence of Virginia Woolf: allow that there are 'less attractive attitudes' and make the best of them. But with the quotations I began with still sticking in my throat, I feel the need to swallow her whole, not spit out the bits of her which I may find distasteful.

I find a stimulating precedent for writing on 'offence' in Christopher Ricks's *T. S. Eliot and Prejudice*, a subtly equivocating discussion of Eliot's anti-Semitism which has some brilliant and witty things to say about bigotry and offence in writers — and readers. Ricks gives anyone writing on such subjects (where, as he says, there is bound to be offence — supposing for instance that you want to speak about gradations of anti-Semitism, some worse than others) a tidy procedural blueprint:

There are four ways of considering the matter of Eliot and anti-Semitism
. . . First, there is the biographical, which would attend to Eliot the man.
Second, the historical, which would attend to the times, the very different
times in which Eliot lived — different not only from our day or from
days previous to his, but differing in themselves, decade from decade.
Third, there is the dissociated, which claims that whatever Eliot's personal
or political doings and sayings may have been, the poems are quite another
matter. And last there is the continuous, which believes that the matter of
anti-Semitism has a particular importance because it cannot be isolated
from the larger issues of categorizing and prejudice in Eliot's poetry, issues
which are as responsible for his greatness as for his rare lapses from
greatness.[35]

If we apply this strategy to Virginia Woolf and her offensiveness,
we find soon enough that the categories stray into each other; all
the same, they are useful.

The first line of biographical defence would usually be to cite
Virginia Woolf's public work, her evening classes at Morley College, her work for the vote in 1910, her Women's Guild meetings
at Richmond, her commitment to the *Well of Loneliness* censorship
case, her membership of the anti-Fascist exhibition committee in
1935, her involvement with the London and National Society for
Women's Service, her attendance at the English branch of Vigilance,
'Intellectual Liberty', in 1936, and other examples of public action.
This line of defence, for all Virginia Woolf's increasing (and under-
recognized) consideration of political issues in the 1930s, is still a
difficult one to take since, although she herself cited her early
public works in her own defence against elitism (in her 1940
correspondence with Ben Nicolson), she was notoriously equivocal
about the value of sitting on platforms, signing petitions, and
marching in processions. And there is a deadly gap, as John Carey is
quick to observe, between her public and intellectual commitment
to feminism and to equal educational opportunities, and the personal
malevolence which he discerns in, for instance, her characterization
of Doris Kilman:

Though she is poor, Miss Kilman is independent, and has gained a degree
in history. She is, in other words, just the sort of woman Virginia Woolf,

as a campaigning feminist might be expected to champion. But the social prejudices of an upper–middle–class intellectual prove stronger than feminism, and Miss Kilman is depicted as a monster of spite, envy, and unfulfilled desire.[36]

To answer this charge by saying, 'But Woolf taught evening classes at Morley College!' doesn't seem very effective. It is more convincing to argue that the 'monstrosity' of Doris Kilman is not the expression of personal spite against a fictional character, but the recognition of a woman's character distorted and made ugly by lack of opportunity, mean social conditions, and exactly the sort of class prejudice which Virginia Woolf is being accused of, but which is, in fact, the subject of her novel.

Part of the biographical defence must be that Virginia Woolf changed. Her class analysis did not stay fixedly in place between, say, *Jacob's Room* and *Three Guineas*. It is in the nature of the 'offended' attacks to treat 'Virginia Woolf' as a static set of attitudes. That is how caricature works. But, again, there is a difficulty with the developmental defence: the offensive quotations with which I began range from 1908 to 1939.

So it is unconvincing to argue that Virginia Woolf progressed towards purer and less offensive attitudes. It makes more sense — and is more interesting — to attend to the ambivalence, self-consciousness, and self-contradictions in — for instance — her behaviour to and feelings about her servants, her social relations to the aristocracy, her attitudes to her Jewish mother-in-law, and her identification with Bloomsbury. There is an unreconciled doubleness in her two very carefully revised letters to Ben Nicolson in 1940, written in reply to his war-time attack on Roger Fry and Bloomsbury and all it stands for. Ben Nicolson described 'Bloomsbury' as a group of people sitting around in armchairs discussing Spinoza. 'Despairing of educating the masses', he said, Bloomsbury 'ignored the stupidity and ignorance surrounding it', in order to 'cultivate the exquisite sensibilities which it alone understood and valued'.[37]

Woolf's reply of 24 August 1940 does two things at once. She is at the same time anxious to separate herself from Fry ('my own education and my own point of view were entirely different from his', she says) and to identify herself with a non-elitist version of Bloomsbury, citing *The Common Reader, A Room of One's Own, Three Guineas,* Leonard's work, Keynes's *The Economic Consequences of the Peace,* Roger Fry's lectures, Lytton Strachey's books, and Duncan Grant's paintings, to 'prove that they [Bloomsbury — and note 'they', not 'we'] have done their very best to make humanity in the mass appreciate what they knew and saw.'[38] The formulation cannot escape from its assumptions about the difference between the educated classes and 'humanity in the mass', which needs educating. This is as far as she can go to breach class boundaries, and she knows it, as her subsequent phrase about Roger Fry makes clear: '[He] did the best he could, given his education, given the society in which he was brought up.'

This is a typically inconclusive and troubled analysis of the limitations of her class position. There are other examples. Some letters to Virginia Woolf (though not their replies) have survived from a self-educated Yorkshire factory woman, Agnes Smith. She complains that Virginia Woolf had not dealt with the working classes in *Three Guineas,* and warms into a friendly and confident correspondence about the need for educational reform. It seems from Agnes Smith's side of the correspondence that Virginia Woolf has accepted the charge about *Three Guineas,* but has blamed the educational system; and that she has gone on to make a strong individual bond with Smith, and has suggested a literary collaboration. Personally and exceptionally, here, the class barrier has been breached; but in general both correspondents agree that it is still in place.

Or take her argument with Desmond MacCarthy in February 1941. MacCarthy had reviewed her essay 'The Leaning Tower' (which looked forward, as she said in the Diary for 11 February 1940, to 'the supersession of aristocratic culture by common readers. Also to the end of class literature').[39] He criticized her in the *Sunday Times* for not owning up to her own 'tower', and for identifying herself 'with an audience of working men'. Citing, as always, differences in the education and the wealth of men and women, she argues in her reply to him that this difference cuts across class: 'So

I'm right to say "we" when I talk to them.'[40] She has difficulties, again, with 'we' and 'them': these examples suggest how painfully and precisely aware she is of her class position.

Even so, the gap between her own identification with the 'common readers', her desire to say 'we', not 'them', and the perception of her as an elitist snob seem absolute, unbridgeable. It is clear that others perceived her as a snob, as they still do. She wouldn't have felt moved to give a paper to the Memoir Club called 'Am I a snob?' unless the labelling of her as such was a running joke. (The paper brilliantly dissolves any serious considera-tion of the charge into a fantastical, witty, and by implication self-justifying account — I am allowed to like the aristocracy because they fire my imagination — of Sybil Colefax's eccentricities.) Throughout her private writings, letters, and diaries, she underscores many of her own most 'unattractive' prejudices, privately voiced, with self-indicting footnotes. The tone of these is not so much 'Am I a snob?' as *Am I a snob!*: it is a mixture of shame and pleasure.

Its partly that I'm a snob. The middle classes are cut so thick, & ring so coarse, when they laugh or express themselves.[41]

[At dinner with Rebecca West and her husband]: Did they differentiate me from other people? No. Or Leonard? But then isnt this Bloomsbury conceit — our d–d refinement?[42]

How I hated marrying a Jew . . . what a snob I was.[43]

I find it hard to distinguish self-esteem from self-blame in these sorts of remarks. In other places the 'middle-class guilt', which can neither escape nor excuse its class limitations, is easier to discern. In 1940: 'Again I'm struck with the helplessness of the lower orders. All of us on top.'[44] Or take the reaction to hearing Tolstoy's daughter Tatiana lecturing in 1926, while she is writing *To the Lighthouse*: 'And I hated us all, for being prosperous and comfort-able; and wished to be a working woman, and wished to be able to excuse my life to Tolstoi.'[45] This emotion finds its way, in *To the Lighthouse*, into the attitude of Charles Tansley towards the Ramsays (more strongly expressed in the draft of the novel) — and might prompt a more sympathetic reading of Doris Kilman than John Carey's. In Virginia Woolf's lifelong argument with herself and others about the effect of class on her imagination, she excoriates and defends herself better than anyone else can. The very prejudices which give so much offence are dealt with in the politics of the novels: in the post-war social divisions in *Mrs Dalloway*, in the legacy of imperialism in *The Voyage Out* and *The Waves*, in the analysis of patriarchal family structures in *The Years* — a novel where the subject is so often class hatred or social injustice.

But to recognize Virginia Woolf's own recognition of her class boundaries is one thing; to come to terms with the Jew in the bath or the vomit-making women in Kensington High Street is another. Certainly her violent seizures of misanthropy and disgust, her cruel and racist stereotypings, come in bouts: you find her sometimes saying 'I hate my kind', 'I do not love my kind. I detest them', and sometimes 'I like everyone', 'I love my kind'.[46] It would seem possible to give a cyclical or symptomatic reading to the eruptions of loathing (as the editors of the letters do, pointing us towards particularly obvious indications of 'lunacy'). And certainly a reading of her stereotypings as indications of instability emphasizes the force of self-disgust and self-hatred which finds expression — or relief? — in the abuse of others. But to appeal to psychopathology as an explanation for misanthropy (as Goldensohn does in her essay) may also be to diminish her. 'Oh, she couldn't help it, she was crazy.' Ricks cites Sander Gilman's *Difference and Pathology: Stereotypes of Sexuality, Race, and Madness* (1985), which describes stereotyping as a process which arises where 'self-integration is threatened', and tries to distinguish between 'pathological stereotyping' (the person who 'sees the entire world in terms of the rigid line of difference') and 'normal' stereotyping, a 'momentary coping mechanism' used by all of us. This distinction seems, itself, to Ricks to be unsatisfactorily and complacently stereotyping ('The Pharisee stood and prayed thus with himself, God, I thank thee, that I am not as other men are, extortioners, unjust, adulterers, or even as this pathological personality'). Simply to believe that 'the bad form of stereotyping is the one done by sick people' is not enough to explain how prejudice works.[47] Goldensohn picks her way uncomfortably here:

Much of the virulence in the world is no doubt pathogenic, and merely present in us in varying and fluctuating proportions as the circumstances of our lives tend to foster or erase it. V W's private river of fear and anxiety about strangers seems only another tributary firmly connected to the great flow of human fury and loathing, and madness seems an awkwardly easy way to rationalize its existence. Still, some lifelong nobble in the brain's chemistry may make all the difference between an intense emotional response and a mad one.[48]

But it is no more satisfactory to explain away the 'Pah' spat out at the Jew in the bath by pointing at 'some lifelong nobble in the brain's chemistry' than it is to account for it as a fictionalized attack on her life with Leonard Woolf. I prefer to think that her marriage to a Jew, and her detestation of Fascism and Nazism, give the lie to the charge of anti-Semitism. To read the disgusted and disgusting passage about the Jew in the bath simply as an anti-Semitic offence does not get close to what is happening in *The Years*. Sara Pargiter is as much an outsider from acceptable society as the Jew, and his presence is meant to intensify our sense in *The Years* of what it means to be 'outside', beyond the pale. Offensive though the moment is, it belongs in the novel's aghast, disenchanted survey of 'civilized' life. '"In time to come," ' Sara says earlier in the book to her sister, ' "people, looking into this room — this cave, this little antre, scooped out of mud and dung, will hold their fingers to their noses" — she held her fingers to her nose — "and say 'Pah! They stink!'"' Her sister repeats 'Pah!' to herself with 'a spasm of disgust', acknowledging the truth of Sara's version of human beings as 'nasty little creatures'.[49] It is not just 'the Jew' who 'stinks'.

In the consideration of class or racial prejudice, the biographical and the historical approach necessarily slide together. If no explanations of context or literary intention seem adequate as excuses for the Jew in the bath and the rude remarks about Leonard Woolf's mother, then a second line of defence could be mounted. It goes like this: Virginia Woolf was no worse than anyone else in her time and class; she couldn't help using the word 'nigger' or having a cook. Henry James, in a 'little dissertation on prejudice', from an

1863 letter, quoted by Ricks, says of prejudice that 'this fatal obliquity of vision inheres not wholly in any individual but is some indefinable property in the social atmosphere'.[50] Ricks is very dubious about the special pleading which attributes all fatal obliquities of vision to indefinable properties in the social atmosphere: as he says of Eliot, 'not everybody was anti-Semitic in the 1920s'.[51] Certainly some were more anti-Semitic than others; some were more anti-democratic than others. When Pound talks about 'democratic sewage', he is more pernicious and offensive than Virginia Woolf talking about how difficult she finds it to identify imaginatively with the man in the street. And there are many other examples of 'hate speech' from figures closer to Virginia Woolf. Fredegond Shove, an old friend of the Stephen girls, writes to Vanessa in 1917 about the first Hogarth Press publication, Virginia Woolf's 'A Mark on the Wall' and Leonard Woolf's 'Three Jews': 'Virginias story and L's have come. *Three* Jews — is not that rather too much of a good thing?'[52] Vita Sackville-West writes to Harold Nicolson in 1945: '*Manifesto*: I hate democracy. I hate la populace. I wish education had never been introduced. I don't like tyranny, but I like an intelligent oligarchy. I wish la populace had never been encouraged to emerge from its rightful place. I should like to see them as well fed and well housed as T.T. cows — but no more thinking than that.'[53] In this context, Virginia Woolf's spasms of offensiveness may seem comparatively mild.

But we cannot 'excuse' her offences by referring to her mental instability, or to her literary intentions, or to the standard attitudes of the time, without acknowledging that she participates in and accedes to many of the current, common prejudices which now cause so much outrage. Virginia Woolf's rabid dislike of the middle classes (a dislike shared by others of her family and friends) does provide grist for John Carey's mill. There is a particularly vitriolic satire (written in response to a broadcast by J. B. Priestley) on the 'middlebrow' chap who is living comfortably on the proceeds of his nice simple ideas: 'Yes you're highly prolific. You're everywhere. When one walks in the garden, what's that on the cabbage? Middle brow. Middle brow infecting the sheep.'[54] In an unpublished version of this sketch, it is even more obvious that the middlebrow — or 'broadbrow' — is a writer, 'one of those simple minded people who write because they cant help it', who 'never commits any indiscretions', who 'dines well but not too well', and who 'believes in the old simple things that last and pay and dont shock and dont make people sit up'. This well-paid contemptible parasite, says Virginia Woolf, is of all people the person she most despises.[55]

Versions of this stereotyping appear whenever she is brought in contact with writers who are of the class just below or adjacent to her own, who are making a living in the market-place of literary journalism and best-selling novels, and who are more embedded in the social conventions of the time than she is herself. So she reserves her special vitriol for characters like J. C. Squire, editor of the *London Mercury*, Bruce Richmond, her editor at the *Times Literary Supplement*, Rose Macaulay, Rebecca West, or Kingsley Martin, the editor of the *New Statesman*: 'undistinguished', 'self obsessed', 'sweeping up his cauliflower on his fork', 'he runs off my mind like a torrent of lukewarm water'.[56]

Leslie Stephen's daughter's scorn for people who are reading the same kind of books as she is, making a living from their literary journalism, or writing novels, but who do not have her background or upbringing, is the sign of a very intensive process of self-definition. The closer they come to her the more she dislikes them: it is necessary for her to be able to say, I am not like them. (*'Did they differentiate me from other people?'*) The fierceness with which she 'differentiates' herself from other people, who might superficially be thought to resemble her (stereotyping them as 'Kensington', 'Chelsea'), is an unpleasant personal snobbery, but it is a snobbery on behalf of her work. She does not want to be censored or compromised by publishers (hence the Hogarth Press) or by literary editors who don't see what she's doing. She does not want to be like Middleton Murry, dropping names and sucking up and making deals in what she calls the literary 'underworld'. The penalty may be isolation, not finding an audience, but the reward is to be able to be 'differentiated from other people'. You can read this haughty withdrawal from the 'middlebrow' culture of her time as a drawing-in of skirts — or as pioneering courage of a Mr Ramsayish

kind. The inextricable mixture of haughty isolationism and courageous individualism is movingly illustrated in this diary entry,
written in response to Wyndham Lewis's attack on her in *Men
without Art* (1934), while she is writing 'The Pargiters':

Fatal, to arrange the Ps so as to meet his criticisms. . . . If there is truth in
W. L. well, face it: I've no doubt I am prudish & peeping, well then live
more boldly. But for God's sake dont try to bend my writing one way or
the other. Not that one can. And there is the odd pleasure too of being
abused: & the feeling of being dismissed into obscurity is also pleasant &
salutary.[57]

We can quote to give offence, or we can quote to please our
own and our audience's prejudices. Rachel Bowlby puts this well:
'Like the Bible, Woolf's texts provide ample support for almost
any position.'[58] I might easily have compiled a more comfortable
list of introductory quotations about the sins of the patriarchy,
hopes for a classless society, and the need for freedom and peace.
Any form of extrapolation is prejudicial. Tom Paulin, quoting
Clarissa Dalloway in *The Voyage Out* ('D'you know, Dick, I
can't help thinking of England . . . Think of the light burning
over the House, Dick!'[59]) in order to prove Virginia Woolf's
imperialism, was falling into the Ayatollah school of literary criticism, whereby authors are condemned to death for their characters' prejudices.

Quoting out of context often causes more offence than the
context allows, or may indeed cause exactly the kind of offence
which the context is repudiating. It is even more prejudicial to
quote offences from diaries, letters, and novels without distinction.
If a defence of Virginia Woolf's offences is to be mounted on
Ricks's third ground of 'dissociation' between the life and work (the
defence which Andrew Motion mounted for Larkin in his biography), then allowance must be made for privacy, for the 'wicked
thoughts' which Virginia Woolf uttered only to her friends or to
herself. After a lethal sketch of Middleton Murry in a letter to Janet
Case, Virginia Woolf adds: 'but this is spiteful. Do not let my views
reach the public.'[60] A long and sensationally furious outburst in a
letter to Ethel Smyth, about a visit from Leonard's relations, which

culminates in '9 Jews, all of whom, with the single exception of Leonard, might well have been drowned without the world wagging one ounce the worse', is then edited by: 'There! Thats a long sentence; and an ill natured.'[61]

That 'There!' tells everything about the role of offence in the letters: its therapeutic benefits, the pleasure of coming to a climax, and the recognition of how frightful, and how frightfully funny it is, to be as killingly sharp as this about other human beings. 'There!' is also short for 'There you are!' or 'There's a good one!' Our reading of these vicious private outbursts is more moralistic than it would be of our own (but which of us, our letters or phone calls or diaries exposed, would 'scape whipping?) and takes no account of the licence that energizes acting up or showing off or letting off steam.

Those who are shocked at these offences, who will not allow for the licence of private speech or the prejudices of the period, argue that Virginia Woolf's 'less attractive' opinions infect and diminish her as a novelist. I have already suggested that the reverse is true: that her own intense self-consciousness and ambivalence about her prejudices enter the fiction in the form of argument and subject-matter, not as unconsidered tinctures of bigotry. But there might be a more interesting way to take on the charge of offensiveness, without having to resort to idealized interpretations of Woolf as a decolonizing revolutionary. I should like to be less bashful and apologetic on her behalf, and to claim for offence an essential, even a desirable role in her work and life.

I want to *praise* her for her malice, and to see it as a vital aspect of her energy and style. Stroll through the pages of the letters and diaries, and you come away with handfuls of shining aphorisms. It is like reading Oscar Wilde, or Dorothy Parker. Once you start looking out for this, you find yourself a hard, glittery, ironical, showy Virginia Woolf, the kind who says to herself before a meeting of the Memoir Club, 'I shall be brilliant as usual': Woolf as dandy, as *flâneur*, as mocking, *dégagée* satirist, described by Hilary Spurling as 'the worldly, racy, posturing, humorous, matter-of-fact and phenomenally observant Virginia Woolf'.[62]

I read the book of Job last night — I dont think God comes well out of it.[63]

Rich men nowadays can be seen divesting themselves of particles of gold with a view to the eye of the needle.[64]

Can one imagine anything less desirable than to be a person who may stay permanently in America — & its hoped she does.[65]

She is quite happy to 'go public' with this tone; she even, at one point, suggests that malice should be systematized and turned into an open sport (this during the course of a spat with Logan Pearsall Smith, himself the most malicious of men):

Why should not Chelsea and Bloomsbury meet and laugh at each other to their faces and quite genuinely enjoy themselves? It seems to me worth trying. Then again, you say 'critics resent criticism, and mockers being mocked.' But do they, if it's done face to face? Surely both sides might benefit greatly if it were done in that way.[66]

Malice and mockery give spice to the fiction and essays, as in the views of the Ramsay children on Charles Tansley in *To the Lighthouse* — 'and he would ask one, did one like his tie? God knows, said Rose, one did not'[67] — or in the footnotes to *Three Guineas*: 'We are led to conclude that a biography of the Deity would resolve itself into a Dictionary of Clerical Biography.'[68] Ridicule in *Three Guineas*, laughter and caricature in *Three Years*, are forceful political weapons. The same energy which might power an 'offence' — a violent attack on humanity in the mass, a scornful caricature of a middle-class journalist — pours into her heroic satires on patriarchy and censorship. Yet we object to the former, and praise the latter.

The second possible way through, rather than round, her offence is to recognize that Virginia Woolf was deeply preoccupied with the very categories and demarcations which bias and inhibit her. If her offence is to put herself above or separate from other people, to be 'I' instead of 'they' or 'we', then this is also her subject-matter. The dilemma of the individual, torn between belonging and sharing, and being apart and egotistical, is expressed in every sphere of her life and writing. Her despair is at never not being herself; but that is also her pride and her refuge. Caricature and offence are very often her ways of keeping herself separate, maintaining outsider status, demarcating herself in particular from the groups, types, and individuals who she feels may be getting too close to her, too like her. But caricature also expresses a powerful desire to apprehend the alien person or group as sharply, as acutely, as closely as possible. She longs to extend her sympathies beyond class boundaries through reading and writing, and the frequent passages where she writes about this provide the best answer to the accusations of snobbery and elitism. Like the examples of offensiveness, they span the whole course of her writing life, from 'Hours in a Library' of 1916 to 'The Leaning Tower' of 1940:

The old hunger to know what the immortals thought has given place to a far more tolerant curiosity to know what our own generation is thinking. What do living men and women feel, what are their houses like and what clothes do they wear, what money have they and what food do they eat, what do they love and hate, what do they see of the surrounding world, and what is the dream that fills the spaces of their active lives?[69]

It is useless to suppose that social distinctions have vanished [from English fiction]. Each may pretend that he knows no such restrictions, and that the compartment in which he lives allows him the run of the world. But it is an illusion . . . There is no animosity, perhaps [between classes] but there is no communication. We are enclosed, and separate, and cut off . . . It seems, therefore, that the novelist, and the English novelist in particular, suffers from a disability which affects no other artist to the same extent. His work is influenced by his birth. He is fated to know intimately, and so to describe with understanding, only those who are of his own social rank. He cannot escape from the box in which he has been bred. [This is changing, she goes on to say.] In another century or so, none of these distinctions may hold good.[70]

The novel of a classless and towerless world should be a better novel than the old novel. The novelist will have more interesting people to describe — people who have had a chance to develop their humour, their gifts, their tastes; real people, not people cramped and squashed into featureless masses by hedges.[71]

But as a reader, as a writer, as a person, she is, also, always locked inside herself. John Carey cites her description of the old beggar woman singing unintelligibly outside Regent's Park Tube station, in *Mrs Dalloway*, as her way 'not of describing but of eliminating old women who beg outside Regent's Park Tube station. By converting her into a peasant or super-peasant . . . Woolf deprives the woman of the distasteful social reality which she would possess as a member of the mass asking for money. The beggar disappears in a primitivist cosmetic haze.'[72]

Another of those beggar women has been sighted before, in the Diary for 8 June 1920: 'An old beggar woman, blind, sat against a stone wall in Kingsway holding a brown mongrel in her arms, & sang aloud. . . . How she came to be there, what scenes she can go through, I can't imagine. O damn it all, I say, why cant I know all that too?'[73]

She is there again in *Jacob's Room*, singing with her back to the stone wall of the Union of London and Smith's Bank, while the workers go home from work, conveyed this way and that through hollow drains lined with yellow light under the streets, and the carriages roll up to the Opera-House, and two thousand people in the audience are arranged in 'a system of classification which is simplicity itself: stalls, boxes, amphitheatre, gallery'.[74] In this remarkable passage the pressure to perceive through caricature and stereotyping, to fall in with the social systems of classification which have created rush hours and seating prices, pushes against the desire to individuate, to get closer, to know more: 'O damn it all, I say, why cant I know all that too?' Caught perpetually between these pressures, and representing in her selection of metropolitan materials (beggars, suburban workers on trains, society out at the opera) precisely the narrow environmental confines she would like to break through, the narrator wanders inside the opera-house between the two thousand people, forced to choose, forced to individuate some and stereotype others: 'Never was there a harsher necessity! or one which entails greater pain, more certain disaster; for wherever I seat myself, I die in exile.'

Notes

1. *The Diary of Virginia Woolf*, ed. Anne Olivier Bell and Andrew McNeillie, 5 vols. (London, 1977–84), ii. 64 (15 Sept. 1920).

2. Ibid. i. 13 (9 Jan. 1915).

3. *The Years* (1937; repr. Oxford, 1992), 322.

4. *Diary*, i. 267–8 (24 Apr. 1919).

5. Virginia Stephen to Vanessa Bell, *The Letters of Virginia Woolf*, ed. Nigel Nicolson and Joanne Trautmann, 6 vols. (London, 1975–80), i. 364 (29 Aug. 1908).

6. *Mrs Dalloway* (1925; repr. Oxford, 1992), 8.

7. *Diary*, iv. 91 (21 Apr. 1932).

8. Ibid. iv. 349 (30 Oct. 1935).

9. V.W. to Vanessa Bell, *Letters*, iii. 265 (19 May 1926).

10. John Carey, *The Intellectuals and the Masses* (London, 1992), 80.

11. Ibid. 210.

12. Ibid. 25.

13. Ibid. 208.

14. James Wood, review of *The Intellectuals and the Masses*, *Guardian*, 2 July 1992.

15. Edward Pearce, ibid., 8 July 1992.

16. Peter F. Alexander, *Leonard and Virginia Woolf: A Literary Partnership* (Hemel Hempstead, 1992), 265.

17. Anthony Burgess, 'Not a Very Lovely Thing to Be', *Literary Review*, Apr. 1993, 5.

18. See David Garnett, *The Flowers of the Forest* (London, 1955), quoted in S. P. Rosenbaum, *The Bloomsbury Group* (London, 1975), 369.

19. Wyndham Lewis, *The Apes of God* (1930), and *Men Without Art* (1934), quoted ibid. 333.

20. Wyndham Lewis, *Men without Art* (1934), in Robin Majumdar and Allen McLaurin (eds.), *Virginia Woolf: The Critical Heritage* (London, 1975), 335.

21. Q. D. Leavis, review, *Scrutiny* (Sept. 1938), ibid. 409–19.

22. John Berger, 'The Artist and Modern Society', *Twentieth Century* (Aug. 1955), 151.

23. T. H. Pear, *English Social Differences* (London, 1955), 131.

24. Jane Marcus, 'A Rose for Him to Rifle', *Feminist Studies*, 4/1 (1978), 68–98.

25. Jane Marcus, 'Introduction: Virginia Woolf Aslant', *Virginia Woolf: A Feminist Slant* (Lincoln, Nebr. and London, 1983), 1.

26. Madeline Moore, *The Short Season between two Silences* (London, 1984), 171.

27. Elaine Showalter, 'Towards a Feminist Poetics' (1981), *The New Feminist Criticism*, ed. Showalter (London, 1986).

28. Andrea Dworkin, *Right Wing Women* (New York and London, 1983), 45–6.

29. Rachel Bowlby, *Virginia Woolf: Feminist Destinations* (Oxford, 1988), 170.

30. Ibid. 178, n. 7.

31. John Mepham, *Virginia Woolf: A Literary Life* (Basingstoke, 1992), 163, 189.

32. Gillian Beer, 'The Island and the Aeroplane: The Case of Virginia Woolf',

in Homi K. Bhabha (ed.), *The Nation and Narration* (London, 1990), 265–90.

33. Alex Zwerdling, 'Class and Money', *Virginia Woolf and the Real World* (Berkeley, Calif. and London, 1986), 87–119.
34. Lorrie Goldensohn, 'The Lives of Virginia Woolf', *Salmagundi*, 74–5 (Spring–Summer 1987), 1–41.
35. Christopher Ricks, *T. S. Eliot and Prejudice* (London, 1988), 61.
36. Carey, *The Intellectuals and the Masses*, 19.
37. Benedict Nicolson to V.W., 19 Aug. 1940, Monk's House Papers, Manuscript Collection, University of Sussex Library.
38. V.W. to Benedict Nicolson, *Letters*, vi. 419 (24 Aug. 1940).
39. *Diary*, v. 266 (11 Feb. 1940).
40. V.W. to Desmond MacCarthy, *Letters*, vi. 467 (2 Feb. 1941).
41. *Diary*, ii. 15 (31 Jan. 1920).
42. *Diary*, iv. 327 (27 June 1935).
43. V.W. to Ethel Smyth, *Letters*, iv. 195 (2 Aug. 1930).
44. *Diary*, v. 291 (3 June 1940).
45. V.W. to Vita Sackville-West, *Letters*, iii. 236 (31 Jan. 1926).
46. *Diary*, iii. 33 (27 June 1925); V.W. to Vita Sackville-West, *Letters*, iv. 380 (16 Sept. 1931); *Diary*, iii. 26 (1 June 1925).
47. Ricks, *T. S. Eliot and Prejudice*, 120.
48. Goldensohn, 'The Lives of Virginia Woolf', 14.
49. *The Years*, 180.
50. Ricks, *T. S. Eliot and Prejudice*, 102–3.
51. Ibid. 64.
52. Fredegond Shove to Vanessa Bell, 19 July 1917, Modern Archive, King's College Library, Cambridge.
53. Vita Sackville-West to Harold Nicolson, *Vita and Harold: The Letters of Vita Sackville-West and Harold Nicolson 1910–1962*, ed. Nigel Nicolson (London, 1992), 361 (7 Feb. 1945).
54. Published in *The Complete Shorter Fiction of Virginia Woolf*, ed. Susan Dick (London, 1985), 246.
55. 'Three Characters', Monk's House Papers, Manuscript Collection, University of Sussex Library.
56. *Diary*, iv. 305 (23 Apr. 1935).
57. Ibid. 252 (14 Oct. 1934).
58. Bowlby, *Virginia Woolf*, 14.
59. *The Voyage Out* (1915; repr. Oxford, 1992), 51.
60. V.W. to Janet Case, *Letters*, ii. 515 (20 Mar. 1922).
61. V.W. to Ethel Smyth, *Letters*, iv. 223 (28 Sept. 1930).
62. Hilary Spurling, review of Lyndall Gordon's *Virginia Woolf*, *Observer*, 11 Nov. 1984.
63. V.W. to Lady Cecil, *Letters*, ii. 585 (12 Nov. 1922).
64. *Diary*, i. 277 (25 May 1919).
65. Ibid. ii. 38 (15 May 1920).

66. V.W. to Logan Pearsall Smith, *Letters*, v. 119 (6 Nov. 1932).
67. *To the Lighthouse* (1927; repr. Harmondsworth, 1992), 12.
68. *Three Guineas* (1938; repr. London, 1986), 172.
69. 'Hours in a Library' (Nov. 1916), *The Essays of Virginia Woolf*, ed. Andrew McNeillie, 6 vols. (London, 1986–   ), ii. 58.
70. 'The Niece of an Earl' (Oct. 1928), *Collected Essays*, ed. Leonard Woolf, 4 vols. (London, 1966–7), i. 219–23.
71. 'The Leaning Tower' (May 1940), ibid. ii. 179.
72. Carey, *The Intellectuals and the Masses*, 37.
73. *Diary*, ii. 47.
74. *Jacob's Room* (1922; repr. London, 1992), 63.

❧ IO ❧

Huxley's Slump: Planning, Eugenics, and the 'Ultimate Need' of Stability

DAVID BRADSHAW

In September 1928 James Joyce received

two most urgent letters in which that extraordinary person Mr Wilson of Willington announces his willingness to pay mine and my wife's expenses up there and back and hotel expenses and what he calls a royal welcome from the miners and for all I know a present of a few tons of coal also. He sent me some sort of gift, I am not sure whether it is a cartridge coach or a case for cigars and cigarettes.[1]

In the event Joyce did not visit Willington, but Wilson was successful in enticing more orthodox men of letters to his County Durham home, such as Laurence Binyon, Lascelles Abercrombie, and Sir Henry Newbolt. As late as 1948 the indefatigable Wilson was badgering Compton Mackenzie for a message which could be read out at a British Legion rally, or, even better, a lecture from the celebrated author of *Whisky Galore* (1947) himself.[2]

Charles Wilson (1891–1969) was a native of Willington and had begun his working life as a miner.[3] By the mid-1920s, however, he had become well known in the region as a freelance journalist and renowned as a kind of one-man adult education bureau. Secretary of the local branch of the Workers' Educational Association and, from 1928, county organizer for the Shakespeare Guild, *The Auckland and County Chronicle* reported that 'study of the best literature as a means of refining the mind and broadening the outlook has had no keener supporter than Mr Wilson, whose study circle has become almost an institution in this part of the country'.[4]

D. H. Lawrence was the recipient of at least six letters, a postcard, two calendars, a nickel cigarette case, and some poems

from 'the irrepressible Durham miner man',[5] between December
1927 and March 1929, all designed to lure the ailing novelist to
Willington.[6] Wilson's letters gave details of the appalling conditions
which were then prevalent in the Durham coalfield, and Lawrence
told Wilson that it 'depresses me very much to hear how badly the
men are working'.[7] Lawrence sent Wilson copies of his books, and
to Wilson's miners he dispatched a 'message' in January 1928[8] and
three short poems the following December as a form of 'New
Years Greetings to the Willington Men — for 1929'.[9]

Aldous Huxley and Lawrence were close friends during the last
three years of Lawrence's life, and it seems certain that both Wilson
and the widely reported social and industrial problems of the
mining regions would have been discussed by the two novelists.
When Huxley was invited to Willington shortly after Lawrence's
death in March 1930 he responded favourably, telling Wilson that
his description of the conditions in the Durham area was 'very
depressing'.[10] Although there was undoubtedly a tuft-hunting streak
in Wilson, it is equally clear that he had a more noble interest in
tempting literary celebrities to the North-East: by the time Huxley
visited the area in October 1930, the Durham coalfield was blighted
with the worst unemployment in England. Wilson would have
been aware of the publicity which a writer of Huxley's stature
might be able to focus on the hardship which was then pervasive in
his part of the country.[11]

Huxley arrived in Willington on Friday, 10 October and delivered a lecture that evening to Wilson's study circle.[12] The following
day Wilson gave Huxley a short tour of the area, and he was
clearly dismayed by what he witnessed:

Of all the more or less wealthy and well-educated men and women who
— in London drawing-rooms, at the Club, over luncheons in the City, in
Government Offices — discuss the Unemployment Problem, the Shrinking
of Dividends, the Dole, the Slump, the Depression in our Basic Industries,
how many, I wonder, have ever taken the trouble to come and look for
themselves at the particular facts summed up by these convenient generalisa-
tions? Uncommonly few ... Mining villages used to be noisy places —
noisy and also melodious; for there was singing in the streets as well as
shouting. Today they are remarkable for their silence. This is true to my

knowledge not only of these Durham villages, but also of the Nottingham-shire and Derbyshire colliery towns. There is a slump in singing as well as a slump in coal. That these two slumps are closely correlated is obvious. Men out of work do not often feel an inner urge to burst into song. The only singing unemployed are those who wander through the streets of the great cities singing for alms from a charitable public ... The material results of prolonged unemployment can easily be calculated. But who will ever be able to compute the sum of psychological mischief, for which it has been and is responsible?[13]

One of the first things Huxley did on returning to London on Sunday, 12 October was to write the following letter to Marshall Diston, then Treasurer of the London Divisional Council of the Independent Labour Party, who was seeking the views of prominent figures, such as H. G. Wells, Arnold Bennett, Bertrand Russell, and Huxley, on how best to solve the current political crisis:

I have never engaged in practical politics and so am not really qualified to express a political opinion. It is delightfully easy to be reasonable and equitable on paper — too easy by half.

Having just returned from the Durham mining district, I feel more than usually diffident of expressing a political opinion. All I know is that I shall be enthusiastically on the side of anyone who gets us out of the social and industrial mess, of which the Durham coal-field provides such a terrifying example. Whether any party will or can get us out of that mess is another question.[14]

With this problem doubtless at the front of his mind, Huxley took his seat in the Strangers' Gallery of the House of Commons on 11 February 1931 when Sir Laming Worthington-Evans moved the Opposition's motion of censure against MacDonald's second Labour Government over its handling of the economy. This debate, during the course of which Philip Snowden, the Chancellor, an-nounced that 'the national position is so grave that drastic and disagreeable measures will have to be taken',[15] was Huxley's first experience of Parliament at work. He did not find the spectacle at all inspiring, and in the article he wrote subsequently about his 'agonising experience ... in the appropriately Gothic hall of the Mother of Parliaments', Huxley arraigned the 'anachronistic bawl-ing' and ponderous ineptitude of the 'Grand Old Men' of British politics with an almost Carlylean rasp.[16] Robert Skidelsky has commented on the 'Jekyll and Hyde' performance of Philip Snowden during this debate, oscillating idiosyncratically between gravity and flippancy,[17] just as Huxley questioned the value of Snowden's oratorical display at the time:

Fiddling while Rome burns is bad enough; but twaddling, it seems to me, is even worse. So long as parliamentary procedure remains what it is, twaddling is unavoidable, prompt and comprehensive action all but impossible. Some such reforms in procedure as those suggested by Sir Oswald Mosley are obviously essential.[18]

On 13 December 1930, with unemployment nearing two and a half million, the Mosley Manifesto had put forward ' "an immediate plan to meet an emergency situation" '. Britain's ' "nineteenth century parliamentary machine" ' would be required to relinquish control of the nation's affairs to a 'Shavian cabinet of five Ministers without portfolio, armed with "power to carry through the emergency policy" subject only to the "general control" of Parliament'. Among other policies, a national plan 'to develop new industries, and to secure the modernization and re-equipment of others', was proposed.[19]

In his autobiography Mosley mentioned that he knew Huxley 'only slightly',[20] but an unpublished letter from the poet Robert Nichols to the neurologist Henry Head, recounting a recent conversation which Nichols had had with Huxley, reveals that Huxley had imbibed the Mosleys' sense of political exasperation in the weeks leading up to their abrupt departure from the Labour Party towards the end of February 1931:

He told me that he'd been seeing Cynthia Mosley. She seemed, he said, very fed up with the Labourite rank and file who, poor souls, are very stodgy and not unnaturally cling to their £400 a year and their chance of comfort and a maid-of-all-work. Later he told me that Mosley is a fearful fellow for women and that there was a row in Paris when two waitresses quarrelled in a restaurant in the presence of his wife, who, however, is devoted to him. Unfortunately, this weakness of his is getting known. Aldous seemed to dislike him and distrust him but said he was very much alive.[21]

Significantly, though, Huxley could not reconcile his admiration of Mosley's political vim with his personal dislike of the man, and he did not, unlike Gerald Heard, Raymond Mortimer, and Christopher Isherwood, contribute to *Action*, the short-lived New Party's newspaper, which, in Huxley's view, consisted of 'articles rejected by *John O'London's*'.[22]

A whistle-stop tour of the industrial Midlands and North of England in mid-February 1931 brought home to Huxley even more graphically the severity of the problems which confronted Britain. He was now convinced that the country faced a catastrophic collapse of its social and political structures and that a radical overhaul of governmental and industrial organization had to be effected as a matter of extreme urgency.

'Planning was the key word of the 1930's', wrote A. J. P. Taylor, 'planned economy, plan for peace, planned families, plan for holidays. The standard was Utopia.'[23] That planning was also Huxley's personal shibboleth during the composition of *Brave New World*, and not something he viewed with libertarian abhorrence, is crucially important. Around the same time he witnessed the 'twaddling paralysis' of the House of Commons, Huxley became involved with an inchoate pressure group, shortly to coalesce as Political and Economic Planning (PEP), which seemed to answer his demand for trenchant action. As Kenneth Lindsay, a founder member of the organization and its first General Secretary, once remarked:

The early birth pangs of PEP occurred during the dying months of the second Labour government; our inception must be measured against the rapidly deteriorating condition of Britain with well over two million unemployed and the prospect of financial bankruptcy. There was also a bankruptcy of political ideas.[24]

Originating in the publication of 'A National Plan for Great Britain' — Max Nicholson's sixteen pages of constructive polemic, 'calculated to secure a maximum of achievement with a minimum of insoluble disagreement' — PEP's function was to provide specific and detailed proposals to facilitate this resurgence.[25]

Following the publication of Nicholson's plan, 'conversations with a view to forming a group went on through February, among those concerned being Aldous Huxley'.[26] Certainly, Huxley was present, with his brother Julian, the architect Clough Williams-Ellis, and others, at a discussion-group dinner the following week, when it was agreed:

That National Planning is an immediate necessity for this country; that the present failure of politicians and others to undertake any serious work towards preparing a Plan and preparing the country to adopt one amounts to a major national danger; that in view of this neglect the meeting accepts the responsibility of preparing and making propaganda for a Plan for the rational re-organisation of our political and economic institutions on a basis of industrial freedom.[27]

Further meetings at which Huxley would most probably have been present were held on 8 and 13 March 1931, followed by a second steering-group dinner two days later when the name PEP was officially adopted.[28] Ironically, the inaugural meeting of PEP proper, at University College, London on 22 March, during the course of which Huxley was elected a provisional Director of the organization, was practically his last association with it. Nicholson later described how 'some agitation was caused by Aldous Huxley drawing a series of caricatures of those present during the meeting; he withdrew from PEP not long afterwards and his only comment was the writing of *Brave New World*'.[29] Huxley was present at the first gathering of the 'Reform of the Machinery of Government' planning group on 30 March, the first of PEP's study groups to be formed, but his name is neither among those present at the first General Meeting of PEP (26 June 1931) nor on a list of members compiled later that year.

Looking back at Huxley's interest in PEP during February and March 1931 Max Nicholson recalled that 'at that time he was positively interested in the potential of a broad and profound approach, based on planning, to the initiation of a new stage in civilisation'.[30] Kenneth Lindsay confirmed that Huxley 'thought it a good thing to join. The word "planning" must have had a mystique at the time. "Intelligent" and "orderly", perhaps "scientific" were freely used for the same purpose.'[31] These testimonies to Huxley's commitment to the embryonic PEP are crucially important in that they contrast with the impression given in the collection of essays published to commemorate the fiftieth anniversary of the organization that Huxley's role was little more than a disinterested observer of PEP. In one of only two glosses, the editor noted that Huxley wrote *Brave New World*, 'after sitting in at early PEP meetings'.[32]

Nicholson's inference that *Brave New World* was Huxley's estranged snook at PEP receives circumstantial support both from the fact that he commenced writing his novel as soon as he returned to France and from his mischievous antics at the University College meeting. But, as we shall see, although Huxley almost certainly became frustrated with the initial dilatoriness of PEP, his belief in the need for planning in fact intensified during the course of the novel's composition, and *Brave New World* is emphatically not the work of a man who was either cynical about or wary of initiatives such as that which PEP represented. Indeed, it is likely that the difficulties which Huxley experienced in writing the novel arose because he veered suddenly from his original intention of writing a satire on material progress and the global triumph of Fordism as the need for national planning became more imperative through the summer of 1931. His first-hand knowledge of the miserable conditions which prevailed in the Depressed Areas, and his heart-sinking experience of the momentous debate in which the Government made plain its inability to remedy the country's problems, accentuated Huxley's hostility to parliamentary democracy during the gestation of *Brave New World* between May and August 1931. If the Huxley of *Brave New World* was as utterly unsympathetic to planning as some critics have argued, then his novel represents a curious tergiversation from the broad drift of his work in 1931. Alternatively, rather than a fictional embodiment of Huxley's supposed loathing of statism, or the legacy of a desultory and disgruntled flirtation with planning, *Brave New World* may be seen as a tentative, paradoxical expression of his fervent interest in the planned state in the early 1930s.

Huxley's abrupt departure from PEP signalled his disillusionment less with planning *per se*, than with the kind of approach which PEP epitomized. Kenneth Lindsay thought Huxley became 'bored' with PEP's dithering, while Max Nicholson's assessment of the wider influence of the group may also help to explain Huxley's behaviour. 'Our group certainly tried to make "Planning" a key issue in the *early* 1930s, but with only limited success, and it never penetrated either the establishment or the man in the street to any extent.'[33] As early as the first discussion-group dinner, when it was proposed to call the venture 'The 1950 Society' (that being the date by which it was hoped the transformation of Britain would be completed), Nicholson complained that 'the Group shows a strong tendency not to move at all'.[34] It is tempting to speculate that, for all PEP's polemical rhetoric, Huxley shared Nicholson's sense of inertia and became rapidly dismayed by its lack of impact. Moreover, it is probable that Huxley found it difficult to reconcile PEP's gradualist, democratic, and tradition-conscious approach to national renewal with his growing bent towards a more authoritarian solution to Britain's problems. Though an early draft of Nicholson's blueprint was called 'The *Week-End Review* Five Year Plan', the published version endorsed 'the retention of the King-in-Parliament as the sovereign omnicompetent body, limited by no written constitution'.[35] Furthermore, although the overhauling of parliamentary procedure was the principal remit of the 'Reform of the Machinery of Government' planning group, they were enjoined by their Directorate to 'keep in mind the historic virtues of Britain's constitution and to avoid excessively radical schemes which would damage the tradition of organic growth and continuity'.[36] Indeed, another of those involved has remarked that some members of the discussion-group were even reluctant to include the word 'planning' in the title of the organization because of the potential confusion of PEP with Soviet and Fascist models of state control. '*Planwirtschaft* spoken with the tone of a Sergeant-Major was replacing the older and quieter Anglo-Saxon word "planning", meaning considering how you got from here to there.'[37]

Huxley was no such pussyfooter. Indeed, during the spring, summer, and autumn of 1931, as the national crisis worsened daily, he repeatedly sanctioned the bypassing of parliamentary opposition to Soviet-style planning as a matter of the utmost gravity and expedience:

There are two national plans at present on the English market — Sir Oswald Mosley's and the rather more fully worked-out plan propounded recently by the *Week-End Review*. Whether either of these plans, or indeed any large-scale plan, could be put rapidly into execution by purely constitutional means, I do not know. It seems to me, I must confess, rather doubtful. The War made it sufficiently clear that rapid large-scale actions and the traditional constitutional methods are not compatible.

So long as there exists a gulf between what is, by the highest human standards, desirable and what is actually desired by a majority or even a minority of human beings, force has got to be used . . . In the present case, a powerful minority, including almost all those now holding political power, may have strong objections to large-scale national planning. But if national planning is, by the highest human standards, desirable, then the actual desires of this minority will have to be overridden and the desirable thing imposed by force. But as this minority at present controls the governmental machines, it follows that the application of force may have to be done unconstitutionally.[38]

David Caute and Paul Hollander have analysed the widespread appeal which the Soviet Union and its Five Year Plan held for Western intellectuals in the late 1920s and early 1930s, and Caute has assembled a montage of pro-Soviet hyperbole from this period which provides an illuminating context for Huxley's enthusiasm:

'The success of the Five Year Plan is the only hope of this world,' said Bernard Shaw. 'But above all I should like to live long enough to see Russia's plan succeed and the states of Europe obliged to accept what they insisted on ignoring . . . My heart applauds that gigantic and yet entirely human undertaking,' said André Gide. The plans, said Julian Huxley, expressed, 'a new spirit, the spirit of science introduced into politics and industry,' . . . For Stephen Spender the plans were instruments for creating a new civilisation.[39]

On another occasion Huxley praised the Soviet Five Year Plan as 'the most significant example of a social experiment',[40] and lauded a gung-ho account of it as 'not merely interesting; it is exciting'.[41] Yet neither Caute nor Hollander mention Aldous Huxley's ardour for the Five Year Plan, and, oddly, only in Caute's book is the

Society for Cultural Relations Between the Peoples of the British
Commonwealth and the USSR accorded two passing references.

Founded in 1924, 'to collect and diffuse information in both
countries on developments in science, education, philosophy, art,
literature, and social and economic life', as J. A. Hobson put it in
moving the resolution for its establishment,[42] the Society for Cultural Relations attracted a wide cross-section of British intellectuals.
Among its earliest supporters were G. B. Shaw, E. M. Forster,
David Garnett, Virginia and Leonard Woolf, H. G. Wells, Bertrand
Russell, and Havelock Ellis, later joined by the likes of L. T.
Hobhouse, Harold Laski, Hugh Walpole, and Julian Huxley. A
request for information about plans for the celebration of Tolstoy's
centenary appears to have been Aldous Huxley's first contact with
the SCR in 1927,[43] and it is quite possible that four years later, as a
recently appointed Vice-President of the Society, Huxley would
have attended a meeting held under its auspices at the London
School of Economics on 23 March 1931, when the Director of the
Supreme Council of the National Economy of the USSR, M. G.
Gurevitch, delivered a stirring address on the interim achievements
of the Five Year Plan.[44]

In the light of Huxley's unacknowledged zest for the Soviet
Union and its Five Year Plan, for which he and his fellow Vice-
Presidents, 'long of hair and throaty of voice', received a thorough
roasting at the hands of the *Daily Mail*,[45] another perennial assertion
about *Brave New World* looks less secure — namely that it *spoofs*
the Soviet Union and its Five Year Plan.

In 'The Victory of Art Over Humanity', Huxley reiterated his
view that a solution to the economic crisis must be 'imposed by
some strong and intelligent central authority. Yes, imposed. For, as
usual, the desirable is not the same as that which is in practice
desired — at any rate by an important section of the population.'
What was needed, according to Huxley, was 'a rejuvenated government, equipped with the necessary institutional weapons, and capable of acting swiftly and with a well-informed and intelligent
ruthlessness'.[46]

Early in May 1931 Huxley told his brother that he would be
'delighted' to accompany him on his impending visit to the Soviet

Union, even though he was, 'very busy here, sweating away at a novel'.[47] A week later, however, Huxley felt compelled 'to renounce the Russian scheme altogether', due to the 'literary catastrophe' he had experienced in writing *Brave New World*: 'Which is sad — but there! I'm afraid there's no alternative. I feel less depressed as it seems, from the literature sent by [the] S C R, that one can do the trip quite fairly easily and without inordinate expense on one's own.'[48]

What was the nature of this 'catastrophe'? It has been noted by Donald Watt that '*Brave New World* was born amid a tangle of lined-out phrases, typed-over words, rearranged passages and tireless autograph insertions', and that Bernard Marx and the Savage seem to have been conceived much more positively when Huxley commenced the novel; 'Huxley qualified to a noticeable extent his initial inclination to lionize John'. Furthermore, Watt concludes that chapters 14 and 15 in the published novel are later interpolations: 'Evidence in the script suggests that Huxley also must have had important second thoughts about the novel's concluding chapters . . . [which] show him fusing what he finally wished to say in the book with the most effective way of saying it.'[49] Does this help to explain why Mustapha Mond has the most persuasive voice in *Brave New World*? It was perhaps Huxley's recognition of this which, years later, prompted him to tell his *Paris Review* interviewer that *Brave New World*

started out as a parody of H. G. Wells's *Men Like Gods*, but gradually it got out of hand and turned into something quite different from what I'd originally intended. As I became more and more interested in the subject, I wandered farther and farther from my original purpose.[50]

Huxley's 'original purpose' in writing *Brave New World* may well have been to travesty *Men Like Gods*, but parody soon gave way to hesitant prescription, with Mustapha Mond acting as Huxley's ideological spokesman. 'Stability,' Mond tells the Director of Hatcheries and Conditioning's party of students in chapter 3, 'stability. No civilization without social stability. No social stability without individual stability . . . stability. The primal and the ultimate need.'[51] Stability was also Huxley's 'ultimate need' in the early 1930s and his friend Gerald Heard managed both to hit the nail on the head regarding the novel's central theme and to distort *Brave New World*'s general reputation at the time, when he wrote that it 'was recognized increasingly as a book which (with almost unique insight into the scientific and social problem) challenged men to choose how much order they would endure to escape how much anarchy'.[52]

Around August Huxley wrote:

At moments like the present — moments of dangerous national crisis — I always find myself thinking of a certain episode in *Gulliver's Travels* . . . Faced by the menace — or worse, by the accomplished fact — of war, or revolution, or national bankruptcy, I feel (with how sickening a sense of utter helplessness!) like Gulliver in the paw of the Brobdingnagian ape.[53]

The following month the National Government slashed unemployment allowance and the salaries of ministers, judges, MPs, and teachers. It also cut the pay of the armed forces, precipitating the Invergordon Mutiny. Huxley had intended visiting America during this month, but the abandonment of the Gold Standard, following close on the tail of these other financial crises and marking 'the watershed of English history between the wars',[54] kept Huxley in a beleaguered London. He told his American publisher:

This startling out-falling of the bottom of old England has made me change my autumn plans — and I have decided that we shan't be coming to New York after all: partly for reasons of expense and partly because I want to be very much on the spot while the crisis is being solved — or not solved! — during the next few weeks and months. One develops a strong sense of patriotism when the moment comes, and I don't at all want to be out of London at this time.[55]

In his biography of Mosley, Skidelsky quotes from a letter which Huxley sent to Lady Cynthia Mosley in September 1931:

Wouldn't it be possible to bring in a Bill of Impeachment against a few of the old politicians who have landed us in this mess by their criminal negligence? I do think it would be a most excellent gesture. And if only one could get one or two shut up in the Tower, how it would encourage the rest![56]

Huxley's attention was not focused exclusively on the domestic scene; he also kept an anxious hawk's eye on the world at large:

In a recent speech, Mussolini announced the possibility, for the coming Winter, of serious and widespread revolutionary movements. It is a prophecy which one does not have to be a man of genius or a reigning dictator to make. The very facts are prophetic; we have only to let them speak.

For central Europe, monetary collapse and a series of national bankrupt-cies are grim possibilities. For the world at large, more unemployment, more poverty, more hunger, are all but certain. There is too much wheat in the world; therefore millions must go without bread; such is the almost divinely paradoxical logic of the present economic circumstances.[57]

After a month's sojourn in London, during which the campaigning for the general election of 27 October intensified, Huxley had 'the impression of being in a lunatic asylum — at the mercy of drivelling imbeciles and dangerous madmen in a state of frenzy — the politicians'.[58] The election resulted in the formation of a second National Government under Ramsay MacDonald, but for Huxley the whole affair served to exacerbate his despair of conventional politics. In 1916 he had poured scorn on Fleet Street's clamour for 'STRONG MEN',[59] yet by late 1931 Huxley was all too ready to add his voice to the growing demand for vigorous, root and branch leadership: 'We may either persist in our present course, which is disastrous, or we must abandon democracy and allow ourselves to be ruled dictatorially by men who will compel us to do and suffer what a rational foresight demands.'[60]

The absorption of biological blueprints into broader plans for the rationalization of society was not uncommon in the 1930s. Greta Jones, who has examined the link between the planning movement and the campaign for improved social hygiene during the decade, cites Julian Huxley's summary of PEP's aims in 1934 as typical of this tendency:

Planning in the sense in which that word is generally used is not enough. It is extremely important to plan out our cities, to rationalize our industries, to guard against exaggerated slumps and booms in the domain of finance, to make provision through co-operative marketing, production quotas, import regulations for a steady flow of agricultural products and a healthy farming industry, to adjust our currency to a flexible world-system, and so on. But this alone is only one aspect of biological and social engineering. In the long run, it is equally important to plan for education, for health, for self-development in adult life, for the intelligent use of the steadily increasing amount of leisure which will be available in a planned society, for quantity of population, for racial improvement.[61]

Aldous Huxley would have concurred with every word of this. Yet, unlike Naomi Mitchison, who was elected a Fellow of the Eugenics Society in July 1925, and W. B. Yeats, who joined as an ordinary member in November 1936, Huxley had no formal connections with the Eugenics Society.[62] This must surely have been because his home in the early 1930s was in France. There is certainly enough evidence to suggest that his interest in eugenics was no less fervid than that of his fellow-writers.

Huxley had discussed Leonard Darwin's *The Need for Eugenic Reform* (1926) in *Proper Studies* (1927), and soon after its publication in 1930, he read a book which was indebted to Leonard Darwin's work, R. A. Fisher's *The Genetical Theory of Natural Selection*.[63] Like Leonard Darwin, Fisher asserted that there was a deleterious inverse relation between social and biological success, in that the prosperous classes, 'being more sensitive to economic and prudential considerations', tended to limit the size of their families. Fisher proposed that a system of 'family allowances on a scale adequate to meet the actual expenditure incurred in respect of children' might help to redress this tendency, and restore the fertility of the 'upper classes'. However, he noted with apprehension that the 'length of time necessarily required before the present agencies causing racial deterioration could be completely annulled, presents, perhaps, the most formidable obstacle to such an attempt'.[64] Fisher's book clearly made an impression on Huxley and he referred to it on a number of occasions in his work in the early 1930s. Writing to Fisher in September 1931, Huxley commented:

after reading in your book about the effects on the human stock of a social organization based on economic reward I think we have a right to a good deal of gloom and alarm! The really depressing thing about such a situation as you describe is that, the evil being of slow maturation and coming to no obvious crisis, there will never be anything in the nature of a panic. And as recent events only too clearly show, it is only in moments of panic that anything gets done.[65]

The other figure in the eugenics movement to whom Huxley owed a great deal, besides Julian Huxley and Fisher, was C. P. Blacker. Blacker was General Secretary of the Eugenics Society from 1931 until 1952, and the principal architect of reform eugenics. It was he who transformed the Eugenics Society 'from a confused, unfocused, amateur organization dabbling uncertainly in the birth control movement into a quasi-professional society committed to family planning and the serious study of population problems'.[66] Blacker and Huxley lunched together at the beginning of January 1932,[67] and it is likely that Huxley's decision to discuss eugenics in his 'Science and Civilization' broadcast of 13 January owed much to this meeting:

So far as our knowledge goes, negative eugenics — or the sterilisation of the unfit — might already be practised with tolerable safety. On the positive side we are still very ignorant — though we know enough thanks to Mr Fisher's admirable work, to foresee the rapid deterioration, unless we take remedial measures, of the whole West European stock. Eugenics are not yet practical politics. But propaganda could easily make them practical politics, while increase of knowledge will make them also purposive and far-sighted politics.[68]

Although the Eugenics Society had begun a campaign to legalize voluntary sterilization following the Wood Report on Mental Deficiency (1929), and had established a committee for the legalization of eugenic sterilization in 1930, in the early 1930s the Eugenics Society began increasingly to focus its attention on birth control. However, with the support of the Eugenics Society, Major A. G. Church M.P. introduced a bill in July 1931 recommending that voluntary sterilization should be legalized. This measure was rejected by the Commons, mainly because of opposition from the Labour Party. Nevertheless, a Government committee chaired by Sir Laurence Brock was set up in 1932 to enquire into the problem of the unfit. To the immense relief of the Society, Brock's committee reported in 1934 in favour of voluntary sterilization (where disorders were indisputably hereditary) but declared that compulsory sterilization could not be justified on any grounds, eugenic or otherwise.

The Brock Report was especially significant coming as it did soon after the Nazis' introduction of compulsory sterilization early in 1933, a development which was viewed with great alarm by Blacker. At the time he wrote:

In view of the publicity which is being given to the German Sterilization Bill and of the misconceptions to which it has given rise in the Press, it is essential that Fellows and Members of this Society should do their best to dissipate the view that to legalize sterilization necessarily implies compulsion or even the smallest infringement of personal liberty.[69]

Nevertheless, the Nazi legislation disquieted many socialists and progressives within the Eugenics Society who were conscious of the inevitable comparisons being made between its espousal of voluntary sterilization and the authoritarian mould of German eugenics.

On 1 December 1933 Huxley wrote the following letter to Blacker:

I have been asked by the editor of *Nash's [Pall] Mall Magazine* to write on the question of eugenics, particularly the sterilization of the unfit. I am tolerably well up in the history of the sterilization movement in other countries and in the evidence in support of sterilization. What I should like to know, however, is this: whether the bill for the legalization of sterilization in England was actually introduced in the House of Commons and if so, what was (and what is likely to be) its fate . . . You will be doing me a great favour if you will let me know very briefly where the question of legislation stands at this moment.[70]

In addition to his reply, Blacker sent Huxley three Eugenics Society pamphlets, all of which had been produced by the Committee for Legalizing Eugenic Sterilization. One was Cecil Binney's *The Law as to Sterilization* [1930] and, another, the anonymous *Better Unborn* [1931], reproduced Church's bill, to which Huxley had alluded. It also printed statements in favour of the bill by, among others,

H. G. Wells, Malinowski, Julian Huxley, and Aldous's old biology master at Eton, M. D. Hill. Blacker also sent Huxley a copy of the *Eugenics Review* for October 1933, which contained the text of the notorious German legislation and Blacker's 'Eugenics in Germany' article which dissociated the Eugenics Society unequivocally from compulsory sterilization. Emphasizing the Society's opposition to sterilization by force, Blacker concluded his letter to Huxley with the complaint that 'the adoption of a drastic eugenics policy by the Nazis has had the not unnatural effect of still further antagonising persons of Labour persuasion against eugenics'.[71]

'What is Happening to Our Population?' the upshot of Huxley's thoughts on sterilization, must have made Blacker very angry. Dismissing the opponents of sterilization as either theologians or 'mystical democrats,' Huxley's article is at once the most wide-ranging and the most narrowly outspoken of his pronouncements on eugenics. Huxley rejects voluntary sterilization as an inadequate means of staunching the multiplication of the unfit and says practically nothing about birth control. Instead, he proposes that the putative hike in mental deficiency should be countered through a combination of the compulsory sterilization of certified defectives — even going so far as to cite the Nazi legislation as a commendable precedent — and the creation of a Fisher-ite system of fiscal allowances to promote the fertility of the professional classes:

> *If conditions remain what they are now, and if the present tendency continues unchecked, we may look forward in a century or two to a time when a quarter of the population of these islands will consist of half-wits. What a curiously squalid and humiliating conclusion to English history!*
>
> What is the remedy for the present deplorable state of affairs? It consists, obviously, in encouraging the normal and super-normal members of the population to have larger families and in preventing the sub-normal from having any families at all.[72]

Huxley incurred the wrath of G. K. Chesterton for his 'sensational' article — 'A good many things have been compulsory in Germany since the beginning of the year; and I shall be surprised if Mr Aldous Huxley approves of them' — and in the context of both the eugenics movement in the 1930s and Huxley's writings in general, 'What is Happening to Our Population?' is an unusually forthright and alarmist piece of writing.[73]

Soon after he wrote this article Huxley underwent a radical change of outlook, and the harbinger of racial decay began to make way for the saintly, reclusive humanist. The decade which had begun with Huxley holding Parliament in contempt for not merely fiddling but 'twaddling' while Rome burned, concluded with him informing Julian that 'Rome burns because it has not been sufficiently fiddled over'.[74]

But if Huxley's work in the early 1930s betrays his chronic ambivalence with regard to the state use of eugenics, the legitimate use of force in society, and the desirability of hierarchical government, this equivocation only enriches a text such as *Brave New World*. Since it was first published in 1932, Huxley's novel has been approached mainly from a dystopian perspective; we can now also recognize that *Brave New World* embodies in an absurd and distorted form ideas and opinions that Huxley framed in earnest beyond his novel's satirical parameters.

Notes

1. *James Joyce: Selected Letters*, ed. Richard Ellmann (London, 1975), 336 (20 Sept. 1928). In 'How To Not Find Joyce Letters,' *James Joyce Quarterly*, 19 (Summer 1982), 455–9, Arnold Goldman described his unsuccessful attempts to locate any letters from Joyce to Wilson. Wilson had also contacted Joyce in 1927.

2. Unpub. letters from Wilson to Compton Mackenzie, Harry Ransom Humanities Research Center, University of Texas at Austin (31 May and 30 Sept. 1948).

3. 'However, before he had been in the mines many years, his indignation was aroused at the tyrannical weapons which were often used against his mining brethren. He therefore avowed himself to be a staunch Trade Unionist, and at the very early age of 18, the Miners found in him a firm, true and solid opposer to oppression, and elected him onto the local lodge committee.

'This was only a beginning, for at the age of 20, the Miners recognized his worth and elected him Secretary of the [Willington] Brancepeth 'C' Pit Branch of the Northumberland and Durham Miners' Association, and he was the youngest office bearer of the two aforementioned societies. However, the Miners still continued to honour him, and at the age of 21, they elected him Assistant Checkweighman, and he had the unique distinction of being the youngest Checkweighman throughout the Northern Counties.' *The Poetical Works of Charles Wilson: The Pitman Poet*, vol. 1 (London, 1916), Introduction. No further volumes were published.

4. 'In the Public Eye: Potted Personalities', *Auckland and County Chronicle*, 16 Oct. 1930, 6. Wilson's only surviving relation stated that 'when he died all his papers were destroyed'. Letter received from Mrs E. Bartlett, 1 May 1985.

5. *The Letters of D. H. Lawrence*, vi, *March 1927–November 1928*, ed. James T. Boulton and Margaret H. Boulton (Cambridge, 1991), 430.

6. See ibid. 229–30, 247–8, 266–7, 279–80, 499; and *The Letters of D. H. Lawrence*, vii, *November 1928–February 1930*, ed. Keith Sagar and James T. Boulton (Cambridge, 1993), 58, 98–104, and 202–3, for Lawrence's replies.

7. *The Letters of D. H. Lawrence*, vi. 248.

8. Ibid. 266–7.

9. *The Letters of D. H. Lawrence*, vii. 99–103.

10. *The Letters of Aldous Huxley*, ed. Grover Smith (London, 1969), 341.

11. According to the *Auckland and County Chronicle*, 30 Oct. 1930, 1, there were 119,000 men and boys on the dole in County Durham.

12. Published as 'Science and Poetry', *Spectator*, 146 (Jan. 1931), 74–5. Repr. as '"And Wanton Optics Roll the Melting Eye"', in Huxley's *Music at Night* (1931), 32–42.

13. 'Abroad in England', *Nash's Pall Mall Magazine*, 87 (May 1931), 16–19, 84. The full text of this article, and other neglected Huxley pieces from this period, have been gathered together in David Bradshaw, ed., *The Hidden Huxley: Contempt and Compassion for the Masses, 1920–1936* (London, 1994).

14. The Poetry/Rare Books Collection, University Libraries, State University of New York at Buffalo (12 Oct. 1930). Excerpts from the replies which Diston received, including Huxley's response, were published in 'What They Think of Us', *The New Leader*, 26 Dec. 1930, 6.

15. *Parliamentary Debates: Official Report. House of Commons*, Vol. 248, 5th ser. (London, 1931), col. 447.

16. 'Greater and Lesser London', *Nash's Pall Mall Magazine*, 88 (Oct. 1931), 48–9, 108. Reprinted in Bradshaw, *Hidden Huxley*.

17. Robert Skidelsky, *Politicians and the Slump: The Labour Government of 1929–1931* (Harmondsworth, 1970), 320.

18. 'Greater and Lesser London'.

19. Robert Skidelsky, *Oswald Mosley* (London, 1975), 237.

20. Oswald Mosley, *My Life* (London, 1968), 225.

21. In the possession of Mrs Anne Charlton (8 Feb. 1931).

22. Quoted in James Lees-Milne, *Harold Nicolson: A Biography*, 2 vols. (London, 1981), ii. 24.

23. A. J. P. Taylor, *English History 1914–1945* (Harmondsworth, 1979), 375.

24. John Pinder (ed.), *Fifty Years of Political and Economic Planning: Looking Forward 1931–1981* (London, 1981), 9.

25. 'A National Plan for Great Britain,' *Week-End Review*, 3, 14 Feb. 1931, Supplement, i.

26. 'Origins of PEP', PEP Papers, British Library of Political and Economic Science, MS Folder UP10 (dated 24 Oct. 1947).

27. 'The Thirties: A Preliminary Survey', PEP Papers, MS Folder UP10.

28. A statement of the aims of PEP was published in the *Week-End Review*, 3, 21 Mar. 1931, 434.

29. 'The Early Days of PEP', PEP Papers, MS Folder UP10. Israel Sieff mentions this incident in his *Memoirs* (London, 1970), 166, though he was not present at the time.

30. Letter received from Max Nicholson (29 Sept. 1985).

31. Letter received from Kenneth Lindsay (22 Oct. 1985).

32. Pinder, *Fifty Years of Political and Economic Planning*, 211.

33. Letter received from Max Nicholson (29 Sept. 1985).

34. '"1950 Society": Notes on Situation Arising from First Ivy [Restaurant] Meeting', PEP Papers, MS 1/7/2.

35. *Week-End Review*, 14 Feb. 1931, Supplement, viii.

36. Quoted in Daniel Ritschel, 'The Non-Socialist Movement for a Planned Economy in Britain in the 1930s' (D.Phil. thesis, Oxford, 1987), 112.

37. Pinder, *Fifty Years of Political and Economic Planning*, 15.

38. 'Abroad in England'.

39. David Caute, *The Fellow-Travellers: A Postscript to the Enlightenment* (London, 1973), 66. See also Paul Hollander, *Political Pilgrims: Travels of Western Intellectuals to the Soviet Union, China and Cuba 1928–1978* (New York and Oxford, 1981), esp. ch. 4, 'The Appeal of Soviet Society: The First Pilgrimage', 102–76.

40. 'Science of Politics?' *Chicago Herald and Examiner*, 4 Mar. 1933, 9.

41. M. Ilin, *Moscow Has a Plan: A Soviet Primer*, trans. G. S. Counts and N. P. Lodge (London, 1931). See Huxley's 'A Soviet School Book', *Chicago Herald and Examiner*, 29 Oct., 11.

42. Quoted in Andrew Rothstein, 'The Foundation of the SCR', *Anglo-Soviet Journal*, 45 (Autumn 1984), 4–6.

43. James Aldridge and Emma Smith, 'The First Ten Years', ibid. 7–9.

44. M. G. Gurevitch, *The Five Year Plan* (London, 1931).

45. Collinson Owen, 'Gentlemen Who Prefer Bombs', *Daily Mail*, 30 June 1931, 11–12.

46. *Nash's Pall Mall Magazine*, 87 (July 1931), 46–9. Reprinted in Bradshaw, *Hidden Huxley*.

47. Unpub. letter in the possession of Lady Huxley (17 May 1931).

48. Huxley, *Letters*, 348–9.

49. Donald Watt, 'The Manuscript Revisions of *Brave New World*', *Journal of English and Germanic Philology*, 77 (July 1978), 367–82.

50. *Writers at Work: The 'Paris Review' Interviews*, 2nd ser. (London, 1963), 165.

51. Aldous Huxley, *Brave New World* (London, 1932), 48.

52. Gerald Heard, *These Hurrying Years: An Historical Outline 1900–1933* (London, 1934), 257.

53. 'Angry Ape', *Nash's Pall Mall Magazine*, 88 (Dec. 1931), 32.

54. Taylor, *English History 1914–1945*, 374.
55. Huxley, *Letters*, 354.
56. Skidelsky, *Oswald Mosley*, 227. I am grateful to Lord Skidelsky for providing me with a photocopy of this letter, dated 26 Sept. 1931. *not 1930, as its use in Skidelsky's text implies.*
57. 'Revolution', *Chicago Herald and Examiner*, 24 Sept. 1931, 9.
58. Huxley, *Letters*, 356.
59. Ibid. 99.
60. 'Forewarned is not Forearmed', *Chicago Herald and Examiner*, 18 Nov. 1931, 9. Repr. in *Nash's Pall Mall Magazine*, 89 (July 1932), 50.
61. Greta Jones, *Social Hygiene in Twentieth Century Britain* (London, 1986), 124.
62. Information obtained from Naomi Mitchison's and W. B. Yeats's membership cards, Galton Institute, London.
63. 'Foreheads Villainous Low', *Week-End Review*, 2, 20 Sept. 1930, 371–2. Repr. in *Music at Night*, 201–10.
64. R. A. Fisher, *The Genetical Theory of Natural Selection* (Oxford, 1930), 263.
65. Quoted in J. H. Bennett (ed.), *Natural Selection, Heredity and Eugenics: Including Selected Correspondence of R. A. Fisher with Leonard Darwin and Others* (Oxford, 1983), 220 (letter dated 26 Sept. 1931).
66. Richard A. Soloway, *Demography and Degeneration: Eugenics and the Declining Birthrate in Twentieth-Century Britain* (Chapel Hill NC and London, 1990), 195. See also 186–7.
67. Unpub. postcard (2 Jan. 1932), Julian Huxley file, C. P. Blacker Archive, Wellcome Unit for the History of Medicine, University of Oxford.
68. 'Science and Civilisation', BBC National Programme, 13 Jan. 1932. Published as 'Science — the Double-Edged Tool', *Listener*, 7, 20 Jan. 1932, [77]–9, 112. Repr. in a slightly revised form as 'Economists, Scientists and Humanists', in Mary Adams (ed.), *Science in the Changing World* (London, 1933), [209]–23. Repr. in Bradshaw, *Hidden Huxley*.
69. C. P. Blacker, 'Eugenics in Germany', *Eugenics Review*, 25 (Oct. 1933), 157–9.
70. Unpub. letter, Julian Huxley file, C. P. Blacker Archive, Wellcome Unit for the History of Medicine, University of Oxford.
71. Carbon copy of unpub. letter (4 Dec. 1933) in the Eugenics Society Archive, Contemporary Medical Archives Centre, Wellcome Institute for the History of Medicine, London. File EUG/C.184 Aldous Huxley.
72. 'What is Happening to Our Population?', *Nash's Pall Mall Magazine*, 93 (Apr. 1934), 12–13, 76–8. Reprinted in Bradshaw, *Hidden Huxley*.
73. G. K. Chesterton, 'The Two Aldous Huxleys', *Nash's Pall Mall Magazine*, 93 (Aug. 1934), 78–9.
74. Huxley, *Letters*, 438.

❧ 11 ❧

Elizabeth Bishop: The Secret Life of a Poet

LINDA ANDERSON

Elizabeth Bishop showed little enthusiasm for attempts to link the writer's work to his or her life. Reviewing a book by Rebecca Patterson entitled *The Riddle of Emily Dickinson* in 1951, she dismissed such works of 'literary detective work' as finally 'just unpleasant'. What she objected to in general was the reductiveness of an approach which subsumed the complexity and open-endedness of both the life and the work into a quest for ultimate revelation: 'In order to reach a single reason for anything as singular and yet manifold as literary creation it is necessary to limit to the point of mutilation the human personality's capacity for growth and redirection.'[1] However, her antipathy to this work in particular may have been fuelled by the specific nature of its claims: that the secret behind Dickinson's life and work was her love for another woman. Always publicly reticent about her own lesbianism, Bishop could well have feared and resented the possibility of such sexual revelations overwhelming the singular and manifold achievement of her own creative work; of the appearance of actively choosing within her own life — her capacity for growth and redirection — being lost beneath the single determinant of sexual choice.

Bishop was equally negative about the value of self-disclosure for the writer. 'You just wish they'd keep some of these things to themselves', was her famous comment about confessional poetry in an interview for *Time* magazine in 1967.[2] In teaching notes she made in 1968 or 1969, she saw Robert Lowell's *Life Studies* as unfortunately marking a 'great change' in contemporary poetry: 'I'm afraid this started the present vogue for CONFESSIONAL POETRY — although he himself didn't confess anything at all shocking — his younger imitators sometimes outdo each other in Telling

All.'³ Until Robert Lowell wrote the poems in *The Dolphin* in 1972 which, for Bishop, simply revealed too much, 'violating a trust' in the use they made of private letters, she enthusiastically endorsed his work;⁴ even afterwards, she always tried to maintain a distinction between Lowell's poetry and the greater excesses of his followers. 'There's all the difference in the world [between] "Life Studies" and those who now out-sex Anne Sexton', she wrote to him in 1974.⁵

Yet Bishop's hostile stance towards confession and public exposure could also be read in another way: not as a simple dismissal of a biographical context for writing but as engaging difficult questions about what it is appropriate or even possible to reveal about oneself or others; and about whether the disclosure of 'secrets' could act as a guarantee of authenticity or truth. In fact in her own poems Bishop is often autobiographical in oblique but sometimes quite obvious ways; she also wrote autobiographical prose, including the disturbing and remarkable account of her early childhood, 'In the Village'.⁶ She was always careful about facts and pleased when she could verify the accuracy of her memories; literal or biographical truth thus retained a significance and meaning for Bishop; never became something she felt free as a writer to distort, discard, or invent. She was also an avid reader of other people's lives and letters; at Harvard in 1971 she designed and taught a course on poets and their letters.⁷

In the series of three prose poems entitled 'Rainy Season; Sub-Tropics', which Bishop completed in 1967, she seems to join her poetic self to displaced and awkward animal bodies: the three monologues are spoken by a Giant Toad, a Strayed Crab, and lastly a Giant Snail:

The sides of my mouth are now my hands. They press the earth and suck it hard. Ah, but I know my shell is beautiful, and high, and glazed, and shining. I know it well, although I have not seen it. Its curled white lip is of the finest enamel. Inside, it is as smooth as silk, and I, I fill it to perfection.

My wide wake shines, now it is growing dark. I leave a lovely opalescent ribbon: I know this.

But O! I am too big. I feel it. Pity me.

If and when I reach the rock, I shall go into a certain crack there for the night. The waterfall below will vibrate through my shell and body all night long. In that steady pulsing I can rest. All night I shall be like a sleeping ear.[8]

The 'lovely opalescent ribbon' which the snail leaves behind could well stand for writing itself, the inscription of the snail's passage through the world, a track or a trace which is 'lovely' — an aesthetic object — but which is also drawn from the snail's body, a residue offering evidence of the corporeality of the subject and its living past. Bishop's snail-artist, who is never far enough from the ground or its body to take possession of them through looking, who cannot transcend its own carnality, is both at home inside its body and its pleasures, and subject to an uncertainty about boundaries and perspectives, about how it occupies space; its journey or desire is towards an interior, hidden place, a space which can maternally·contain it. For Bishop, it would seem, the body could not simply be overcome or even surveyed from some transcendental place; it shapes subjectivity and leaves its mark on artistic production. And because our bodies are also inevitably gendered, Bishop's symbology of the body is distinctly feminine, as is also, perhaps, her image of the body's traces with its associations of viscosity or mucosity.[9]

What I want to explore in this essay, taking Bishop's snail as my starting-point, is a model of the relation between biography and poetic creation which neither sacrifices the life to the text — the anonymous textuality of post-structuralist theory — nor assumes that life and text can be simply linked in a narrative of cause and effect: that biography is a prior or privileged narrative which can enfold the time of writing into its own ordering of origins and ends. In her recently published biography of Elizabeth Bishop, Brett Millier admits that 'hard facts about Elizabeth Bishop's childhood, as about anyone's, are few'. 'And yet,' she goes on,

few writers have been as consistent and complete in writing about childhood. Bishop claimed a very literal sort of accuracy as her highest poetic value, and is rarely caught in an error or contradiction. Her own accounts, in poetry and prose both published and unpublished, are the main source of information about her earliest years.[10]

This, of course, provides reassuring confirmation of my own assertion that Bishop was an ardent and careful autobiographer in both her poetry and her prose. But it also turns back on itself: for if Bishop's own accounts are 'the main source of information about her earliest years', how can they also stand outside or before the time of her own written texts; how can they also provide the basis for this different, explanatory narrative about her? The draft of an unpublished poem, 'A Drunkard', a poem which Millier uses in her biography as evidence of an early traumatic incident in Bishop's childhood and in her relationship with her mother, ends with the line: 'And all I'm telling you may be a lie'.[11] This statement seems to stand as a warning or a rebuke to the reader who may have been drawn too easily into complicity with 'a drunkard's' story. It could also point to Bishop's own uncertainty, her inability to verify her own memory, her recognition of the unreliable or equivocal nature of any act of self-representation. 'If we could only get through our own *figurativeness*', she wrote in her notebook in 1935,[12] acknowledging to herself with some frustration the entanglement of identity with the irreducibly figurative or fictive nature of language itself.

To return for a moment to Bishop's snail. Both the snail itself, and its 'lovely opalescent ribbon' are, of course, figures for the poet–subject and the traces of her body in the production of a text, rather than those traces themselves. What they cover over or mask as figures (whilst serving as metaphors for it) is the process of signifying itself, what is involved in the emergence of a sign or a figure — if you like, the moment of identification which calls the sign into being as its object.

What I want to do here is to try to understand a little better what is involved in this process of signifying and how it is carried within the sign not as representation — the way in which the snail and its opalescent ribbon could be said to be figures for representation itself — but rather as trace. In order to do this I want to turn first of all to a notable feature of Bishop's writing career: the prolonged period of gestation for many of her poems. The most famous instance in this respect is 'The Moose', begun in 1946 and not completed until 1972; it was eventually published in the volume *Geography 111* in 1976, some thirty years after its conception.[13] This slow — even snail-like — pace of composition creates a problem for her biographer since it is hard to fit it to the swifter cadence of life events. In Bishop's notebooks, observations and descriptions frequently appear which will find their way into poems decades afterwards: for example, references to Robinson Crusoe and a fascination with the idea of living on an island — making do in a difficult situation — occur in her notebook in 1934: 'On an island you live all the time in this Robinson Crusoe atmosphere; making this do for that, and contriving and inserting . . .'[14] She also reads in the same month Parington's *Colonial Mind* and notes with interest the idea of Robinson Crusoe as middle class, 'even his umbrella is extremely bourgeois', she observes.[15] Her poem 'Crusoe in England', which has Crusoe in old age looking back at his island experience, was begun by Bishop in 1963 or 1964; she finished it in 1970. By being written years before, carried with her in memory and notebooks over the years, images and ideas which eventually find their way into her poems could accordingly take on, I suggest, something of the materiality of objects.

In a passage in her notebook reminiscent of Virginia Woolf's description of her diary as 'some deep old desk, or capacious hold-all, in which one flings a mass of odds & ends without looking them through',[16] Bishop imagined a place in which she could store a mass of disparate objects acquired at different times throughout her life:

Sometimes I wish I had a junk-room, store-room an attic where I could keep and had kept, all my life the odds & ends that took my fancy . . . *Everything and Anything*: If one had such a place to throw things into, like a sort of extra brain, and a chair in the middle of it to go and sit on once in a while, it might be a great help — particularly as it all decayed and fell together and took on a general odor.[17]

Inconsequential objects — like the seemingly irrelevant details of memory itself — could carry with them an unconscious significance. For Bishop such objects take on the trace or 'general odor' of all the other meanings stored in the 'junk-room' of her unconscious. As with Woolf, Bishop wanted both the familiarity and the precise detail of objects and the estrangement wrought on them by the passage of time, their 'ghosts' and 'distortions';[18] she wanted to imagine them through the process of a return.

One object which we can see Bishop making such a return to was a kite — writing first about it in her notebook in 1938 and then including it as a ghostly figure in her late poem, 'The End of March', in 1974. In 1938, some days after writing about 'the sound of the waves on the sand-bar, rushing like white-handwriting',[19] she described the pleasure of flying a kite: 'When there is a wind it is out of your hand & up in the air almost before you lug it out of the house. It stands in the air steadily — moving very slightly from side to side once in a while.'[20] In 'The End of March' she comes across on her walk 'A kite string? — But no kite', 'lengths and lengths, endless, of wet white string, / looping up to the tide line, down to the water, over and over'. The poem, which itself records a visit to somewhere she has been before, and which is structured around an outward journey and a return, ends by reanimating the tracks or traces she encountered before, both the paw-prints and the kite string:

> On the way back our faces froze on the other side.
> The sun came out for just a minute.
> For just a minute, set in their bezels of sand,
> the drab, damp, scattered stones
> were multi-colored,
> and all those high enough threw out long shadows,
> individual shadows, then pulled them in again.
> They could have been teasing the lion sun,
> except that now he was behind them
> — a sun who'd walked the beach the last low tide,
> making those big, majestic paw-prints,
> who perhaps had batted a kite out of the sky to play with.[21]

If I am right and that kite makes its appearance in this poem having already been written about years before, then it not only represents a real object but is a figure for writing itself — its wet string also working as a visual equivalent, like the white handwriting Bishop had already read in the tide's edge in 1938. But having been written about, it also carries with it something of the materiality of that past: paw-prints and kite string could be seen as traces or as traced through with a previous meaning; about them hovers the question: have I already done this, have I already been here? In a sense Bishop is able to stabilize the meaning of these images at the end of the poem, the blurring of the borderline between past and present, remembering and forgetting, by refiguring them, freeing them into a realm of sheer invention or play, letting them take on a life of their own, a life which is separate from her.

What I am attempting to describe in Bishop's writing is something close to the idea of displacement. According to Freud displacement is the 'psychological process by which . . . indifferent experiences take the place of psychically significant ones';[22] this explains, for Freud, the way that 'worthless fragments' or the 'unimportant details of waking life' are frequently used by the unconscious as the manifest content of dreams.[23] In an entry in her notebook for 1940 Bishop recorded her dislike for the mountains of North Carolina. 'I hate masses of things you can't see the shape of, no formality anywhere', she wrote, revealing how her mind was quick to register the analogy between geographical and psychical landscapes. She went on:

Every time I look at the mountains I think of the expression 'at the back of my mind'. This sensation they give is so strong that I feel a physical compulsion to turn my back and then with them *there*, to go on looking at the ferns, roots, etc.[24]

Bishop turns to the detail in the foreground as a strategy of displacement, just as she frequently focused on seemingly inconsequential but psychically charged objects in her writing. But the mountains, or the unconscious meanings looming in the background, are, as Bishop says, still there. However, we could also think about this scene in terms of Julia Kristeva's idea of abjection, since it is the shapelessness or formlessness of the mountains that seem to threaten Bishop, that must be kept separate or at a distance in order to protect her identity. The abject, says Kristeva in a metaphor that maps well on to Bishop's landscape, 'is a land of oblivion which is constantly remembered'; it beckons but it must be constantly separated from.[25] As Kristeva defines it, the abject is the unspoken or unrepresentable underside of the symbolic; it is what threatens the subject's stable speaking position in the symbolic with the dissolution of boundaries, with a falling back into the body, into materiality and chaos. 'We may call it a border,' Kristeva writes; 'abjection is above all ambiguity. Because while releasing a hold, it does not radically cut off the subject from what threatens it.'[26] Abjection takes us to the edge, to the very place or moment when identity or the autonomy of subject and language becomes possible or impossible, to the threshold between language and the body.

'In The Waiting Room', again one of Bishop's later poems, seems to hover on just such a threshold, threatening the subject at the very moment of identification with a terrifying loss of boundaries. Hearing her aunt's cry of pain 'from inside' whilst outside in the dentist's waiting-room, the child speaker of the poem becomes unsure whether the cry is her own or her aunt's:

> What took me
> completely by surprise
> was that it was *me*:
> my voice, in my mouth.
> Without thinking at all
> I was my foolish aunt,
> I — we — were falling, falling,
> our eyes glued to the cover
> of the *National Geographic*,
> February, 1918.[27]

Here the child's concentration on the cover of the magazine, on the surface or outside, does not stave off the pain coming from the inside, in the sense of both her aunt's cry and her already troubled identification with the representations of the body and of femininity inside the magazine. Her moment of identification and self-naming: 'you are an I, You are an *Elizabeth*, you are one of *them*' is fragile, ambiguous. As Kristeva points out, '*I am* only *like* someone else'; thus the 'territory I can call my own' is ambiguous since the Other 'points it out to me through loathing'; since, in other words, it can only be reached through the process of abjection. Within the poem the child speaker struggles with the 'Otherness' of her own identity, an Otherness which, in Kristeva's terms, both 'precedes' and 'possesses' her and 'causes her to be'.[28] She experiences a moment of vertigo and revulsion — the very moment of abjection — when she stands at the boundary between being an embodied subject and what that means symbolically.

It is difficult to read this poem without thinking of that other 'cry' in Bishop's writing, the mother's scream in the story 'In the Village'. That scream dominates the narrator's memory of her childhood in an almost visual sense, unforgettable, ineradicable as a stain: 'A scream, the echo of a scream, hangs over that Nova Scotian village. No one hears it; it hangs there forever, a slight stain in those pure blue skies.'[29] Throughout the story the careful, detailed attention to place and to objects threatens to give way, to reveal itself as only the fragile exterior to other unconscious regions, the sounds which have preceded the signs and which linger in the descriptions as a 'stain' or a trace. The narrator's power to demarcate a territory for herself, a territory she can 'call her own', is both realized in the story through the kind of minute description she is engaged in and under threat from what she cannot see, a fear she can never completely separate herself from and which make the boundaries of her world themselves permeable. Even the 'clang' that issues from the anvil of Nate, the blacksmith, the sound of a masculine creativity, is less 'a solace and a refuge'[30] from the mother's scream than a container for it, gathering within itself the 'affect' or 'fascination' of that other sound.[31]

Bishop is a writer who has frequently been praised for her powers of observation — for her 'eye' — but what is apparent is that her images are frequently layered, calling attention to an anterior relation to sound. In this way she summons up what has already been traced within the signs, a more archaic relation to the body. To end this essay I want to return to where I started, to Bishop's snail. She describes the snail at the end of the prose poem as a sleeping ear: 'All night I shall be like a sleeping ear'. She employs, in other words, an image which is visually appropriate —

but, as I have tried to show, the body's significance is also there in another way; it is also there as a trace or an echo to be heard.

Notes

1. Published in *New Republic*, 127/7 (18 Aug. 1952), 20.
2. *Time*, 2 June 1967, 35–42 (p. 42).
3. 'Three American Poets', typescript, Vassar College Library.
4. See Ian Hamilton, *Robert Lowell: A Biography* (London, 1983), 422–3.
5. Quoted in Brett Millier, *Elizabeth Bishop: Life and the Memory of It* (Berkeley, Calif. and Los Angeles, 1993), 490.
6. See Elizabeth Bishop, *Collected Prose* (New York, 1984), 251–74.
7. See Millier, *Elizabeth Bishop*, 453.
8. See *Elizabeth Bishop: The Complete Poems 1927–1979* (New York, 1983), 140–1. I am indebted to Helen Vendler's article, 'The Poems of Elizabeth Bishop', *Critical Inquiry*, 13 (Summer 1987), 825–38 for drawing my attention to this poem and its metaphorical possibilities.
9. 'Mucosity' is an important term within Luce Irigaray's writing and her attempt to rethink sexual difference. She uses it not simply in a referential way but to invoke what cannot be thought within phallocentric paradigms. Thus it crosses as a term a series of important conceptual boundaries: it is neither solid nor fluid; it can expand but its shape is unstable; it marks a threshold between inside and outside. See Luce Irigaray, 'Sexual Difference', in Margaret Whitford (ed.), *The Irigaray Reader* (Oxford, 1991), 165–77 (p. 175), and Margaret Whitford, *Luce Irigaray: Philosophy in the Feminine* (London and New York, 1991), 163.
10. Millier, *Elizabeth Bishop*, 1–2.
11. Typescript 1971, Vassar College Library.
12. 'Recorded Observations', 12 June 1935, Vassar College Library.
13. See Lorrie Goldensohn, *Elizabeth Bishop: The Biography of a Poetry* (New York, 1992), 252–9, for an interesting discussion of the process of composition of this poem.
14. 'Recorded Observations', July 1934, Vassar College Library.
15. 'Recorded Observations', 25 July 1934, Vassar College Library.
16. *The Diary of Virginia Woolf*, ed. Anne Olivier Bell and Andrew McNeillie, 5 vols. (London, 1977–84), i. 266 (20 Apr. 1919).
17. 'Recorded Observations', 17 Aug. 1935, Vassar College Library.
18. Ibid.
19. 'Travel Diary', 17 Aug. 1938, Vassar College Library.
20. 'Travel Diary', 6 Sept. 1938, Vassar College Library.
21. *Complete Poems*, 180.
22. Sigmund Freud, *The Interpretation of Dreams*, Pelican Freud Library, 15 vols., iv (Harmondsworth, 1976), 263.
23. Ibid. 260.
24. 'Travel Diary', 10/26 Aug. 1940, Vassar College Library.

25. Julia Kristeva, *Powers of Horror*, trans. Leon S. Roudiez (New York, 1982), 8.

26. Ibid. 9.

27. *Complete Poems*, 160.

28. Kristeva, *Powers of Horror*, 10.

29. *Collected Prose*, 251.

30. Robert Griroux, Introduction to *Collected Prose*, p. x.

31. See Patricia Yaeger, *Honey-Mad Women* (New York, 1988), 134–46, for an interesting discussion of this story.

PART III

Life and Art: The Biographer at Work
and the
Writer as Biographer

Jane Austen, Matthew Arnold, Shakespeare: The Problem of the Opus

PARK HONAN

'Sticks and stones may break our bones', Richard Wilson writes in an essay on the New Historicism in literary studies, 'but words will surely kill us.'[1]

That is a comment on the theory that Indians of the New World were destroyed not by bullets and cold steel, but by Spanish writing. Well, we have had the Holocaust of the 1930s and 1940s; words preceded it, prepared it. Yet even so, Wilson's comment might have looked odd in an essay on literary criticism written much before our own time. Matters changed around 1970. Since then, literary theory, under the effect of structuralist, post-structuralist, several kinds of historicist, deconstructive, and feminist and gender critics among others, has changed radically from its old formalist basis. A poem, play, or novel — or the *opus* — is seen to be enmeshed in a complex web of social and historical factors by those who grant that 'literary' texts have any real existence.

If we live in a storm of theory, what has this done to the writing of literary biography? This genre is pragmatic. As if to ward off an assault of theories, biographers in the 1980s announced their own rules and 'musts'. Some are sweepingly prescriptive. Suppose we hope to write a life of Honoré de Balzac. We are told we must relate Balzac to his novels 'meaningfully and profoundly'. Or in a biography, we must include a 'sensitive evaluation' of *Eugénie Grandet*, if not of the whole *Comédie humaine* (or of everything from *Les Chouans* in 1829 on). Or with help of the Interpreter's Freud — if not of the Clinician's Freud, too — we must psychoanalyse Balzac deeply enough to show the tensions and traumas in his work.

Freud can be useful. But others throw up their hands over the notion of thinking too much about biography, and there is something to be said for this. Lord Blake tells about the principles that helped him to write his *Disraeli*, but he isn't unreasonable in adding that arguably 'one might write better biographies by not thinking too much or too self-consciously about the correct way of doing it'.[2]

Sometimes while engaged in research, and just to clear my head, test new evidence, or explore some aspect of a form, I have succumbed to writing short biographical essays myself and have usually sent them off to a specialized journal — with the hope that if I have said something quite woolly or wrong, not many will notice the folly. Coming across Ira Bruce Nadel's (quite fair and accurate) comments on a piece called 'The Theory of Biography', I was put off by my own prescriptiveness; at least this piece, slightly revised and retitled 'After Boswell', sits better in a book which *has* no doctrinal unity, a collection of my experimental essays called *Authors' Lives*. Are there really any hard and fast axioms for biography other than Desmond MacCarthy's to the effect that we are 'under oath' and ought to respect factuality? (Without that, biography stops.) The form thrives on variety, and that is why it is one of the liveliest and most exciting of genres today; of course if we write of Balzac's life, we don't need to psychoanalyse him, we don't need to evaluate *Père Goriot* or anything else, we don't need necessarily to discuss his fiction at all. Is Boswell's *Johnson* worse for scanting Dr Johnson's art? Is a 'documentary life' of Shakespeare worse for saying little of the plays, even less about the Reformation or Renaissance?

But there is some evolution of forms. I think practices may have changed on the whole in about two ways since the 1970s, in that we are more modest about 'inclusiveness' and more alert to multivalence in evidence.

As we give up the 'definitive' aim, we see better how new works can supplement those we have. David Nokes's agile *Jonathan Swift* of the 1980s builds on Ehrenpreis's 'monumental' *Swift*. With its fine sense of the Victorian religious mind Ian Ker's 'intellectual' biography *John Henry Newman* (1988) supplements Meriol Trevor's colourful volumes on Newman's locales and milieux. Delving into a social matrix, Katherine Duncan-Jones's *Sir Philip Sidney* (1991) replies to biographies which had taken 'political ideas' as the link between Sidney's art and life.

Theories tell us about the difficulty of hermeneutics, and we find history and personal identity more obscure. Leeds Barroll writes of the 'still immature study of historical personality', and shows that Shakespeare's rhythm of creativity may be related to details about *Yersina pestis* and rat-fleas; but the plague was only one of many factors bearing on Jacobean theatre-interdictions, which must have affected the creative rhythms of poets.[3] In our era of microbiology, the only occasions we have had to study at first hand some conditions that may have affected the writing of *King Lear* have been in Mongolia, Korea, and China early in this century. It seems there have been no major outbreaks of bubonic plague since. If history gets that complex, then all biographers may be involved in a co-operative enterprise. And we begin to see how helpful it is to take the document as multivalent — of as much value in telling us about history, society, and group codes, as about one person.

It helps, too, at a time of jostling literary theories, to see how the theories can be useful to biographers. Let us try to illustrate that briefly by taking up a novelist, a poet, and a playwright in the light of a few of the ideas of deconstruction, the New Criticism, and the New Historicism.

The authors here — Austen, Arnold, Shakespeare — are three whom I've tried to see in a biographical light. As for the theories, I may be naïve. I'm not worried. What are they good for, if not for an easy, free play of mind?

To begin with Jane Austen's *Mansfield Park* and Jacques Derrida will seem an odd pairing — for Derrida has been *l'enfant terrible* among modern French critics. His relation to Heidegger's phenomenology should mean more to me than it does, since two of Heidegger's Berlin pupils, Kurt and Alice Bergel, were once my teachers and are now my friends. But we want only Derrida's suggestiveness for Jane Austen.

189

One of his ideas seems to be that we may dissolve the notion of the artistic 'author' or 'text', but also reconstitute any such a notion, as Derrida surely does in his delightful aphoristic essay 'L'aphorisme à contretemps' on *Romeo and Juliet*.[4] Another idea is that it is useful to question even the obvious linkage between an author's *proper name* and a *text* — from which one might conclude that *naming* might be of special interest to a literary biographer.[5]

In fact — and curiously — Jane Austen's proper name and the text of *Mansfield Park* were never linked in print during her own lifetime. This novel appeared, in 1814, as 'by the Author of "Sense and Sensibility", and "Pride and Prejudice"', and the first of *those* had appeared three years earlier as 'by a Lady', after notices which called the author only: 'a Lady', 'Lady — ', and 'Lady A— '.

Did Jane Austen write *Mansfield Park*? No one else wrote any of it. But Derrida doesn't question authorship; he seems to ask about *naming*. Now, the author's experiences in Kent among the names 'Mansfield' and 'Yates' seem to bear on themes and motifs in *Mansfield Park*. But her preference for 'real' names extends far beyond that. Why do her brothers' Christian names parade through her novels? After slightly neglecting Charles Austen in this way, she put six 'Charles'es in one work, to the possible confusion of the reader because four have the same surname, 'Musgrove', which was the name of a gentleman in the family of one of her godmothers when Jane Austen was christened — or when she became 'Jane Austen'. She put another gentleman's name from that family, 'Mr John Knightley', straight into *Emma*; she used her own name and her sister Cassandra Elizabeth's second for the two liveliest Bennets in *Pride and Prejudice*, and so on.

There may not be a case, in the whole history of fiction, of a writer who was so deliberately *un*inventive with names as Jane Austen. How might this concern a biographer? Suppose playfully, taking a hint from Derrida, we were for a while to dissolve the idea of 'author', so that we might look with a certain new freedom and realism into a creative situation back in a Hampshire rectory in the 1780s. Just then, Jane Austen's brothers were bringing home comic, Tory tales that play on words such as 'sensibility', or on 'prejudice' and 'pride'.

We have heard Jane Austen had no political opinions. But there is good evidence, now, that she was one of the strongest Tories in her household. How would politics have affected a creative situation in which she was supposed to be an entertainer? How would the personalities around her have impinged? In the 1980s new material about these persons came to light, so we are by no means quite in the dark. Isn't it possible that *naming* had a much more vital role in her early life than has been supposed?

We won't find her less independent than we have believed, I'm sure, but we may find her even more playful and intelligent. By dissolving static notions, and asking us to look into what seems simple, but is not, Derrida might help biographers in one great way. He can keep us from taking things for granted as in this case when we look into the nature of a novelist's creativity.

For our second example, we look into the New Criticism, which according to Paul de Man had its real heyday from about 1935 into the 1950s. It had some origins in earlier writings of T. S. Eliot and I. A. Richards. According to this view, the poem or *opus* is a self-contained, autonomous structure. It is cut off from the author. It may be examined for its own 'tension', 'irony', 'paradoxes', and the like.

I remember when this theory was popular. Leavis, Empson, and others who were not 'New Critics' swelled its authority. As a student at Chicago University around 1950 (before I began to study in London), I recall that friends such as Paul Carroll, C. R. Moyer, Joan DuBrow, and Larry Ragan (some of whom became poets, critics, or essayists) were too struck by lyrics to have time for love-affairs, and we recited or argued over Donne or Browning long into the night. We were pleased to have T. S. Eliot teach a poetry seminar and recite *The Waste Land* to our English Club, and I suppose we felt safe from Eliot because we had undoctrinaire critics (who also exalted the poem) such as Norman Maclean. His last words to me in his eighties may suggest his tone. 'Good to see you, Honan. Good to see you. But I've got to meet that bastard Robert Redford — who wants to make a FILM out of *A River Runs Through It!*'

And such a practical spirit made us run to the library for biographies. These we found dreadful. But in 1950, we were at the edge of a renaissance. Oddly, a New Critical paradigm for biography had been suggested by Eliot himself, when in the same year as 'Tradition and the Individual Talent' he had said in the essay 'Ben Jonson' that the creating of a stage-character 'consists in the process of transfusion of the personality, or, in a deeper sense, the life, of the author into the character. . . . The ways in which the passions and desires of the creator may be satisfied in the work of art are complex and devious.'[6] In my present thumb-nail sketch, I'm not trying to write (or rewrite) our century's literary history about which I know too little, and yet I try not to be glib or over-simple. Eliot's plan or paradigm is often implicit in New Critical essays, which admit that the two *objects* of prime interest in Western literature must be the author (with 'passions', 'desires' as in Eliot's phrase) and the marvel of the poem or *opus*. Eliot implies the ways between them are complex, devious, obscure, but they stand like bridge-piers on either side of a stream, and the biographer's challenge was to span the ways between.

And making use of Freudian or Jungian psychology often, and of letters, social details, and exhaustive research always, this is what the most brilliant biographies of the 1950s did. It may be that this genre has never shown better architectonics than it shows in Richard Ellmann's *James Joyce* (1959), with its fine weaving back and forth between author and *opus*, or than it shows in George Painter's *Marcel Proust* (1959, 1965), in which the second volume, on *A la recherche*, is so beautifully prepared for by the first. Have we seen much better books about these particular authors than Leon Edel's *Henry James*, L. A. Marchand's *Byron*, or Gordon N. Ray's *Thackeray*, and I have almost added Edgar Johnson's *Dickens* (though we would expect Dickens biographies to have improved in the light of Kathleen Tillotson's and her fellow editors' volumes of the Letters, as indeed they have improved)? I know too well such attacks on biography as in René Wellek's seventh chapter in *Theory of Literature* (1942), and these are sometimes associated with New Critical theory. I know, too, from their talk and their work, that both Ellmann and Ray were in amused opposition to such formalism.

But the implicit New Critical paradigm helped to make great biographies such as Painter's and Ellmann's possible.

To descend abruptly from such heights to a brief, anticlimactic illustration, around 1970 I set out to write a full and concise life of Matthew Arnold; I was twice warmly encouraged by I. A. Richards himself; and I collected letters, and explored myths. The best-known myth about Arnold is that he had had a love-affair with a French chambermaid or language-teacher in the Alps in 1848, because he writes about a 'Marguerite' in his *Switzerland* lyrics. No detailed life of Arnold had been written. In ten years of work I collected journals, letters, and diaries and much else; I had no wish to prove or disprove anything about Arnold, but over seven years it became clear that, for a variety of reasons, it is unlikely that he wrote literally of a love-affair in the Bernese Oberland. No scrap of evidence about such a Frenchwoman in the Alps has ever come to light, not in gossipy letters or diaries by Arnold's near or distant friends who knew the 'Marguerite' lyrics; he could not have censored writing that was going all over the world.

In the Alps, however, he had written to Clough about a plan to linger one day at Thun to see 'blue eyes' in a hotel there. In the Arnold set, in the Lake District, there was a French Protestant exile in her twenties who had been baptized in the French community at Friedrichstadt; she had relatives in Switzerland. She wrote amateur works in imitation of Jean Paul and Ugo Foscolo. Most observers happened to praise her physical beauty, and to one she was the most beautiful person he had seen. She was witty; she refused on principle to attend church; she could be as obstinate as a brother, Louis, whom her mother typically found 'occupé a faire *des riens*'. She scorned a meeting with others at a 'point de reunion'. She took tea with the Arnolds, went on waterfall scrambles with Arnold men, and became lost on the fells.

Her name was Mary Claude. Her close friend Anne Clough had visited Thun in the Alps; Mary Claude left the Lake District just before Arnold did in 1848, and she would have had reasons, as we know, for visiting Geneva and Thun. One aspect of her appearance is singled out by her mother — Mary Claude's dark blue eyes.

What of Arnold's plan to see 'blue eyes' at Thun? When he came home, he was ridiculed by friends; he must have talked to his married sister because that lady wrote about him to a brother in New Zealand, who said that what amused him most was the account of 'Matt's romantic passion for the Cruel Invisible, Mary Claude'. In his first poem about 'Marguerite', he gives the fictive lady several of Mary Claude's known traits.

There is not much of 'Marguerite' in the later *Switzerland* lyrics because the fictive lady dwindles to become a locus for complex ideas about the will, the self, human isolation, and the like. Arnold and his Swiss guide, on a tight travel-schedule, may have found a blue-eyed 'Marguerite' behind every glacier in 1848. But the only *known* model for the lady in the first poem is the Friedrichstadt exile Mary Claude, and this imposed a biographical problem. It is quite untrue that this lady *was* 'Marguerite', because Arnold's fictive construct is at once more, and less, than a human being. Mary may have little relation to the later 'Marguerite' poems; we simply don't know.

In this case, what I have called the New Critical paradigm seemed helpful. By keeping 'author' and *'opus'* (Arnold and the 'Marguerite' lyrics) chiefly in view, one could recount what is known about the Claudes and 'Matt's romantic passion' without letting what seems to have been a romance of short duration get undue emphasis. It is true that a minor romance may have felt like a major one to Arnold, and the best choice seemed to be to tell the facts we have, and not to speculate, but to relate these to what we know about the author and his poems.

In brief, the New Critical paradigm is workable here. Still, Arnold's life could be presented in other ways; the house of biography has many windows. And the 'Eliot' or New Critical paradigm may be less useful if we lack an author's letters.

If we turn to Shakespeare and the New Historicism in this modest survey, we may have a case in point.

Why is it, just now, that 'Shakespeare information' seems to be in advance of 'Shakespeare biography'? The New Critical or Eliot paradigm did little for Renaissance subjects, and bridging in a Painter-like or Ellmann-like way between author and *opus* seems idle if we know much about the works and far less about the author. Romantic speculation about Shakespeare has a long history. In this century, the best works about his life have been counter-biographical in attacking myths about him and cleaning the bones of documents.

Our forms lag behind the state of biographical information, all the same. At present, we know more about Shakespeare's youth, parents, schooling, and Stratford, more about Hathaways and the Shottery circle, more about actors, playing companies, and Shakespeare's London — by far — than has yet appeared in any reliable account. One trouble is that the 'letter' has been a locus round which our biographical forms have organized themselves. Proust's or Joyce's letters make 'Proust' or 'Joyce' fairly stable in our minds. Texts don't change much. It is otherwise with Marlowe, Shakespeare, or Jonson. These authors are comets, in blurred motion all the time.

The reason is, of course, that local history studies, urban studies of the Tudor capital's wards and parishes, studies of virtually all aspects of Tudor and Jacobean endeavour appear month by month. Just now I have at hand Gurr, Mulryne, and Shewring's report on archaeological evidence for the Globe which asks the reader to interpret '*ad quadratum*' and 'sill and wall plate' sketches.[7] I have seen the virtue of reading in one Washington library in the daytime, at another in the evenings, and taking to bed for six weeks three heavy volumes of the Folger's manuscript catalogues to read, bit by bit, 40,000 card-entries before falling asleep. Further, not some, but literally all new comments on Shakespeare's works affect our images of him. It is the same for Marlowe or Jonson. When documentary evidence of the person is limited, and especially when letters are few or lacking, then our image of the 'author' is unfixed and will be affected by everything said or discovered about his works or time.

New biographical forms are needed to accommodate what we glean. Difficult, problematic material as in E. A. J. Honigmann's *Shakespeare: The 'Lost Years'* (1985), which makes it more likely but not certain that the young Stratford man at first worked for Hoghton in Lancashire, has not been accommodated in Shakespeare biographies partly because we respond too simply to a 'Lancashire theory' with a yes or a no. We need a method of alternative narrative, which might show us factually what a young Stratford person would have found in Hoghton's circle in the -north. But alternative narrative would require more care with form than we have shown since Ellmann and Painter's time. In this case the new material is important, well researched, and of no small relevance to what we know of Shakespeare. The Hoghton–Hesketh circle included figures such as Lord Strange, whose company produced some of Shakespeare's early work, and Lady Hesketh, to whom his career at the time of the Globe can be factually linked.

Partly because it might guide us towards new forms in Renaissance biography, the New Historicism is important. Every theory has its day. Critics of the future may link this one with the 1980s, days of the Cold War, Mrs Thatcher, Reagan, and leftist bitterness, and the New Historicism has sounded a political note. Its catch-terms such as 'social energy', 'power', and 'negotiation' can be grating; but it refreshed Shakespeare criticism quite as much as feminism refreshed Jane Austen or Brontë studies. It is a formalist theory which denies that the *opus* can be autonomous. Historical contingencies in this view resonate within a Shakespeare play, which is partly brought into being by the social practices of its time even as it contributes to them.

At their best, New Historicist critics ask us to look into historical contexts in new ways. Stephen Greenblatt, whose own work launched the theory, in his *Shakespearean Negotiations* (1988) takes up *King Lear* in relation to one of the play's known sources, Samuel Harsnett's *A Declaration of Egregious Popish Impostures*, for example. Harsnett had impugned the exorcisms of some English Catholic priests in the 1580s. Now, Greenblatt shows that Shakespeare did not just borrow terms from this book, but hugged it closely. *King Lear* runs parallel with Harsnett. Both works are involved in redefining major values of society, in particular the definition of the sacred; and yet whereas Harsnett only shows corrupt individuals and a corrupt Church, Shakespeare shows an intensity of evil and corruption which neither individuals nor institutions can adequately contain; the only 'answer' to this evil is in extreme suffering.

Two ideas for biography emerge from this. One is that an influence, as from one author to another, is not just a straight line. Both authors in parallel may 'face out' to society. The second idea, I think, is that the term 'influence' is deceptive. Here we may need Derrida's ludic scrutiny of terms. When Shakespeare is (or seems) most humbly influenced, when he hugs a source, he most devastatingly transforms the source.

Another way in which New Historicist theory is useful is this. By seeing the *opus* as splintered or broken open by multiple discourses, it acknowledges that in the *opus* we may see the author. I think it has encouraged biographical comment on Shakespeare's works. We had had this before, but it gave its own sanction to the biographical insights of Kenneth Muir, G. K. Hunter, R. A. Foakes, Stanley Wells, Muriel Bradbrook, or E. A. J. Honigmann, who, I think, were not its disciples; and one might add Philip Edwards, who wrote in 1987 that 'inferences from documents' in Shakespeare's case 'are far more dangerously insecure than inferences' from works of Shakespeare's pen.[8] And after the 1980s, we ask better questions.

Ian Donaldson, for example, in a review of David Riggs's life of Ben Jonson asks: 'If Jonson's writings do indeed reveal something about their author's life, how exactly (and how dependably) do they do their revealing?' Or 'What kind of relationship can we assume to exist between Jonson's texts and Jonson's life, and through what filters and distorting lenses do we read the latter in the former?'[9] The reviewer admits these queries may be unanswerable. One sighs with relief. After all, what if Jonson's 'kind of relationship' changed each time he wrote? What if his works 'do their revealing' in six, sixty, or 600 ways? Very precise questions can imply axiomatic answers, and these can cut off some lines of enquiry. But Donaldson is quite right in asking questions that seem to put us in the white coats of the biologist's laboratory, because he reminds us that we need system as well as intuition.

We also need in biography what may be called intermediate approaches. New Historicists themselves, not getting too embroiled in persons, suggest this. For the Sonnets, we need to ask again not, perhaps, who the Young Man, Rival Poet, or Dark Lady might be,

but what the Speaker is really like. An intermediate approach
would not assume that the Speaker is the poet or author; in a way,
it would be indifferent to the question as to whether Shakespeare
the man has anything to 'do' with the Sonnets, and so might build
upon D. K. Weiser's findings in *Mind and Character* (1987). In
another way, it would coolly correlate with data about the man
and with what can be learned about the implied author of the play-
texts.

We need intermediacy in our approach to the plays, for example
in our regard for the fact that at their centre is the topic of familial
bonds. Why are these at the centre? The 'family' with its intimacy,
its potentially great tensions, interested Greeks and Elizabethans.
Othello, *Macbeth*, even *Hamlet* are not much more 'familial' than
one of *Hamlet*'s presumed sources or Kyd's *The Spanish Tragedy*.
With this approach we might ask how the author's situations on
stage correlate with what he knew at Stratford, and I suppose we
would see that *The Comedy of Errors* has the closest relation to
known details of his marriage and that *The Merry Wives of Windsor*
is second in the running. Closeness-to-the-life, for him, results in
farcical comedy (though the comedy may be poignant). We would
ask with this approach why he is so painfully slow in mastering the
tragic, or why out of the twenty-one plays or so he had written by
his mid-thirties only three or four are proper tragedies (if we
include, with some strain, *Richard II*). With a lambent, impression-
able mind he could be slow and halting, not very flexible. When a
couplet 'turns' a theme in the Sonnets the result is often lame,
though when it reinforces or restates a theme the result can be
brilliant.

New Historicist theory takes us through the pathway of the *opus*
to matters outside the creator's control, and so it can perhaps help
us to see beyond Shakespeare, or to judge the limits of his 'universal'
mind. Constraints limited him, and some of them limited his age.
All in all, to its credit, New Historicism as effectively as any other
theory since the time of the New Critics broke down the binary
hegemony of 'author' and '*opus*', and so began to make the Renaissance much more available to literary biographers.

Greenblatt — who fathered the theory — once began a book

with a special authorial confession, so let me end this with one. At 18 or 19, I read the Furness Variorum *Hamlet* and concluded that Shakespeare was a semi-divine being, a miracle. (He could not have been a mere man.) I read *Pride and Prejudice* with a sensation of amazement, anger, and a weird pained delight because the sun had landed at my feet. I read Matthew Arnold, and wept on the streets night after night over 'Thyrsis'.

About adolescent crushes over 'authors', there is nothing good to say except this. A connectedness begins, even in confusion which may not quickly dissipate itself. A biographer need not have struggled for years to come to rational terms with an author, of course, but don't we need to be a little inward, or to allow time for naïve imagination and intuition to contend with a subject before we try to be biographically objective about it? Even then, we may see too little, and that is why I have been recommending our exposure to theories of our time (or of the recent past). Still, we need to 'take in' author and *opus*: the actors, someone noted of Peter Brook's rehearsals of *A Midsummer Night's Dream*, 'were encouraged to have their own deeply personal link with the material, which could then evolve and grow during the run, like any valid relationship'.[10]

Notes

1. Richard Wilson and Richard Dutton (eds.), *New Historicism and Renaissance Drama* (London and New York, 1992), 6.
2. Robert Blake, 'The Art of Biography', in Eric Homberger and John Charmley (eds.), *The Troubled Face of Biography* (London, 1988), 75.
3. Leeds Barroll, *Politics, Plague, and Shakespeare's Theater* (Ithaca, NY and London, 1991), 209, and see ch. 3.
4. This was first published by Jacques Derrida in *Roméo et Juliette* (Paris, 1986).
5. See Jacques Derrida, *Signéponge/Signsponge*, trans. Richard Rand (New York, 1984).
6. T. S. Eliot, 'Ben Jonson' (1919), *Selected Essays* (London, 1972), 157–8.
7. Andrew Gurr, Ronnie Mulryne, and Margaret Shewring, *The Design of the Globe* (Coventry, 1993).
8. Philip Edwards, *Shakespeare: A Writer's Progress* (Oxford, 1987), 12–13.
9. Ian Donaldson, 'Life into Text', *Essays in Criticism*, 41 (July 1991), 260–1.
10. *Peter Brook: A Theatrical Casebook*, compiled by David Williams (London, 1992), 162–3.

Starting Again: One of the Problems of the Biographer

ANN THWAITE

When I was first approached to contribute to these papers, it was assumed that I would want to focus on my new subject. I am working on a biography of Emily Tennyson, the poet's wife, which Faber will publish in 1996, one hundred years after her death. But I have no wish or need at this moment to pin Emily down, as if I were a Victorian lepidopterist. She is alive in my mind, incandescent — mysterious — and I want her to stay that way while I read around and about her and all the words I can find that she wrote herself. I shall hesitate to form paragraphs about her for quite a while. I try to avoid answering questions about her, though sometimes it is difficult. I have formulated a few routine sentences about why I am 'doing' her and try to leave it at that.

'Was she a writer herself?' people ask. 'She wrote letters and a journal', I say, 'which makes it possible, I think, to retrieve her life in a way that is often difficult with wives. I am interested in wives, in poets' wives, in Victorian women. They deserve celebration.' Clever people then ask me if I will use Philip Larkin's lines as my epigraph.

> Mrs Alfred Tennyson
> Answered
>   begging letters
>   admiring letters
>   insulting letters
>   enquiring letters
>   business letters
>   and publishers' letters.
> She also

> looked after his clothes
> saw to his food and drink
> entertained visitors
> protected him from gossip and criticism
> And finally
> (apart from running the household)
> Brought up and educated the children.
>
> While all this was going on
> Mister Alfred Tennyson sat like a baby
> Doing his poetic business.

I am not at all sure about using Larkin's lines as an epigraph for my biography — though certainly they sum up a part of Emily Tennyson's attraction for me. I feel involved in examining the nineteenth century to do more justice to women's role in it. Men's lives of men so often leave women in the shadows. And seeing justice done has always been a strong motivating force for me.

But the decision to write about Emily Tennyson is a complex one and Larkin's lines in no way encapsulate the essence of the life that floats alluringly in my mind. A subject for a biography needs 'vitality of soul', Henry Sidgwick once wrote to Edmund Gosse — and that has certainly got something to do with my choice of Emily Tennyson. I have a great sense of her immortal soul, of her determination to live a life well lived. Twenty years ago, in his *Truth to Life*, A. O. J. Cockshut drew attention to the advantages of nineteenth-century biographers with their confidence that they were writing about immortal souls — and now Robert Skidelsky has suggested that in a way the wheel has come full circle:

As biographers we are once more in the business of writing exemplary lives. But now the example is the life itself, not what the life enabled the person to achieve. Or, more precisely, the life *is* the achievement . . . Quite obviously on this criterion a much wider range of lives is opened up to biography, paucity of achievement in the traditional sense being no barrier to being written about.

A question mark slipped into the original subtitle of my paper: 'Starting again — one of the problems of the biographer?' It made me think. How does the problem of choosing a new subject —

starting again after years immersed in a totally different life — how does that problem compare, as problems go, with all the other problems of writing biography? The title of a book devoted to the papers from a previous biography conference, at the University of East Anglia in 1985, was called *The Troubled Face of Biography* and suggested that the whole enterprise is riddled with problems and that biographers spend their own lives (such as they are) with perpetually frowning brows.

A great deal has been said and written about the problems of the 'true representation of a fellow human being', of the impossibility of really understanding someone else's life ('How intimately can we know the self of another person?' as Richard Ellmann put it) and about the practical problems of finding out, of filling in the gaps, about the problems of copyright and invasion of privacy, about the unreliability of witness, spoken and written, and the constant rewriting of history by everyone, main characters and bit players alike. There is the basic problem of illegible handwriting. Then there are the problems of time and money, of pacing, form and structure. There is simply — and most complicatedly — the problem of trying to get it right, to tell a good story, to provide a compelling narrative that neither distorts nor compromises. There is the problem of trying to achieve (and it cannot be achieved by thinking about it, any more than we can, by thinking, add a cubit to our physical stature) — the mysterious transition from craftsman to artist. We know that even Virginia Woolf could not make her mind up about that one. (In 1927 the biographer could cease to be a 'chronicler; he has become an artist' but twelve years later she had decided 'his work is not a work of art but something betwixt and between'.) However, there is no doubt or dispute that we need to share with the creative writer a compulsion to write, which carries us on when any sensible person would have given up long ago.

A great deal has also been written about the problems of over-whelming material. We have a glimpse of Boswell, in his diary, so overcome by the number of his notes, when he started to put them together, that he would sit in London coffee-houses, with tears pouring down his cheeks. And Virginia Woolf was dismayed by the 'thick hedge' of Roger Fry's letters, 'three large brown boxes of

Fry' and 'a whole room full more'. But that is of course nothing compared with the forty tons of documents that confronted Franklin Roosevelt's biographer or (to confine the discussion to literary subjects) the paper mountains of Mark Twain or Browning letters.

I remember myself, half-way through *Edmund Gosse*, thinking it was impossible. The sheer amount of material threatened to engulf me. With *A. A. Milne*, one of the initial attractions, I fear, was that there seemed to be so much less to go on, that there was, I knew, no great archive of family papers. 'All had been destroyed', Christopher Milne wrote in *The Path Through the Trees*. I even dreamed whimsically that I might be able to write a perfect, slim volume, slim enough not to get stuck, like Pooh, if posted into Rabbit's burrow. Little did I know . . .

I am actually attracted to the suggestion Henry James once made that 'the art of the biographer, a devilish art! — is somehow practically *thinning*. It simplifies even while seeking to enrich.' I like that and, with Emily Tennyson, I dream again of a slim volume, of distilling the essence, not detailing every daily movement this time. Emily's journal, after all (inevitably and tantalizingly), tends to detail Alfred's daily movements rather than her own. This idea of the form and flavour of an unwritten book is very strong, however much it has to be modified in practice, as the research goes on.

Leon Edel has famously said that the only imagination the biographer can be allowed is the imagination of form and structure. I want to suggest that by far the most important use of the biographer's imagination is in the crucial first step — in imagining what the choice of a particular subject might actually mean. I called this crucial act 'starting again' in my title, because that is what it is for me — but perhaps it should have been called 'choosing a subject'. I have a good collection of books about biography and it seems no one has really addressed this matter, of why particular writers have chosen particular subjects, though, of course, a good deal has been said about the interaction of writer and subject, about empathy and sympathy and a 'discerning love', once the subject has been chosen. The two must, after all, as Michael Millgate has put it, be 'ineluctably intertwined', even if the ideal state for a biographer is — in Michael Holroyd's phrase — 'a passionate detachment'.

But how to decide on a subject with whom we are prepared to be 'ineluctably intertwined' — for year after year after year? 'I live all day in the company of Jeremy Taylor and dream of him at night', Edmund Gosse wrote ninety years ago. How can we find a subject worth that degree of involvement? It was nine years after I had first thought of writing about Gosse himself that my biography of him was finally published, so I know what a long commitment can feel like.

It has always been something that has interested me — how/why a particular biography came to be written. I remember the late, much-mourned George MacBeth saying something to me as he read the first few words of my Introduction to my A. A. Milne biography ('I am often asked how I came to write this book' — echoing, though I didn't realize it at the time, similar words in my first biography). George MacBeth said ruefully, 'Oh, no one ever asks *me* that'. The reason has something to do with the difference between novelists and poets — and biographers. The creative process is too mysterious for the lay person to query it — but biographers? That's different. How does it come about that he/she has acquired this lovely bit of literary property? *Why* is she/he having this chance to cash in on the fame of A. A. Milne, Trollope, P. G. Wodehouse or whoever it may be — certainly writers far more famous than their biographers are themselves?

As Edmund Gosse put it in an essay: 'The popular idea seems to be that no-one is too great a fool or too complete an amateur . . . to undertake the "life" of an eminent person.' And Phyllis Grosskurth — biographer of John Addington Symonds, Havelock Ellis, and Melanie Klein — has recorded that the tax authorities in Canada once defined the writing of biography as a 'hobby'. If we, as professional biographers, protest at these attitudes, I feel they do perhaps account for the extraordinary figure of 2,164 biographies (about 40 a week) apparently published in Britain in 1990, the year my *A. A. Milne* came out. And biographers do seem often to find themselves as such by accident. 'I have never heard of a child saying "When I grow up I want to be a biographer",' as Grosskurth put it.

In recent years there has been some attempt to raise the status of biography in the universities. (And, after all, no one grows up saying 'I want to be a deconstructionist', either.) Michael Millgate has expressed it thus:

If scarcely fashionable within the academy biography still commands, together with other remnants of essentially historical thinking a certain grudging acceptance — not unrelated, perhaps, to the frequency [I would have said inevitability] with which even the most austere of theorists find themselves living disconcertingly chronological and indeed finite lives.

Phyllis Grosskurth herself started her work on Symonds as a result of a casual suggestion from her supervisor, Geoffrey Tillotson, discouraging her from another doctoral thesis on a more major writer, Matthew Arnold. She was spurred on to investigate the life of John Addington Symonds, himself a character in Edmund Gosse's story, by reading Horatio Brown's biography, which, not surprisingly, omits all reference to Symonds's homosexuality as it was published only two years after Symonds's death in 1893. It was, in fact, to a large extent a censored version of Symonds's autobiography. We know this because, by a miracle, that was not destroyed, as so much original material was destroyed by the Victorians — not least by Hallam Tennyson — when producing their own sanitized and often deliberately misleading versions of lives. Symonds's memoirs survived safely, locked up in the London Library. Grosskurth's original thesis concentrated on Symonds as 'representative of certain nineteenth-century aesthetic theories' — a respectable academic subject. It was someone at Longmans, the publishers, who suggested a biography.

It is to me surprising how often the binding of biographer and subject is not because (as some might assume) the writer is burning to write about a particular person. Biographies are very often written at the suggestion of other interested parties: publishers, agents, families. Often the first biography is — as Hilary Spurling described her first, of Ivy Compton-Burnett — 'an affair of the heart'. Subsequent books are more likely to be 'marriages of convenience', as she described her *Paul Scott* and the life of Matisse she is now working on.

I count myself lucky to have been allowed three 'affairs of the heart'. Only A. A. Milne was suggested to me. When, nearly twenty years ago, Elizabeth Jane Howard reviewed my life of Frances Hodgson Burnett in the *Sunday Times*, she wrote: 'Mrs Thwaite is first to be congratulated upon finding somebody so extraordinary and so neglected to write about.' (In 1994, I'm glad to say, Faber brought it back into print as a paperback.) I'm not sure it is exactly a matter for congratulation, but I certainly consider Edmund Gosse was also 'extraordinary and neglected'. I have never been interested in writing about someone who has already been 'done', over and over again. Starting again, I would never contemplate for a moment writing yet another biography of Charles Dickens, of Charlotte Brontë, or of Jane Austen. Someone has calculated that Byron's life has been written 200 times and at this moment there are several more Robert Louis Stevensons in production — to add to all those already on the shelf. There are even, apparently, *nine* biographies of Dorothy L. Sayers.

The life of a writer needs to be examined again by each succeeding generation, it has been decided, and sometimes it seems as if the years of a generation can be counted on one hand. One explanation of this could be contained in something Victoria Glendinning wrote in the *TLS* in 1985 in a review of Ira Bruce Nadel's *Biography: Fiction, Fact and Form*. She wrote: 'It is probable that compulsive biographers immerse themselves in other people's lives as a way of indirectly examining their own' — though they must beware, Glendinning warns, of suggesting 'mythic parity' with their subjects. Similarly, Peter Ackroyd once 'chuckled', according to a journalist, that 'the subject of a biography is the biographer, not the subject'.

Like a good novel, Glendinning says, 'a life can be re-interpreted endlessly'. That is certainly true but I am myself much more interested in discovery rather than re-interpretation. One of the great pleasures, with all my subjects, has been the sensation of reading letters that no one else has read since the moment, perhaps a hundred years earlier, when the intended recipient has neatly slit open the envelope with an ivory paper-knife. (I allow myself here a moment of fantasy, of guessing, I would never allow myself in a biography. I don't *know* that any of the hundreds of recipients of letters I have read actually possessed ivory paper-knives.)

In my Emily Tennyson research the moment, so far, which I recall with most pleasure was when Susan Gates, the librarian at the Tennyson Research Centre in Lincoln, said to me of a couple of boxes marked 'EMILY TENNYSON', 'No one has looked through those boxes before'. I must add that when, very recently, I told Robert Bernard Martin this story he naturally protested. I'm sure he did indeed open the boxes but, not surprisingly, there is no trace of the contents in his *Tennyson*. The Tennyson material is as vast and overwhelming as any literary archive. Why should anyone, writing about the great poet, worry about his wife's address book with the size of the poet's head neatly listed under the address of his hatter?

'These little things are my delight', Edmund Gosse once wrote — and they are mine too. He was writing, at that point, of the fact that Samuel Butler, when he travelled abroad, kept diarrhoea pills in a special pocket in the handle of his Gladstone bag. I suppose it was Dr Johnson who first admitted the satisfaction of curiosity as a legitimate aim for a biographer, suggesting he should 'lead the thoughts into domestic privacies and to display the minute details of daily life'. Much more recently Michael Holroyd has said it was 'the intimacy of private life that attracted me to biography'. They seem — these details, these little things — to have a lot to do with discovering the essence of the character under examination — and little to do with one's own.

But Julian Symons in his Introduction to *The Quest for Corvo*, his brother's book about Frederick Rolfe, subscribes to Victoria Glendinning's theory, even when the subject is comparatively obscure. 'A good biography', he wrote, 'is prompted not by the inherent qualities of its subject, but by the biographer's consciously or unconsciously realized opportunity for self-expression' — the imagination of choice I suggested earlier. How can we deny this when Symons suggests the interrelation may be unconscious — however much we would rather lean to Robert Gittings's idea of the biographer in the wings, out of sight, letting the story appear to tell itself? Certainly I feel there should be some deep connection between biographer and subject — though this begins to seem unlikely when one investigates in how casual and arbitrary a way the connection so often comes into being. As Hilary Spurling suggested, 'arranged marriages' are far more common than affairs of the heart, and many books, even extremely good ones, result from other people's suggestions.

Nigel Nicolson invited both the biographers of his parents — James Lees-Milne to write about Harold Nicolson and Victoria Glendinning to tackle *Vita*. Graham Greene notoriously (and perhaps without sufficient care and attention) 'appointed' Norman Sherry as his own biographer — 'an instinctive decision', Sherry called it. Greene's own explanation was that 'he has the great advantage of not knowing me' — unlike Christopher Sykes on Evelyn Waugh or Frances Donaldson on P. G. Wodehouse. There can be odder reasons. Paul Ferris wrote a biography of Dylan Thomas, he said, because he was born in a suburb of Swansea, only a mile from Thomas's childhood home.

His publishers suggested to Ronald Hayman 'when I was nearing the end of my Kafka biography . . . Brecht should be my next subject'. Elizabeth Longford was commissioned to write her life of the 'extraordinary and neglected' Wilfred Scawen Blunt. (She calls the other sort of biography 'spontaneous'.) Andrew Motion's biography of the Lamberts is dedicated to his publisher, Carmen Callil, 'who gave me the idea for this book'. With the new three-author D. H. Lawrence biography, the whole enterprise must obviously be masterminded by Cambridge University Press, though there is no indication in the Introduction to John Worthen's first volume how the three authors came to be chosen.

Deirdre Bair, like Phyllis Grosskurth many years earlier, was struggling to find a Ph.D. subject when she became 'ineluctably intertwined'. It was an unpromising beginning to what turned out to be a particularly challenging and rewarding union with Samuel Beckett. No one who has read it will ever forget her account of the conditions under which she worked, the conditions Beckett himself laid down.

The respectable reason (far more respectable than simple curiosity, the eagerness to know) that is often given for writing a writer's life is that the life will illuminate the work. This respectability is obviously particularly necessary when there is officially not supposed to be a biography at all. Lyndall Gordon came to biography through criticism.

The more I found out about Eliot's life, the more it appeared that life and work were, in this poet, inseparable. For the patterning of the poetry on the familiar model of spiritual biography was reflected in a life that was, to a curious degree, patterned itself, almost as though Eliot's life were an invention complementary to his work.

Peter Ackroyd too had written of Eliot: 'The connection between the life and the work is explicitly made, and it will be the purpose of this book to attempt to elucidate the mystery of that connection.' So widespread is this idea of the prime purpose of literary biography that I was actually expected by some people to have written my life of A. A. Milne, entirely and ridiculously, in order to 'illuminate' *Winnie-the-Pooh*. This was far from the case and I hope no one will suggest I am writing Emily Tennyson's life in order to illuminate further Alfred Tennyson's poems.

Henry James once said, 'In our opinion the life and the works are two different matters, and an intimate knowledge of the one is not at all necessary for the genial enjoyment of the other' — which could be made to work both ways. Certainly one can *imagine* readers enjoying Edel's *James* or Holroyd's *Shaw* without having read a word written by either, but it seems rather unlikely.

I am glad I have never had the task of writing a biography of a major writer. I should worry about the danger of distracting the reader from the work. With the three writers I have 'done', their lives and times were certainly as interesting and worth examining as their books — though all of them wrote books more famous than they are themselves — and *Father and Son* provided some interesting problems.

There is no question in my mind that, with a major writer, what counts is the work. And, as Julian Barnes has put it: 'The work can easily be blurred, or half-buried, by the life. Think of Byron, Wilde, Robert Lowell, Samuel Johnson . . . What novelist, given the choice, wouldn't prefer you to re-read one of his novels rather than read his biography?' That was in the same essay in the *New York Times* in 1985 that told the story of Flaubert's two stuffed parrots, the 'droll, deflating moment, part Monty Python, part moral tale', when Julian Barnes realized the huge elusiveness of biographical truth and which was the *donnée* for his novel *Flaubert's Parrot*. Flaubert himself once wrote, 'The artist must manage to make posterity believe that he never existed', and, in 1853, 'Man is nothing, the work of art everything'.

Sometimes, amazingly, it seems that even biographers believe this, that they feel the need to justify writing biography, that they feel perhaps literary biography is only justifiable when the biography is itself a work of art. As I start again (having made a New Year's resolution — too easily broken — to have nothing further to say to anyone about A. A. Milne and *Winnie-the-Pooh*), as I become more and more deeply involved in Emily Tennyson's life, theories of biography bother me very little. I shall allow an experienced instinct to tell me how to deal with the material I find.

❧ 14 ❧

Pieties and Literary Biography

NORMAN WHITE

Other essays in this collection have discussed ambiguities and paradoxes inherent in the writing of a biography: ambiguities and
paradoxes which question and disturb the validity of biography's
basic claim, to tell another person's life. 'A Life for a Life.' There is
that word 'Life', meaning a person's existence between birth and
death; but there is also the word 'Life' meaning what a biographer
tells you was another person's existence. In spite of scholarly notes
about sources and authorial limitations you can't get away from the
fact that biography claims the two are the same, though plainly
they are not. We *do* invent what we call the truth. There is a poem
by Christopher Reid called 'Your Biographer':

> Inevitably
> your biographer
> is getting it all wrong.
>
> His little screen
> recapitulates
> the few known facts.
>
> With rapidly dabbing
> fingertips he coaxes
> a workable pattern, till
>
> there it is —
> the truth at last!
> And you stand condemned
>
> to centuries
> of ignominy,
> your well-polished plea unheard.[1]

If falsification is integral to the nature of biography, then the
biographer must be a scoundrel. The charges against biographers

are well rehearsed. The potential subjects of literary biographies have almost always been suspicious of the idea of a book about themselves. Sometimes this has been demonstrated in forms of protectionism. Wordsworth censored many autobiographical parts of *The Prelude*. Thomas Hardy wrote his own *Life*, with instructions that its authorship should be credited to his wife. James Joyce selected his own biographer, Herbert Gorman, and then directed him in his research. When Gorman's manuscript was complete, Joyce virtually rewrote it, deleting passages and inserting footnotes. It has been asserted that the starchy exteriors and facial hair of men of letters at the turn of the twentieth century — Hardy, Barrie, Kipling, Bridges — were expressive of this 'don't come too close' complex. Then there's what Edmund Gosse defined as the 'Widow' factor: the Widow, anxious to conceal the faults of the deceased. Tom Moore destroyed Byron's autobiographical memoir and prudently distorted his own *Life* of Byron; Mary Shelley presented her husband as a paragon of interesting virtue, an angelic and inspirational poet, a misunderstood philanthropist and simple genius.

Henry James manifested biographical suspicion in several ways: he consigned to a roaring fire the correspondence of some forty years, and he also wrote his parable of the biographer's desire to become omniscient, *The Aspern Papers*. The unnamed narrator will stop at nothing to obtain a famous dead poet's papers, now in the possession of an elderly woman who had once been the poet's lover; he moves into the woman's desolate Venetian *palazzo* as her lodger. She surprises him in the act of opening a desk where he supposes the papers to be hidden; and she denounces him as a 'publishing scoundrel'. All biographers must feel themselves accused. Mr Valiant-for-Truth is really Peeping Tom in disguise.[2]

What I want to do in this essay is to counter-attack: to say that the villain of this basic biographical dilemma is sometimes not the writer but his or her audience. What often gets in the way of telling truths about someone's life is not the biographer's distortions or myopia, but the reader's preconceptions about what should be there, the way it should be told, and the conclusions which should be drawn. I've written only one biography and so I'll not generalize much, but instead I'll use experiences from the making of *Hopkins: A Literary Biography*.[3]

I'm using the word 'pieties' in my title partly because of its ambiguous and floating nature, and partly because of its relevance to the biographizing of the life of a writer who was also a priest. The three primary meanings of 'pious' are: (i) showing devotion to religious duties; (ii) dutiful, loyal; and (iii) marked by hypocritical virtue, sanctimonious. The last two usages are moralistic, one implied morally good ('dutiful, loyal') and the other ('hypocritical, sanctimonious') bad. It's a convenient word because I want to talk about a kind of conflict that recurs in creating biographies, that between the 'truthful' picture of the subject that the biographer sees and the 'desirable' picture proposed by interested other parties — guardians of conventions and proprieties; in particular, the conflict between the warts-and-all image proposed by modern secular biographers, and the hagiographic tradition of portraying an exemplary picture of an ideal, as a guide for emulation. It has been considered that the hagiography and its descendants were dealt their death-blow in the early twentieth century with Lytton Strachey's *Eminent Victorians* and Edmund Gosse's *Father and Son*, and that the flag of truthfulness to all the available facts would now flutter forever. But remnants from the hagiographic tradition are still often thrust at a writer if his or her subject is seen as representative of a particular ideology which still has currency.

The first piety which I see as having to be counteracted is the received version of someone's life. Even though until two years ago there were no comprehensive biographies of Gerard Hopkins, there were nevertheless commonly acknowledged facts and received opinions, repeated in almost every school textbook and anthology introduction, which were either downright wrong or else could at least be looked at again. To begin with, his name. I have always felt uneasy with 'Gerard Manley Hopkins'. There is an artificiality about the Manley part. It belongs to Hopkinsian criticism rather than to Hopkins, though at times it seems to have almost more currency than Gerard — at the annual Summer School at Monasterevin in Ireland you often hear him referred to as 'Manley Hopkins', while on a BBC quiz he was called General Manley Hopkins. In his lifetime he was commonly known as Gerard, and referred to by people who knew him well as 'Gerry'. (At school he was also called 'Skin' and at Oxford 'Poppy', while in Dublin, where he spent the last five years of his life, he was more often than not referred to as 'Gerald'.) The 'Manley' was not frequently used until after 1918, when he had been dead for almost thirty years. By that time there was another Gerard Hopkins in the family, the poet's nephew, who later became well known as translator of François Mauriac; Robert Bridges decided jointly with the Hopkins family to add 'Manley' to the title-page of the first edition of *Poems* to distinguish the two. There would be ample justification for a biographer to call his subject Gerard Hopkins, but there would be scores of objections after seventy-five years of stressing the 'Manley'.

There were several examples of other common but questionable assumptions in a BBC television film of Hopkins's life, 'To seem the stranger', written by John Wain.[4] It started, for instance: 'During the lifetime of Gerard Manley Hopkins not even six people knew that he wrote poetry.' If a number is considered important enough to be given, some counting should be done: Hopkins had two parents, three sisters, four brothers, and several aunts and uncles; there were four or five maids in the family at different times who could hardly have avoided seeing a carefully written copy of one of his poems above his mother's bed; there were fellow-students at school and at Oxford, the Jesuits in the various houses in England and Wales, the editors to whom he submitted poems which they refused, the editors who accepted, besides his colleagues in Dublin, where one of the reasons given for his appointment was his skill in composing verse; all of these in addition to his pen-friends Dixon, Bridges, and Patmore, all of whom showed his poems to friends. Even if one were to say 'not six *hundred* people knew that Hopkins wrote poetry' the counting would have to be done carefully and might easily produce an underestimate.

But a list of similar common mistakes would be tedious; sufficient to say that they abound ('for seven years [1868–75] he wrote no poetry at all',[5] and so on). The fact is that biographical untruths are accepted by audiences if they have been said two or three times and fit in with expectations. There are sanctions of disapproval if you offer truths which are uncanonical; you can't start a talk or paper by saying, for instance, 'Gerard Hopkins was a homosexual midget'.

A recent review of a Hopkins book said: 'it remains rather a mystery why so many biographers tramp around in this small, shaded garden.' But in fact biographical coverage of Hopkins has been extraordinarily sparse. There was a short book published in 1930 by a Canadian Jesuit, who did it in a few months in his spare time; there was a study by an English Jesuit of the background to Hopkins's Jesuit training; and there have been three shorter books, all in some ways lacking fresh research and material.[6] There was no entry in the old *Dictionary of National Biography* — the *DNB*'s most notorious omission. And there have been only two full-length biographies, both in the last two years. Why is this when Hopkins's popularity cannot be denied? His fame has continually increased since the 1920s, fed by a variety of factors: the sense of excitement and challenges in his poetry, the idea that his poetry shows original technical skills, Roman Catholic religious interests, his acceptance into the canon of school and university syllabuses, and the boost given by the hundredth anniversary of his death. His poems have been set to music by eminent composers; some are in hymn-books; there is a cold plaque, next to Auden's, in Poets' Corner of Westminster Abbey. His usually dull and often incorrect music has been recorded; there have been numerous parodies and translations published ('My ain hert lat me nae conter aye, lat / Me efterhend til my glum sel byde kind'[7]); a recent book discussed his influence on twenty-five poets, and castigated him for 'constituting a lethal influence on modern Nigerian poetry;[8] Hopkins is greeted by Whitman with 'You're the first pagan Jesuit I've ever met' in another publication;[9] while Anthony Burgess's *The Clockwork Testament*[10] pictures a Hollywood film version of 'The Wreck of the Deutschland', adapted to show the tall nun (played by a Swede), having torn off her Franciscan habit to make bandages during the storm scenes on the Kentish Knock, in 'an ambiguous moment when, storms bugling, though somewhat subdued, Death's fame in the background, she cried orgasmatically: "O Christ, Christ, come quickly" — Hopkins's own words, so one could hardly complain' (the film got 'a very restrictive showing rating, nobody under sixteen', and was the subject of a court case in Ashton-under-Lyne). With all this interest in the diminutive, effeminate priest, with his high-pitched voice, toffee-nosed manner, and remarkable poetic talent, why is there the most curious reticence about his life? After all, there have been almost thirty full-length biographies of George Eliot.

The main blockage I see as the difficulty of being adequate to both the primary areas of Hopkins interest — the poetry and the religion. It appears to many people that only a Jesuit could write about Hopkins's 24-hours-a-day life as a Jesuit. The great Hopkins scholar Humphry House planned to write a biography of the early life, which finished on the day that Hopkins entered the Jesuit novitiate; his life after that, House considered, could be written only by a Jesuit. How can an outsider know, let alone understand, what goes on in a Jesuit community?

But a Jesuit approach may have limitations *sui generis*: in many respects a Jesuit way of looking at poetry is likely to be different from that of secular universities and secular people — there is a centuries-old gap. The intense and far-reaching implications of the magnificent and terrible motto and war-cry, 'Ad Maiorem Dei Gloriam', 'to the greater glory of God', are not generally realized. Perhaps the most obvious obstacle for a Jesuit author, and one that caused Hopkins himself a great deal of trouble, is censorship — 'all that we Jesuits publish (even anonymously) must be seen by censors and this is a barrier which I do not know how anything of mine on a large scale would ever pass.'[11] There must be inevitable pressures to write a hagiography, according to orthodox ideas of how the Society of Jesus, and Father Hopkins within that, should be portrayed, and with a binding limitation as to what can and cannot be published.

The religious element in Hopkins's life also causes the problem of alternative versions of events; for example, his death. There is a long-standing tradition that his last words were 'I am so happy', repeated three times. On the other hand, Hopkins's last years in Dublin were marked by deep depressions and he died from a particularly nasty and painful illness (peritonitis setting in after typhoid), a realistic picture of which, in horrifying detail, was given in Mann's novel *Buddenbrooks*. There are two kinds of validity here — the very moving Catholic tradition of the 'good death', and the physical actuality. Plainly here it is a matter not of choice, but of two aspects.

Then Hopkins's sexuality was until recently a considerable biographical problem because of his religious affiliation. He was exceedingly attracted to physical beauty and presences — mainly in males, men and boys, but (and this is not so often mentioned) also women and girls, even a horse and a dog (his black retriever, Rover), so strongly that he counted the experience a sin. He sometimes felt the wrong sort of feeling on looking at crucifixes. This quivering responsiveness is important because it is at one with the experiences behind a great deal of his poetry, his responses to nature as well as to humans and fauna, and with some part of the attraction his poems have for some readers. As is now commonly known, there exist diaries which Hopkins wrote while an Oxford undergraduate which detail everything he did which he considered sinful — in the ten months of this part of the diary he estimated that he had committed 1,564 sins, or on average about five a day. Of these, 238 were sexual sins. They show him to be sexually immature: he often records looking up dirty words in the dictionary or lexicon or medical journal when he was nearly 21. (I imagine most people have exhausted this branch of philology well before that age.) The notes show that he was mainly, but not exclusively, attracted by his own sex; from the evidence of public-school and university mores of the 1860s, this was not abnormal. There are no sexual acts with other people recorded, only feelings and instances of attraction. These notes are not in the slightest scandalous — as far as Hopkins's sexuality is concerned they give evidence of naïvety and innocence above anything else. But in other ways they give biographical information, mainly as to where and with whom he was during an important ten-month period. But until recently these notes had not been published[12] because of the guarded attitude of the Roman Catholic Church towards sexuality, and so (unlike most of his poems and letters) they are still in copyright. An important source was thus difficult to utilize.

It is of course well known that the Church's attitude towards Hopkins's poetry — its assignment to the category of mere aestheticism — has resulted in grievous losses to the literary world. Quite often, it seems to me, the problem caused by the incompatibility of secular and religious approaches is not faced, and a watery compromise stance is adopted for the sake of its inoffensiveness. I hope that the limitations of my approach are apparent at the outset of the Life of Hopkins; it is the biography of a poet and does not intend to satisfy those readers to whom Hopkins's spiritual life is of prior importance. The authorial stance as regards the religious elements is that of an outsider who has to make some explanation and sense of what he sees; thus, Jesuits may well be seen as the strange creatures which indeed they are within a much larger and very different society. A similar stance was used for the Oxford University sections: Oxford looked at as though by a visiting amateur anthropologist discovering a strange tribe — and 1860s Oxford society was decidedly strange, although Oxford people writing about it don't seem to realize its many oddnesses.

There is too much admiration of a wrong kind for Hopkins; objectivity has become difficult. The Dictionary of Accepted Ideas about Hopkins is full; those who read Hopkins's poems to confirm their views of the universe seem to expect his *Life* to provide uplift, biography as a brassière.[13] It is very difficult to write objectively about a religious order which believes as toughly as the Jesuits; and there is also the pressure of the fact that Hopkins is often considered by his co-religionists as almost a saint.

On 8 December 1975 the memorial to Hopkins was unveiled and dedicated in Poets' Corner of Westminster Abbey.[14] In the Abbey that day there was an odd sense of a second laying to rest, as if the first, at Glasnevin in 1889, had been so unsatisfactory and temporary that Gerard's ghost had been hovering for the last eighty-six years, unsettled in some half-ecclesiastical, half-poetic limbo (making though, according to Robert Bridges' prefatory sonnet to the first edition of his Poems, an excursion across St George's Channel to Chilswell, near Oxford, in the winter of 1917–18, to thank his editor). Although the Westminster Abbey stone says 'Buried at

Glasnevin, Dublin', it yet seems to imply that the body itself, or at least the essence of Hopkins, lies beneath.

London newspapers confirmed the ceremony as a laying to rest: 'A heaven haven memorial' (*The Times* said); 'Corner stone at last for Hopkins', and 'Gerard Manley Hopkins finds his place' (said two editions of the *Guardian*); the difference between a gravestone and a memorial stone seemed blurred. Poets' Corner was seen as a remarkably fitting last resting-place for Hopkins (or for all that is vital of him). An odd and peculiarly English place for religion and art to meet — hadn't Abraham Cowley written 'Poet and Saint! to thee alone are given / The two most sacred names of earth and Heaven'? Byron in white stone four feet away from Hopkins in black, sanctified together, and united further by the adjoining memorial to Saint W. H. Auden, who appreciated both of them (byronically replying to Hopkins's 'Look at the stars! look, look up at the skies!' with 'Looking up at the stars, I know quite well / That, for all they care, I can go to hell').[15]

But this Corner nags into mind other corners of this and many other English churches, corners with statues in militaristic poses, and overhanging tattered smelly flags in dusty grey net. Imperial heroes from the Crimean or Zulu or Sudan or Boxer or Punjab or hundreds of other wars and mutinies and rebellions, killed by 'marauding savages' who might have been blown to pieces tied to the mouths of cannons in reprisal; churches have always known how to bring heroes from other walks of life into their fold, by giving them an odour of sanctity, and providing a patronizing last canopy of 'time is the great leveller'. Many people today must feel cynical when they see military memorials from the imperial age, and wonder how a church that preached Love ever squared its conscience. Did it ever really bridge the gap, or did it just give the signs of doing so, the memorials, and hope they would convince the people who saw them that all awkward questions had been answered? (Lacunae may also be noticed in the logic of Hopkins's own poetic contributions to militaristic jingoism, 'The Soldier' and 'What shall I do for the land that bred me?', his 'recruiting song for soldiers'.)

Literary giants have always produced followers who wanted to

sanctify them when dead. Saint Byron, Saint Shelley, are largely
accepted now; in their lifetimes they weren't and didn't want to be.
The sanctification has more to do with the psychological needs of
their pygmy fans than with the nature of the giants themselves.
But, you might reply, although there is something quirky, not to
say inappropriate, about Byron and Shelley in a church, Hopkins, a
professional priest, is evidently a different case, isn't he?

Several layers of irony could be uncovered from that Westminster
Abbey ceremony. The main strange and dramatic and moving fact
was the collection under one roof of representatives, the blood and
spiritual descendants, of all kinds of people associated with elements
of Hopkins's life: relatives, close friends, borough and school
officials, Jesuits, other Roman Catholic and Anglican priests and
laymen, poets, scholars; representatives of several of the elements
that warred against each other in his life and afterwards, all taking
part, amicably enough it seemed, in one religious ceremony, —
Hopkins's 'rare talent' no longer in disdain, to use Robert Bridges'
tenderly indignant words, but now with innumerable jostling
brokers.

The main irony at one level — the lack of recognition while
Hopkins was alive, compared with the trumpeting of his fame now
(and there was trumpet-music of Hopkins's favourite composer,
Purcell, played on Purcell's own organ, to assist the process) — was
embodied in the fact of the ceremony itself, and also expounded
very sensitively in the form it took: the theme of individual fame
and sacrifice, interspersed with vivid poetic examples of Hopkins's
perception of, as the programme put it, 'the beauty of the eternal in
and through the temporal'. (Another minor irony was the curious
sight of a row of literary critics who normally wouldn't be seen
dead at a church service — in Hopkins studies one's religious
affiliations don't remain secret so easily — standing in the choir-
stalls singing Newman's hymn 'Praise to the holiest in the height'.)

The memorial was unveiled, a wreath placed by Hopkins's great-
nephew, and an address given by the famous living Jesuit poet and
Greek scholar (another irony) Peter Levi (who has since left the
Society); processions of robed dignitaries, prayers, hymns, readings
from Hopkins and the Bible. Then in the historic Jerusalem

Chamber sherry and rustling robes, Anglican and Roman Catholic difficult to distinguish: a strange Tudor English atmosphere. It connects with some of Hopkins's own deep emotions and wishes.

Many sorts of poignant echoes were there for anyone concerned with Hopkins. And yet I felt considerable disquiet at both the fact of the ceremony and its particular form. It was a religious service, which included some items, like prayers and the blessing, which were entirely ecclesiastical; others which were almost entirely so, like Bible readings and hymns, where artistic interest was either subordinated or a lucky gratuity; and interspersed were four Hopkins poems and stanzas from 'The Wreck of the Deutschland'. The poetry was enclosed within a special religious context, and used for a religious purpose. The many varieties of Hopkins people there were all made to appear parts of a vast Panharmonicon. Assumptions were made there, if I am not mistaken, about Hopkins's poetry as a whole, which were confirmed by the precedence given to priest over poet on the memorial slab: that its primary nature and value are homiletic; that its treasures are prescriptions; that it should be used as an aid to bringing people towards one particular philosophy of life.

Hopkins claimed, as many Victorians did, to give answers to ultimate questions. He comes from an age when, as John Holloway said, one after another of the more gifted and thoughtful members of that society decided that they must make a new start, coming to terms afresh with fundamentals. Almost all the best thinkers, though, were anti-traditional. Hopkins's religion is anti-traditional only in the minor sense that he discarded recent Anglican traditions. His conversion was one of thousands, and he was one of hundreds who became a Jesuit. As a prescriptive sage, Hopkins is nowhere near the class of Newman, the main exception to the anti-traditional norm. What most readers find of interest in Hopkins is not primarily the doctrinal, not the message, but the observation and manner of expression. We don't look to Hopkins for notions about man's place in the world, and how one should live.

I wouldn't go so far as to call Hopkins's religion a 'faint theatrical Catholicism', as did W. B. Yeats, who hadn't read Hopkins's letters, where there is much down-to-earth religion; but I think that the more one is interested in Hopkins for his religion's sake, the less one is being true to, first, the whole complex nature of his poetry, and second, the many and complex cultural, social, and psychological influences which his poetry comprehends; his religion is only one of many parts of his total context. Furthermore, the more he becomes a sacred oracle the less likely it will be that normal critical antennae will be able to explore and delve; the poetry will become of less and narrower interest and significance except within the enclave; and the more people will be inclined towards the kind of fulsome and sentimental, essentially woolly and distant, praise of which Hopkins has already had too much. One of Hopkins's main appeals to the literary mind is, I think, his complexity, the fact that there is no easy homogeneity. If we reduce him to a saint, then his complexities, his total reality, are much less likely to be valued and explored.

Let us not forget that it is his poetry that has made Hopkins famous, not his religion; and that the main force of his poetry — what has created and justified his status as a major poet — is not, however much his co-religionists may wish it, the Christian and homiletic parts of the poems, but the artistic and literary powers of his observation and expression. We do not read 'The Starlight Night' for 'Christ and his mother and all his hallows', and that rather muddled sestet, but for the stars and the night and the human excitement; nor 'Spring' for the sentimental and largely traditional priestly appeal to Christ, but for the poet's spring feast. The power of his poems lies in the images, rather than in their application, which is often clumsy and jarring and over-sentimental. (I believe that Hopkins was prone to deceive himself and many of his readers as to how much his descriptive observations were merely illustrations of something else, and how much they were in fact the major subject.) The desolate Dublin sonnets, which are sometimes ignored or devalued on non-poetic grounds (they had no part in this memorial service, for instance, although they are an essential factor in any balanced view of the Hopkins canon), are read not for their occasional religious reference, but for their human cries of the continually jaded and harassed mind, 'thy sainted sense trammel'd in ghostly pain'. It is Hopkins's *distinctive* qualities that make him worth reading and exploring: not what he has in *common* with thousands of other servants of the Church, his priestly function; where he speaks as a poet, in his *own* voice, not where he speaks as a priest, as the voice of the Church.

Notes

1. *London Review of Books*, 26 July 1990, 5.
2. To borrow terms from Alan Shelston, *Biography* (London, 1977), 3.
3. Norman White, *Hopkins: A Literary Biography* (Oxford, 1992). Parts of this essay have been adapted from Norman White, 'Hopkins: Problems in the Biography', *Studies in the Literary Imagination*, 21/1 (Spring 1988), 109–19.
4. Shown on BBC 1, Sunday, 5 Jan. 1986.
5. Denis Donoghue, 'The Heart in Hiding', *New York Review of Books*, 27 Sept. 1979, 51.
6. G. F. Lahey, SJ, *Gerard Manley Hopkins* (London, 1930); Alfred Thomas, SJ, *Hopkins the Jesuit* (London, 1969); Eleanor Ruggles, *Gerard Manley Hopkins* (London, 1947); Bernard Bergonzi, *Gerard Manley Hopkins* (London, 1977); Paddy Kitchen, *Gerard Manley Hopkins* (London, 1978).
7. Edith Anne Robertson, *Translations into the Scots Tongue of Poems by Gerard Manley Hopkins* (Aberdeen, 1968), 41.
8. Richard F. Giles (ed.), *Hopkins Among the Poets* (Hamilton, Ont., 1985), 114–23.
9. Philip Dacey, *Gerard Manley Hopkins Meets Walt Whitman in Heaven, and other Poems* (Great Barrington, Mass., 1982), 70.
10. Anthony Burgess, *The Clockwork Testament* (New York, 1976), 13.
11. *The Letters of Gerard Manley Hopkins to Robert Bridges*, ed. Claude Colleer Abbott (London, 1955), 200.
12. *The Early Poetic Manuscripts and Note-books of Gerard Manley Hopkins in Facsimile*, ed. Norman H. MacKenzie (New York and London, 1989).
13. Term borrowed from Julian Barnes, *Flaubert's Parrot* (London, 1984), 136.
14. For a fuller account of this ceremony and its implications see Norman White, 'Saint Gerard Manley Hopkins?', *Yale Review* (Spring 1980), 473–80.
15. Hopkins, 'The Starlight Night'; Auden, 'The More Loving One'.

❧ 15 ❧

The Necessary Ignorance of a Biographer

JOHN WORTHEN

My title offers neither paradox nor false modesty. I am attempting to bring back into the debate about biography a fact which many of us (and all our publishers) desire to conceal. Not only do biographers necessarily remain profoundly ignorant of many things in the lives of their subjects, but the narrative of a biography is in almost every case designed to conceal the different kinds of ignorance from which we suffer. As with all forms of knowledge we might roughly call 'historical', biographical knowledge exists simultaneously with (and I believe should never be allowed to obscure) inescapable ignorance: what I call necessary ignorance.

In D. H. Lawrence's early address book, it is often possible to tell precisely when he made entries. In the 'B' section, for example, following the names of two sisters he met for the first time in January 1912, an entry reads:

> Pauline
> Major Street
> Mansfield Road.[1]

Major Street is off the Mansfield Road in Nottingham; and as Lawrence left England early in May 1912, it seems probable that he entered the 'Pauline' name and address sometime between February (when he returned to the Midlands) and April. Only two other people in the address book lack surnames. One is a girl named Gussie we know he was attracted to in 1911. The other was his best friend, Alan Chambers. This suggests a certain intimacy about Lawrence's relationship with Pauline B. But of her, we know nothing: except that he either wrote to her, or meant to visit her. Most of the houses in Major Street were lodging-houses. Lawrence was in Nottingham a number of times during February, March, and April. Pauline may have been simply a passing acquaintance: but in that case why did he not enter her surname? She may have been someone he was close to: in which case the fact that we don't know anything about her reveals how much in the dark we often are, concerning other people's lives.

But as a biographer, I feel oddly inadequate at not being able to tell you who she was. I feel obliged to speculate: to wrap her in narrative phrases which will turn her from someone I am actually ignorant about into someone whose significance might be assessed. And how many other Pauline Bs are there, whose names I do not even know? This is a precipice over which the biographer must peer, appalled.

What the last two decades have witnessed is the increasing dominance of the idea of the biography as (ideally, anyway) definitive and comprehensive. Certainly it is getting harder and harder to publish biographies that claim less than omniscience: the day of the biographical monograph or the short biography is long gone.[2] Impressiveness and weight are necessary, if we are to be taken seriously. My publisher and I once met to discuss the size of my biography.[3] Embarrassed at the length of my manuscript, and learning that we would be using an especially large page size, I remarked innocently on the excellence of the idea: my book would not look so long. 'In that case', said my publisher, scandalized, 'we would print it on thicker paper.' He *wanted* it comprehensive-looking, definitive-looking. Ask yourselves why Michael Shelden's 1991 biography of George Orwell (subtitled *The Authorised Biography*) was printed on paper like thin cardboard, with extra wide margins, and with even its index in a single column.[4]

A narrative depending upon the reader's illusion of omniscient knowledge tends, too, to fall back for its narrative links on the convenient concept of the inevitable. If you do not know why something happened in a life, nothing is (all the same) easier than to show that it was inevitable. Because from the biographer's point of view it *is* inevitable. The biographer knows what is coming next in his or her narrative; and when you know what is going to happen next in a life, you know you are justified in explaining exactly how and why it must inevitably have happened. If the person you are writing about couldn't, poor thing, see it coming, you — with hindsight — most certainly can.

On Saturday, 3 December 1910, on a train between Leicester and Quorn, Lawrence asked his old friend Louie Burrows to marry him. She was astonished, but she said yes. Most of his and her family and friends were staggered. Lawrence professed *himself* astonished at what he had done: but insisted that it was a good idea. 'I'm jolly glad I asked her. What made me do it, I cannot tell. Twas an inspiration.'[5] No one believed the relationship would last. It survived just fourteen months.

How should a biographer introduce this sudden and unexpected development — unexpected even to the parties involved? The usual way, of course, is to explain it as inevitable. Jeffrey Meyers in his 1990 biography of Lawrence explains it in terms of the failure of Lawrence's relationships with other women. 'Lawrence's break with Agnes Holt in 1908, with Jessie [Chambers] in 1910 and with Helen [Corke] in 1911 propelled him towards the dark, attractive and apparently passionate Louie Burrows.'[6] Biographies unfortunately make us used to such sentences; sentences working hard to give a sense both of sequence, and of what people are like, all in a few short phrases. What Meyers is saying is still quite extraordinary: three 'breaks' with other women, over a period of three years, propelled Lawrence towards proposing to a fourth woman. It's the kind of logic which works only — if at all — as a narrative device. It is not an account of emotional experience; especially when you realize that one of the breaks (that with Helen Corke) actually took place six months *after* it supposedly propelled Lawrence towards Louie Burrows. To be fair, Meyers goes on to suggest other reasons why Lawrence turned to Louie Burrows. But his first instinct was to suggest that it happened inevitably; the failures elsewhere 'propelled' Lawrence to Louie; he did not choose, he was inevitably moved.

Another, more complex example. On or about 3 March 1912 Lawrence met a married woman, Frieda Weekley, at the house of her husband Professor Ernest Weekley. What happened then is known to every Lawrentian and to many other people too. Lawrence and Frieda went away together two months later, at the start of May. That simple meeting, therefore, changed both their lives dramatically. She gave up her husband — which was apparently easy — and her children, which was much harder. He in his turn ended his unsatisfactory relationships with other women. He had to start to earn his (and her) living by writing, and so became a professional writer. He also began to write over and over again about Frieda's experience: she had had considerable experience of men, apart from her husband. She also had some smatterings of psychoanalytical theory (gleaned from pillow talk with the analyst Otto Gross) which Lawrence found extremely useful in writing the final version of *Sons and Lovers*, and which he could probably not have found in any other way. They had to live abroad at the start of their relationship, because Weekley would not (before the divorce) have stood for their living together in England. Lawrence thus went to Italy for the first time, to live as cheaply as possible, and immediately used it to write symbolically about un- or pre- or sub-conscious modes of life. The meeting with Frieda Weekley, therefore, can be said to have changed his life and his writing irrevocably. Its consequences have — shall we say — a certain sublime necessity about them, in retrospect.

It comes therefore as something of a shock to register that when Lawrence and Frieda went away on 3 May 1912, they did not elope (though almost every biographical account will tell you that they did).[7] Far from making an inevitable break with her bourgeois life, Frieda had every intention of returning to her husband and children at the end of a summer holiday which she regularly spent in Germany with her parents and her sisters. When they went away, Lawrence was looking forward to — at best — a week's love-affair with her: she would almost certainly have gone back to her husband if Lawrence hadn't burnt her bridges by writing and telling Weekley that he was in love with her, and she with him (a letter used to dramatic effect in the divorce proceedings). Far from being committed to Lawrence, or to the new life, Frieda had an affair with another man at the end of her first week with Lawrence; talked of going back for months; had at least one further affair later in the summer, while she and Lawrence were walking to Italy together. These things don't fit at all well with that story of the inevitable meeting, love, elopement, and change which not only biographers but — significantly — the protagonists themselves were happy, after the event, to turn their experience into.

But, even discounting the great elopement story, are we really to think of Lawrence's meeting with Frieda as a fortunate accident? Is it possible — or sensible — for a biographer to try to describe Lawrence's life as if we did *not* know what was going to happen next? Can we avoid the paragraph starting 'Little did Lawrence know, as he entered the cosy suburban Nottingham drawing-room that sunny but breezy March morning, that he was embarking upon the most important relationship of his life'?

I would say that we certainly can. The Cambridge Lawrence biographers — of whom I am the first[8] — are not allowing themselves hindsight. When Lawrence enters the drawing-room, the reader — like the historical Lawrence — does *not* know what he or she is getting into. But what biography has traditionally done is — knowing such a moment as the so-called elopement was looming — to prepare us for it: so that the new development, while remaining exciting, silently becomes part of the emergent pattern.

It's an oddly child-like aesthetic which rates the virtues of consistency and inevitability so high: which cannot cope with things like luck and chance meetings and goings-away together and casual affairs which were not intended to be final, or were not even particularly well understood by those who were engaged in them: or, indeed, with characters who simply did not know what they were doing. The fact that we *want* an emergent sense of the inevitable development suggests the enormously soothing quality which biographies have come to have in our age. Not only do biographies suggest that things as difficult as human lives can — for all their obvious complexity — be summed up, known, comprehended: they reassure us that, while we are reading, a world will be created in which there are few or no unclear motives, muddled decisions, or (indeed) loose ends. Leon Edel once wrote disarmingly of how the random accumulated detail thrown up by the biographer's researches 'must flow from his pen in an orderly fashion . . . must be fitted into a narrative calm and measured and judicial'.[9]

Ignorance is banished, while we are in the grip of that calm and measured explanatory narrative: we comprehend all sides, command all points of view, know all there is to be known. This apparently seamless and omniscient narrative is, however, constructed out of a random survival of facts and letters and memoirs, and a random survival of relationships that can be known about.

Let me use Lawrence as my example again. If we look at Lawrence's life in the early spring of 1912, what we see and what we shall almost certainly describe — if we know that he is going to elope with Frieda — is a man coming to the end of his previous relationships, someone preparing for a new life. On 4 February 1912, for example, he broke off his engagement to Louie Burrows. Lawrence's biographer Harry T. Moore writes like this about the end of Lawrence's relationship with Louie:

Lawrence had plainly cast her off, although she magnetised him physically . . . the following February he sent her a note . . . in which he firmly indicated that he was breaking away. He was unconsciously preparing himself for the woman with whom his difficult temperament could establish a relationship in which they would be . . . 'two stars in balanced conjunction'.[10]

That is, he was unconsciously preparing himself to meet Frieda Weekley. And — brilliantly, he did, just a month later. Clever Lawrence. Well done, Harry T. Moore. It's not often that we find a biographer being *quite* so blatant. It is normally done, of course, in the final paragraph before the new chapter introducing the new relationship. Here is Jeffrey Meyers approaching the arrival of Frieda in his narrative. Three pages earlier, he had told us that in breaking off from Louie, Lawrence 'had rejected his old life, but was not quite ready for a new experience'.[11] We then get a couple of pages about Edward Garnett and Ford Madox Hueffer. And then the chapter ends like this:

In the spring of 1912, the end of the Croydon years, Lawrence was cut off from his family and fiancée in the Midlands and from the teaching profession . . . But . . . He had met distinguished, bohemian men, who lived with women who were not their wives and carried on adulterous affairs. He craved complete participation in life and was ready, at last, for Frieda Weekley. She led him out of his sexual impasse and helped him realize his greatness as a man and as a writer.[12]

So — unlike Harry T. Moore's Lawrence, prepared at the start of February to meet Frieda — Meyers's Lawrence is explicitly 'not quite ready' in February. But some thinking about the bohemian lives of Garnett and Hueffer (there is no evidence at all that Lawrence did any such thinking between February and March) successfully prepared him for Frieda: and thus made him ready 'at last' for the new relationship.

It was not, of course, actually Lawrence who was 'not quite ready' to meet Frieda. It was Jeffrey Meyers who was not quite ready, because he had some things he still wanted to tell us. When he's told us what he wants us to know — then, hey presto, Lawrence is ready and waiting for Frieda: and he meets her on the following page.

Such an approach seems to me, I have to say, a recipe for the very worst kind of biography: one which is apparently serious and concerned, but which actually imposes upon a life the story which it is to tell, and then fills in the details (like someone doing painting by numbers) with the necessarily random facts which happen to come down to us. This can certainly make for a revealing and coherent life, one in which — of course — all the facts go to support the central narrative, and create what Leon Edel called 'the essence', indeed 'the story' of that life.[13] But the priority of such a biographical method is very clearly the convenience of the biographer, and *not* the experience of the person whose life it is about.

Not only Lawrence biographers do this. Here is a biographer confronting the problem of making things fit together and seem inevitable: the biographer of William Carlos Williams, Paul Mariani.

it is axiomatic that the biographer must always be true to the facts — the literary remains — which he keeps finding, trying to make sense of it all in something like a final ordering . . . to feel then the dust of all those words we call 'facts' begin to take form, like the shape of the rose (to borrow an

image from Ezra Pound) emerging out of the steel-dust particles when a
magnet has been placed beneath their surface.[14]

Mariani wants what he ominously calls a 'final ordering' into
which all the known facts fit. He argues that if you manage to get
such a shape, then it will be because you've got the right one. He
describes the moment of illumination when the inner life of the
biographical subject is revealed, at last:

I think most successful biographers will tell you (or at least *could* tell you)
that there was that moment of light when the inner life of their subject
was suddenly revealed. At that point the earlier, partial images fell away
and the inner consistency of their subject was impressed in upon the
biographer.[15]

That is, the successful biographer reveals 'the essence', 'the story' of
which Edel wrote. This strikes me as — at best — terribly naïve.
But there can be no doubt that such consistencies of narrative and
texture are what many readers have learned to look for in biography; and it is the biographer's desire to present them, combined
with the reader's need to find them, which most vitiates the
development of a post-nineteenth-century biography.

Consider that very common habit of spelling out, in the first
moments of a biography, what is going to happen chronologically
towards the end — a death. Jay Martin began his biography of
Nathanael West with the death of West and his wife in a car crash:
the chapter is called 'December 22, 1941': the car is wrecked, the
dog running wild. The first words are 'Eileen's watch stopped at
2.50.' 'Having killed off his subject, Martin explained a few years
ago at a session on biography at . . . Harvard, he could get on with
the business of recounting West's life that would lead up to this
irrevocable terminus.'[16] That's a fine example of a biographer
ignoring his ignorance and heading blithely towards understanding.
Peter Ostwald starts his biography of Robert Schumann with an
appearance even more dramatic than Schumann's actual death:

Just past noon on Monday, 27 February 1854, a hulking figure suddenly
emerged from a house on Bilkerstrasse and turned left on the cobbled

street. Although it was a cold, rainy day in Düsseldorf, the man wore only a thin robe and slippers. His face was pasty, his eyes were downcast, and he was sobbing. Walking unsteadily, as if on tiptoe, he headed for the Rhine River . . . rushed down the incline leading to the bridge, ran part way across, paused briefly, and threw himself headlong into the icy torrent.[17]

Schumann was in fact rescued, and died in an asylum two years later. But Ostwald's book is based on his theory that madness appears throughout Schumann's life; and this grotesque, hulking, pasty-faced and sobbing figure implicitly confirms the direction the biography is about to take.

And here is Peter Ackroyd on the first page of his *Dickens*.

CHARLES DICKENS was dead. He lay on a narrow green sofa — but there was room enough for him, so spare had he become — in the dining room of Gad's Hill Place. He had died in the house which he had first seen as a small boy and which his father had pointed out to him as a suitable object of his ambitions; so great was his father's hold upon his life that, forty years later, he had bought it. Now he had gone.[18]

What this does, of course, is sanction the vision of a life seen as inevitable progress to that final point; it informs us that this life is to be comprehended in terms of its ironically achieved ambitions, and of the power of the father.

Deaths in biographies are very often — by their very position in the narrative — seen not just as the necessarily final things to happen to the subjects of biographies but as culminating points, which can be used to sum up and confirm what the lives have really been about. (Supposing Philip Larkin were still alive, for example.) When Lockhart wrote about the death of Scott, for example, he was under the handicap that Scott had lapsed into a coma — in which his mind was what Lockhart called 'hopelessly obscured'[19] — several weeks before he actually died. If you read Edgar Johnson's life of Scott, you will find that Scott is in that coma uninterruptedly up to the death-bed scene itself (of which more a little later). Almost all, however, that Johnson knows about this passage of three weeks culminating in Scott's death is described by Lockhart, who was himself at Abbotsford. But one thing Johnson leaves out: and that is the extraordinary episode in Lockhart's biography in which Scott, early one morning four days before he died, came round for a few minutes, and asked to see Lockhart.

His eye was clear and calm — every trace of the wild fire of delirium extinguished. 'Lockhart,' he said, 'I may have but a minute to speak to you. My dear, be a good man — be virtuous — be religious — be a good man. Nothing else will give you any comfort when you come to lie here.' He paused, and I said — 'Shall I send for Sophia and Anne [Scott's daughters]?' — 'No,' said he, 'don't disturb them. Poor souls! I know they were up all night — God bless you all.' With this he sank into a very tranquil sleep and indeed he scarcely afterwards gave any sign of consciousness . . .[20]

It is impossible to escape the conclusion that Lockhart saw it his duty as a biographer to ensure that Scott got the chance for a ritual final utterance. This was the point towards which the biography had been moving; but, unfortunately, Scott's coma denied him public statement. However, Lockhart's private communication from Scott (it is very striking that Scott, having been in a coma for three weeks, immediately knew to whom he should talk) — this private conversation allowed Lockhart's narrative to contain the crucial element of summary, the final words of wisdom, the convenient (but characteristically thoughtful) exclusion of the daughters on the grounds of their tiredness — how did Scott know they'd been up all night if he'd only just come round? — and the final 'God bless you all!'

Edgar Johnson does not believe that those final words were ever spoken. He is not, after all, writing that *kind* of biography. Accordingly, and I think sensibly, he leaves the episode out of his narrative.[21] However, lest you start thinking of him as an unsentimental realist, let me point out some interesting differences between Johnson and Lockhart's description of the subsequent death-bed scene. This is Lockhart describing Scott's final moments:

It was a beautiful day — so warm, that every window was wide open — and so perfectly still, that the sound of all others most delicious to his ear, the gentle ripple of the Tweed over its pebbles, was distinctly audible as we knelt around the bed, and his eldest son kissed and closed his eyes.[22]

When he came to describe the scene (for which Lockhart was

almost his only source), Johnson — either consciously or unconsciously — reacted against the idea of kissing a dead man's open
eyes. He altered Lockhart's 'kissed and closed his eyes' to 'closed
and kissed his eyes'.[23] That is modern squeamishness, not realism.
Secondly, like Lockhart he mentions the sound of the Tweed —
but he explicitly makes it the last sound Scott ever hears, and not
the sound heard by the people in the room. I regard that as simply
sentimental. And, finally, not content with Lockhart's description
of it as 'a beautiful day', Johnson adds some description of his own:
'Outdoors the autumn foliage was a glory of russet, crimson and
gold.'[24] Autumnal splendour: how appropriate. But this is 21 September. Do autumn colours come so early in the Scottish lowlands?
I was once at Abbotsford, as it happened, late in September at the
end of a dryish summer; and the foliage was solid, if dusty green.
The fading autumn glory is just as manipulative a piece of biographer's narrative piety as Lockhart's account of Scott's final testament
of faith.

So-called documentary facts (I don't know what else to call
them) in a biography may be no more than materials manipulated
by the biographer into an apparently and ideally seamless web of
cause and effect, of inevitable and seamless progression. The metal
particles described by Paul Mariani are never permitted to remain
scattered at random; the biographer ensures that his centralizing
magnet groups them to form the shape of the rose: the life and its
progress to a death. Death itself is not so much a documentary fact,
more of a biographical opportunity.

But in fact, of course, biographers are always — like Lockhart and
Johnson — stuck with a fairly random survival of materials; and
the story which those materials can be induced to tell is limited by
what they happen to be. This unfortunate fact is one that biographers do their very best to stop you thinking about. The impression
they want you to gain, of course, is that the facts which we happen
to know are also necessarily the important ones. This is often quite
untrue: and the whirligigs of time sometimes have a nice way of
demonstrating it.

The relationship between Lawrence and Louie Burrows for

nearly forty years played almost no part in Lawrence biography. If you pick up a 1950s biography — Richard Aldington, *Portrait of a Genius, But . . .*, for instance — you will find almost no reference to Louie; she appears by name just once in the text, and her surname does not appear in the index. She is simply a girl with whom Aldington describes Lawrence as being in 'a bit of a tangle' with.[25] There is no reference to an engagement between them. But the fact was that almost nothing was known about her (I suspect Aldington did not actually know her surname) for the simple reason that she had refused to talk to biographers and had refused to allow Aldous Huxley access to her Lawrence letters in 1932;[26] and had thereby succeeded (much to her relief) in marginalizing herself in Lawrence biography for nearly forty years. Without the letters from Lawrence to her, there was in Huxley's collection just a handful of references to her — including, however, one to the fact that Lawrence called her 'My girl' in December 1911.[27] But Huxley reduced her name on the three occasions she appeared in his text to the initial 'L': and she was omitted from his index.[28]

By the mid-1930s, everyone — every biographer — knew that the important women in Lawrence's early life were Jessie Chambers and Helen Corke. Both of them had written books about how important they had been.[29] And discussions of Jessie and Helen dominated the early biographies — including Harry T. Moore's own first biography, of 1951.[30] The random survival of facts and the willingness of certain people (but not others) to write memoirs successfully created what documentary biographical fact actually *was*.

Over the years there had in fact been a few attempts to bring what was known about Louie Burrows into the picture: she was at least mentioned in Moore's 1951 biography ('a Midlands girl to whom he was engaged for a while'[31]) and played a slightly larger role in his 1955 biography *The Intelligent Heart*; Moore added comments such as the fact that at Christmas 1911 — when Lawrence was recovering from pneumonia and people were coming to see him — 'Louie Burrows also appeared':[32] the casualness of the phrase demonstrating the insignificance of the visit. She received a careful

and accurate note in Edward Nehls's *Composite Biography* of Lawrence in 1957.[33] But the *Collected Letters of D. H. Lawrence* of 1962,
edited by Harry T. Moore — though containing a number of
letters specifically referring to her, and editorial interpolations which
on three occasions identified her by name — again failed to contain
an index entry for her.[34] The reason, I am sure, is that Moore had
grown up knowing that Louie was unimportant; he had written
two biographies in which she hardly appeared; and he went on
behaving as if she did not exist. She thus remained marginalized:
there was no way in which her presence could disturb (or be
allowed to disturb) the existing structure and pattern, the consistency and beautiful inevitability, of the standard account of
Lawrence's early relationships.

But the very year when the *Collected Letters* came out, Louie
Burrows died; and it turned out that not only had she kept almost
everything Lawrence had ever written her, but her executors had
sold the collection to the University of Nottingham. And there it
was, blowing a great hole in the previously unchallengeable right-
ness and balance of Lawrence early biography: 165 new letters and
cards. Almost half of all Lawrence's surviving correspondence of
1911 was addressed to her. His letters to her utterly transformed
our understanding of what he went through that year: and I would
say, of him too.[35]

When Moore created his updated biography of Lawrence — *The
Priest of Love* — in 1974, he could no longer leave Louie out. But as
he had the years 1906–12 nicely mapped out already, he didn't
allow her to disturb his account of those years. He simply provided
some quotations from letters to her, and added some details of the
circumstances of their final meeting (his previous version had
simply referred to Lawrence's 'amusing and lively description of
Louie' in a restaurant when she had been 'coy, coquettish, and
vague').[36] He added that sentence I quoted earlier, for example,
starting 'Lawrence had plainly cast her off, although she magnetised
him physically'.[37] He did not believe that Louie Burrows could
ever have been important to Lawrence: simply because, when he
grew up as a biographer, she wasn't and couldn't have been.

It was not until 1979 that her correspondence appeared at last in the full context of all the rest of Lawrence's early letters, in the Cambridge edition of the letters.[38] But even then, Jeffrey Meyers in his 1990 biography of Lawrence could not help conforming to the old picture that Lawrence's engagement to Louie was a side-issue. He could not take it seriously: he commented that 'Lawrence, like any new fiancé, soon had second thoughts':[39] a remark that reveals Jeffrey Meyers even more than it does Lawrence. The fact that Lawrence and Louie were engaged; the fact that he wrote so much to her; the fact that she answered at least one profound impulse in him to be ordinary and normal and happy and conventional — all this has been ignored in biography. It was not, I would argue, until the following year, when my own biography of Lawrence appeared, that anything like a full appreciation of Louie Burrows and her place in Lawrence's life was attempted.[40]

But I have no reason for complacency. What cache of manuscripts is out there, lying in wait to ambush me, waiting to blow a hole in the side of my biographical understanding? To prove that my carefully balanced and responsible portrait is based upon ignorance and folly? I even know what that cache might be. There have been rumours for years that Lawrence's letters to his mother survive, within the family. And there I might find a letter saying 'Louie isn't important to me, mother: only Jessie is'. I sit and wait: and what I wait for may, one day, come.[41]

Biographical writing is very often indeed a species of confidence trick — in spite of its continual claim to be rooted in documentary evidence. What it says is: 'Drop your guard: allow the spell of "essence" and "story" to take over: allow yourself to be moved into a version of human affairs where everything is tied up and explained, into narrative which is essentially problem-less.' Such problems as are allowed to remain in the narrative stay there primarily so as to display the skill of the biographer in solving them before your very eyes, as in conjuring — or in detective fiction, which is actually an interesting parallel genre. I am increasingly struck with how escapist modern biography is, for all its apparently ruthless search for documents and evidence and its new, imagined 1990s toughness in being either hard-hittingly authentic — i.e.

'authorized' — or better still (for this guarantees scandal and sales) 'unauthorized'.[42] What contemporary biography primarily creates, I suggest, is not only fiction (which has often been said) but a particularly escapist and uninteresting kind of fiction. The created lives within most contemporary literary biographies, in fact, make television soaps look minor miracles of complexity.

When we read a biography, we must always tell ourselves that the author has us in his or her power: to make us feel not only that what we are getting is true, but that there is no other truth which matters. And that — neither they nor we can know. We must remind ourselves that the biographer is ignorant: not just accidentally ignorant, but ignorant by the very nature of the biographer's trade; necessarily ignorant, hamstrung by the accidental survival of materials, obliged to make and impose a pattern where none exists, forced to construct a narrative where the only materials he or she possesses have also to be the only significant events within it, pressured by his or her publisher *not* to keep putting in sentences describing his or her ignorance.

I very much admire the biographer who none the less does this. I should like to cite Claire Tomalin, whose biography of Ellen Ternan is a model of how to incorporate, not to hide, absence and ignorance. She gives you a summary of the probable events of the years 1861–5 of the joint life of Ellen Ternan and Dickens: years when it seems probable that

Nelly became pregnant by Dickens and . . . he moved her to France, probably somewhere in the Paris area; that she had her baby there, with her mother in attendance, some time in 1862; that the baby died, probably during the summer of 1863; and that she then stayed on in France or spent most of her time abroad until June 1865, when the Staplehurst railway accident happened.[43]

Most biographers would have been happy with that summary. But she prefaces what she has done like this: 'This chapter has tried to make some sense of the known facts of the years between 1861 and 1865, and suggested a simple outline of a narrative to fit them . . .'[44] That is what biographers nearly always actually do, but very few confess to it. She then starts a new paragraph, and I cheer her for her courage and good sense: 'Some or all of this may be wrong. She may not have had a baby; she may not have lived in France but only visited it for brief holidays.'[45] 'Some or all of this may be wrong.' I suggest that those words might usefully be affixed to all literary biographies, as a kind of Government Health Warning. Ignorance is implicit in the nature of our business: and we should embrace its necessities.

Notes

1. Address Book at the Bancroft Library, University of California at Berkeley.

2. Leon Edel argued in the mid-1950s for three significant types of biography: the 'Stracheyan' psychological life, the brief 'portrait' life, and the documentary, 'chronicle' biography. See Leon Edel, *Literary Biography* (London, 1957), 82–9. Such arguments bear no weight today: the 'portrait' life is as dead as mutton.

3. John Worthen, *D. H. Lawrence: The Early Years 1885–1912* (Cambridge, 1991).

4. Michael Shelden, *George Orwell: The Authorised Biography* (London, 1991).

5. *The Letters of D. H. Lawrence, i. September 1901–May 1913*, ed. James T. Boulton (Cambridge, 1979), 193.

6. Jeffrey Meyers, *D. H. Lawrence* (Basingstoke and London, 1990), 65–6.

7. See e.g. Mark Schorer, *D. H. Lawrence* (New York, 1968), 14 ('Hardly a month later they had fled to Germany together'); Paul Delany, *D. H. Lawrence's Nightmare* (New York, 1978), 4 ('Lawrence had fled England with a woman who seemed to offer him, by the immediate and spontaneous gift of herself, freedom'); and the 'Chronology' to most volumes in the Cambridge University Press Edition of the Works of D. H. Lawrence, e.g. *Lady Chatterley's Lover*, ed. Michael Squires (Cambridge, 1993), p. xi ('March 1912 Meets Frieda Weekley; they elope to Germany on 3 May'); cf. Worthen, *D. H. Lawrence: The Early Years*, 393–9.

8. Vol. ii (1912–22) is being written by Mark Kinkead-Weekes, vol. iii (1922–30) by David Ellis.

9. Edel, *Literary Biography*, 81.

10. H. T. Moore, *The Priest of Love* (London, 1974), 138–9.

11. Meyers, *D. H. Lawrence*, 74.

12. Ibid.

13. Edel, *Literary Biography*, 3, 82: the whole sentences read: 'What is the essence of a life, and how do we disengage that essence from the eternal clutter of days and years, the inexorable tick of the clock — and yet restore the sense of that very tick?' 'And in what manner is the story to be told?'

14. Paul Mariani, 'William Carlos Williams', in Jeffrey Meyers (ed.), *The Craft of Literary Biography* (Basingstoke and London, 1985), 133–4.

15. Ibid. 139. And cf. 'My experience has been that if this moment of light rings "true" to the biographer, then all subsequent finds will accommodate themselves to this pattern' (p. 139). One may be sure that they will.

16. Jay Martin, *Nathanael West: The Art of His Life* (New York, 1970), 3–6; Paul Mariani, 'William Carlos Williams', *The Craft of Literary Biography*, 148. Mariani also gives an account of the opening of Martin's biography which, however, offers a spectacular catalogue of errors. The crash happened in 1940, not '1941' (as Mariani states): in December, not in 'summer'; West and his wife Eileen were both thrown out of the car, but Mariani has them 'slumped over in their new stationwagon' (it was not new); Mariani claims that West's body was 'resting on the horn, still sounding', but Martin had described West being thrown into the road: the horn was not sounding, West's car was not 'demolished'. And where Mariani has 'the two of them dead', West actually lived for another 75 minutes, Eileen for another 60. The errors make one hope Mariani is never called as a witness to a car crash or to give testimony for a biography.

17. Peter Ostwald, *Schumann: Music and Madness* (London, 1985), 1.

18. Peter Ackroyd, *Dickens* (London, 1990), xi.

19. J. G. Lockhart, *The Life of Sir Walter Scott Bart.* (abridged edn., 1848; repr. Edinburgh, 1879), 726.

20. Ibid. 779.

21. He does record part of it, however (omitting its second half), in n. 82 of his biography *Sir Walter Scott*, 2 vols. (London, 1970), 1337–8.

22. Lockhart, *Life of Scott*, 779–80.

23. Johnson, *Sir Walter Scott*, 1276. Johnson's other sources for the event were letters written by Scott's daughter Sophia on 16 and 26 Sept. 1832, and a doctor's account and report (p. 1338 n. 85).

24. Ibid. 1276.

25. Richard Aldington, *Portrait of a Genius, But . . .* (London, 1950), 103.

26. *The Letters of D. H. Lawrence*, ed. Aldous Huxley (London, 1932).

27. Ibid. 17.

28. Ibid. 24, 25, 27.

29. E. T. [Jessie Chambers], *D. H. Lawrence: A Personal Record* (London, 1935); Helen Corke, *D. H. Lawrence and Apocalypse* (London, 1933).

30. Harry T. Moore, *The Life and Works of D. H. Lawrence* (London, 1951), 31–2, 71.

31. Ibid. 71.

32. Harry T. Moore, *The Intelligent Heart* (rev. edn., Harmondsworth, 1960), 148.

33. Edward Nehls (ed.), *D. H. Lawrence: A Composite Biography*, 3 vols. (Madison, Wis., 1957–9), i. 556.

34. *The Collected Letters of D. H. Lawrence*, ed. H. T. Moore, 2 vols. (London,

1962), 71, 77, [78], [99], 100 (bracketed numbers denote pages where Louie's name is used but she is not identified).

35. The correspondence was first published in *Lawrence in Love*, ed. James T. Boulton (Nottingham, 1967).
36. Moore, *The Intelligent Heart*, 152.
37. Moore, *The Priest of Love*, 138.
38. *The Letters of D. H. Lawrence*, ed. Boulton, vol. i.
39. Meyers, *D. H. Lawrence*, 66.
40. Worthen, *D. H. Lawrence: The Early Years*, 288–324, 334–41.
41. Cf. *Sons and Lovers*, ed. Helen and Carl Baron (Cambridge, 1992), p. 14, line 29.
42. e.g. Michael Shelden's *George Orwell: The Authorised Biography* (London, 1991) and Kitty Kelley, *Nancy Reagan: The Unauthorised Biography* (New York, 1991). I saw *Armand Hammer: The Thoroughly Unauthorised Biography* displayed for sale in New Zealand in September 1992, but have unfortunately been unable to trace the title in Europe.
43. Claire Tomalin, *The Invisible Woman* (edn. with additional material, Harmondsworth, 1991), 147–8.
44. Ibid. 147.
45. Ibid. 148.

Virginia Woolf and 'The Proper Writing of Lives'

JULIA BRIGGS

'I should like to write a very subtle work on the proper writing of lives. What it is that you can write — and what writing is. It comes over me that I know nothing of the art', Virginia Stephen confided in her brother-in-law, Clive Bell, in 1908.[1] Many years later she would fulfil her ambition, writing subtle essays on 'The New Biography' (1927) and 'The Art of Biography' (1940), but her earliest writings are preoccupied with the problems it posed, exploring them through her writing practice and her comments on its possibilities and constraints. Biography could be seen as an exemplary form in combining history and imagination, fact and fantasy, constraint and freedom, but at the same time she did not subscribe to its rationale, indeed its exemplary nature in that other sense of holding up moral examples. From an early stage, she was committed to extending its range and increasing its flexibility, to writing against it as well as within it, as she would later do with fiction. In her second novel, *Night and Day*, fiction and biography are used to mirror one another, but the novel was completed while the inset biography remained unfinished.

That the young Virginia Stephen should equate the possibilities of and constraints upon writing with the writing of biography is scarcely surprising given her status as 'daughter of the *DNB*'. Leslie Stephen had gained his knighthood primarily for his editorship of the *Dictionary of National Biography*. Not only in the household in which she grew up, but in the wider family group, biography was accorded high status as a literary form, and much practised: 'when one of them dies the chances are· that another of them writes his biography'.[2] Leslie Stephen's commitment to his massive task was

245

at once respected and resented: according to family legend or joke, the *Dictionary* had been produced at the expense of his younger children's stability: 'Poor old Adrian!' wrote Woolf of her younger brother, 'the *DNB* crushed his life out before he was born. It gave me a twist of the head too. I shouldn't have been so clever, but I should have been more stable, without that contribution to the history of England', and it amused her to attribute her poor health to 'those 68 black books'.[3] At the end of her life, when she was writing her autobiography, she read Freud, and borrowed from him the term 'ambivalence'[4] to describe the blend of love and hatred that she felt for her father. Something of those conflicting feelings extended to the literary form with which Stephen was most closely and consistently associated. Her earliest work paid homage to it, and accepted it as a literary yardstick even as it sought to modify its influence.

Leslie Stephen had accepted the editorship of the *DNB* in 1882, the year Virginia was born; its purpose was to keep a national record of the lives of great men, the heroes who 'had sailed with Sir John Franklin to the North Pole, and ridden with Havelock to the Relief of Lucknow',[5] the great British writers, statesmen, and thinkers; yet fired though it was by a Carlylean sense of the inspiration that such lives might provide, that ethos was already beginning to be questioned. It was during the 1880s and 1890s, the years when Stephen was working on his *Dictionary* that modern biography was born: Woolf herself pointed out many years later that 'Froude's [biography of] Carlyle is by no means a wax mask . . . And following Froude there was Sir Edmund Gosse, who dared to say that his own father was a fallible human being'.[6] A cultural shift in the nature of biography had begun. Both Woolf's later essays on biography analyse this process, in which Lytton Strachey played a key role. Over time, she recognized, it would bring the intimate, domestic view, with its 'accent on sex', to the centre of biography, the place it occupies today.[7]

Virginia Stephen's first encounter with biography might have been designed to illustrate the gap between the authorized version and the backstairs view. In the autumn following her father's death (in February 1904) the historian Frederic Maitland invited her to contribute to his biography of her father. The resulting sketch, published in *The Life and Letters of Leslie Stephen* (1906), portrays him sailing a toy boat with his children on the Round Pond and reading to them in the evening[8] — intimate scenes from the great man's domestic life, yet, as such, carefully selected. Familiar only to the women in his life were the violent uninhibited rages and tantrums that seemed so 'brutal'.[9] His mother, his sister Caroline, his two wives, and his daughters had put up with them, each accepting them as the price of his 'genius'; in Woolf's later view, each 'bowing to it, increased the load for the other'. Fred Maitland, she recalled, had 'resolutely refused to believe, though tactfully instructed by Carry, that Leslie's tempers were more than what he called (in his biography) coloured showers of sparks'.[10]

Men and women, then, might see the same individual from very different angles. The intimate and sometimes sordid secrets of a man's life, that he 'threw boots at the maid's head, had a mistress at Islington, or was found drunk in a ditch after a night's debauch'[11] were often only too apparent to his wife, his maid, even his daughter, yet as Woolf recognized, truths of that kind were not yet tolerated in middle-class society. Trawling through her father's letters for his biographer, she was urged by an old family friend, 'Whatever you do, *don't* publish anything too intimate'.[12] 'The sensibilities of conventional people' demanded that the male subject be portrayed in such a way that he continued to command respect within his family: 'One of the objects of biography is to make men appear as they ought to be, for they are husbands and brothers.'[13]

Not only were the perspectives of public and private life very different, but women were confined to roles whose most characteristic activities and experiences were often considered too trivial for fiction, let alone for biography, defined in terms of 'the lives of great men'. Living mainly at home, feeding rabbits, visiting old ladies, shopping or reading, young middle-class women were virtually invisible, as they went about their 'curious silent unrepresented life'.[14] One of the chief problems that Woolf confronted as a biographer was how to write the lives that the *Dictionary* had ignored, those lives of the obscure that remained unrecorded, that were lived out, unconsidered and unvalued in the shadows. As reader, reviewer, and writer, she committed herself to an exploration of women's lives. Her many biographical sketches of women writers made a counter-claim to her father's writings, as if setting up a posthumous interrogation of his principles of inclusion, or drawing attention to the major omissions in his coverage.

She was particularly interested in the lives marginalized by the *Dictionary*, lives of women, of outsiders, of the obscure. In 1915 she proposed writing 'a book of "Eccentrics". Mrs Grote shall be one. Lady Hester Stanhope. Margaret Fuller. Duchess of Newcastle. Aunt Julia?' An essay of 1919, 'The Eccentrics',[15] attempted to revive the idea, and she did indeed write brief lives of three of the five at different times.[16] All were women who in one way or another had refused to accept traditional social pressures and had put their own dreams and visions first, as the writer has to do. The category of lives of the obscure was altogether more problematic: eccentrics usually attracted the attention of their contemporaries, of diarists or later memoirs, but obscure lives, and ordinary people, the people that historians overlooked for so long and are even now combing the records for, have seldom left any account of themselves. When they did, it was largely by chance, as with the letters preserved in the Paston family. From Woolf's short story of 1906, 'The Journal of Mistress Joan Martyn', to *Between the Acts* and her late, unfinished essay 'Anon',[17] she recorded her search for the voices of those that history and literary historians had failed to represent. Their silence created a supreme difficulty, but also an artistic opportunity for the writer who could picture their lives or find words for them to speak.

For her earliest experiments in biography, however, Woolf turned to friends and members of her family, who provided her with subjects and a strictly limited but familiar audience. In doing so, she was following a family tradition, for not only did her relatives write each other's official lives, but they also left private papers addressed to one another, and letters, diaries, and other family papers were brought out and reread on occasion.[18] After his wife's death, Leslie Stephen wrote an account of her addressed to her children, which they referred to as the 'Mausoleum Book'. In so doing, he may have had in mind his grandfather's memoir of himself 'for the Use of His Children'.[19] Woolf began (late in 1904) by writing comic lives of her paternal aunt Caroline Stephen and her maternal aunt Mary Fisher (Frederic Maitland's mother-in-law).[20] Though these have not survived, the operatically interfering aunts in her novel *Night and Day*, Cousin Caroline and Mrs Milvain, are probably their descendants. Her two accounts of her eccentric great-aunt, the photographer Julia Margaret Cameron — an essay introducing her photographs and her comedy, 'Freshwater' — may belong to the same tradition.[21]

Her first serious attempt at life-writing was that of her sister Vanessa, probably begun in the late summer of 1907, and the subject of her letter to Clive Bell quoted at the start of this chapter.[22] This was precisely the kind of life that challenged *DNB* principles — that of a young woman who had lived at home, studied at art school, and recently married. Even so, the voice she adopted was still her father's, though her father's at its closest approach to domestic intimacy (it was still not close enough to discuss the really intimate crisis): the sentimental tones of the 'Mausoleum Book'. Addressing his children there, his dead wife becomes 'Your Mother'; Woolf managed to use the same device by addressing herself to the child that Vanessa was now expecting. She also adopted her father's mournful tone (she was more hurt than she could admit by her sister's departure). The memoir recalls their earliest games together — 'the great extent and mystery of the dark land under the nursery table, where a continuous romance seemed to go forward',[23] — and sets out Vanessa's truthfulness and sense of responsibility for her younger siblings. It is chiefly concerned, however, with their mother and their step-sister Stella, and their untimely deaths ten and more years previously.

While the memoir might have provided Virginia with an opportunity to reconsider the account of Leslie Stephen given in Maitland's official biography, it is his portrait of their mother that is deemed inadequate: 'You will not find in what I say, or again in those sincere but conventional phrases in the life of your grandfather, or in the noble lamentations with which he fills the pages of his autobiography, any semblance of a woman whom you can love'. The difficulty lies, it seems, in the nature of 'written words' which 'drape themselves in smooth folds annulling all evidence of life'.[24] Her analysis is acute: the style she was using continually translated Julia Stephen into an abstract, heroic mode, entirely lacking in intimacy: 'She rose to the heights, wide-eyed and nobly free from all illusion or sentiment, her second love shining pure as starlight, the rosy mists of the first rapture dispelled for ever'; or 'she sank, like an exhausted swimmer, deeper and deeper in the water, and could only at moments descry some restful shore on the horizon'.[25] It seemed impossible to portray Julia Stephen and Stella Duckworth as familiar, lovable people: their lives had been swallowed up in their care for others. Their tragic fates overshadowed them, precluding humanizing laughter or particularity, and occasioning a deeper fear that, in inheriting their roles as bride and mother, Vanessa might be similarly swallowed up. In her mourning for them, Woolf concealed her own mourning for the loss of Vanessa, her own echoes of her father's resentful demands. The warmth of Mrs Ramsay lay twenty years and four novels ahead.

Virginia's letter to Clive Bell about 'the proper writing of lives', quoted in my opening lines, reveals her desire to recover Vanessa vicariously, through writing her life, but what strikes her most about her effort is its inadequacy: 'I have been writing Nessa's life; and I am going to send you 2 chapters in a day or two. It might have been so good! As it is, I am too near, and too far; and it seems to be blurred, and I ask myself why write at all? seeing I never shall recapture what you have, by your side this minute.'[26] She had not achieved the speaking likeness she had aimed at, and at the first point where scandal threatened, when Vanessa fell in love with Stella's distraught widower, Jack Hills, the narrative ended abruptly. Even in a document intended only for the family circle there was much that biography could not yet say.

In marked contrast to the life of Vanessa, though written slightly earlier, and out of a comparable emotional need, is the life of her friend Violet Dickinson, entitled 'Friendship's Gallery' (August 1907).[27] Violet Dickinson was an older woman who had given Virginia motherly love and support, and to whom Virginia, in turn, was passionately devoted. Though in no obvious way exceptional, Violet fitted few of the Victorian stereotypes of womanhood:

well-bred, clever, affectionate, and cheerful, she was also single, middle-aged, and enjoyed making herself useful. She encouraged the young Virginia to write reviews for a clerical weekly called the *Guardian*, shared holidays with the family, and nursed her devotedly through a major breakdown. 'Friendship's Gallery' was a love-gift for her, typed out in violet ink and bound in violet leather. But here, Violet's humorous approach to life set the tone, releasing Virginia into fantasy and parody that comfortably accommodated the prosaic details of her friend's life by making fun of them.

Though the three chapters differ from one another, the predominant mode is mock-heroic, inflating its subject to the proportions required to justify the celebration of Violet's life, while covertly alluding to her exceptional height: though not a 'great man', she qualified as 'great' in the most literal sense (according to Leslie Stephen, 'her only fault is that she is 6 feet high').[28] Woolf makes the most of a new-found imaginative freedom, beginning in the vein of another mock-biography, that of *Tristram Shandy*. After Violet's Shandean baptism, with its search for a suitable name, we are hurried through the schoolroom to a detailed account of her first season:

I suspect that my artistic skill would have been more consummate had I thrown these first pages into the waste paper basket or enclosed them within the arms of a parenthesis. For when you are writing the life of a woman you should surely begin
Her First Season
and leave such details as birth parentage education and the first seventeen years of her life to be taken for granted . . . But then this Biography is no novel but a sober chronicle; and if Life will begin seventeen years before it is needed it is our task to say so valiantly and make the best of it.[29]

Here different aspects of her early life are not even distinguished from one another by commas, and only her arrival in 'society', the announcement of her marriageable status, is deemed worthy of record. 'Making the best of it' becomes a keynote, characterizing both the author's approach to her form and her subject's approach to her circumstances.

The second chapter takes place in a wonderful garden in which Violet and her friends Nelly (Lady Robert) Cecil and Kitty Maxse are distanced and enlarged into 'gigantic women lying like Greek marbles in easy chairs; draped so that the wind bared little gleaming spaces on their shoulders; who laughed as they helped themselves to strawberries and cream as though they looked upon a vision of a jocund world'.[30] Their size reflects the status attributed to them, as it might in the fantasies of Pope or Swift, lending an affectionate absurdity to Violet's prosaic preoccupations with drains and operations. In the third section, a fairy-tale version of Violet and Nelly's world tour of 1905, the two are promoted to goddesses who rescue the city of Tokyo from an invasion of sea monsters with the tips of their umbrellas. Dickinson's size and power within the fantasy register her relative importance and maternal role, and compensate for the failure of conventional biography to value her special talents as they deserved.

As *Orlando* would do twenty years later, 'Friendship's Garland' solved the problem of how to write the life of an intimate friend by substituting fantasy for realism, by writing it in a manner that proclaimed its fictiveness. Reviewing a new life of Sterne in 1909, Woolf took the opportunity to weigh up the attractions and obstacles that biography afforded. Her experience already suggested to her that a degree of intimacy with a subject might, given contemporary sensibilities, demand disguise in fiction: 'A certain stigma is attached to the biography which deals mainly with a man's personal history, and the writer who sees him most clearly in that light is driven to represent him under the cover of fiction.'[31] At the same time, she recognized that fiction was at a disadvantage compared with biography in that it was taken less seriously by the reader — it lacked 'the aesthetic effect of truth': 'the bare statement of facts has an indisputable power, if we have reason to think them true . . . a real life is wonderfully prolific; it passes through such strange places and draws along with it a train of adventures [so] that no novelist can better them, if only he can deal with them as with his own inventions.'[32] To rewrite personal history as fiction, to use the materials of real life as if they were her own inventions — these were the lessons that she learned from her early experiments with biography.

Although real lives were potentially 'wonderfully prolific',

Woolf's next exploration of the subject moved decisively away from the lives of friends and family, while employing the knowledge she had gained from her earlier experiments, that determining factors in the writing of biography were the style, which dictated what it was possible to discuss, and the relationship between biographer and subject, conventionally kept out of sight, but often setting up its own hidden agenda. She also drew on her professional experience as a reviewer with a particular interest in women's memoirs. The result was her most complex and ambitious fiction yet, a short story which sets out two competing biographical narratives, and in so doing exemplifies the advantages of the new biography over the old nine years before Lytton Strachey was to do so in *Eminent Victorians* (1918).

'Memoirs of a Novelist' (1909) presents itself as a review of an obscure volume of life-and-letters ('the book which one may still buy with luck in the Charing Cross Road');[33] its subject is an even more obscure mid-Victorian sentimental novelist, Miss Willatt, whose works are now only to be found on the dusty top shelves of seaside libraries (in fact, both the volume of memoirs and the novelist are imaginary). Miss Willatt, it seems, was a person of powerful and determined character who in life easily dominated her friend and future biographer, Miss Linsett. Timid and conventional, Miss Linsett was nevertheless pleased to discover that the power dynamic of their relationship had altered with Miss Willatt's death, transferring control over her friend's 'life' to her. She finds 'how pleasant mere writing is, how important and unreal people become in print so that it is a credit to have known them; how one's own figure can have justice done to it'.[34] Yet far from revealing the facts, Miss Linsett flinched from them, reducing the impact of her friend's life by filtering it through the medium of her own lesser personality. Above all, she had nothing to say when she reached Miss Willatt's sole experience of passion: 'The most interesting event in Miss Willatt's life, owing to the nervous prudery and the dreary literary conventions of her friend, is thus a blank.'[35] Only towards the end does the framework loosen, and the reviewer briefly becomes the narrator in order to expose the pretentiousness of Miss Linsett's response to her friend's death: 'But afterwards, when she went home and had her breakfast, she felt lonely, for they had been in the habit of going to Kew Gardens together on Sundays.'[36]

This moment of spontaneous feeling emphasizes Miss Linsett's literary self-indulgence by contrast; it also marks the end of the alternative biography of Miss Willatt that the reviewer has been imagining, reconstructing her from her letters and photograph: 'The sight of that large selfish face, with the capable forehead and the surly but intelligent eyes, discredits all the platitudes on the opposite page; she looks quite capable of having deceived Miss Linsett.'[37] The revised version exposes the inadequacy of the original biography, substituting instead an analysis of the nature of the relationship between the biographer and the novelist. In this new reading, Miss Willatt's silly novels and Miss Linsett's pious biography deserve attention for what can be learnt from or read into them. Out of their thinness, the reviewer has built a new and altogether more compelling narrative, demonstrating how the new biography can be made by dismantling the old. This story brings together criticism, biography, and fiction with a sophistication that the simple oppositions of the essay on Sterne had not allowed for. While it seems to illustrate a process in which dead books can be rendered down into the facts required for a new story, the books themselves were imaginary in the first place, and the story's focus on the process of narrative construction tends to qualify our response to that final moment of truth.

'Memoirs of a Novelist' was submitted to Reginald Smith, editor of the *Cornhill*, for whom she had been reviewing memoirs. It was intended as the first of a series. Understandably, if unforgivably, he found it 'cleverness itself, but . . .'.[38] It was put away for good, but its lessons were not forgotten: the imaginary biography of an imaginary writer surfaced again in her second novel, *Night and Day*, and its exploration of the boundaries between fiction and biography opened the way for further experiments with existing forms. Rescuing or reconstructing Miss Willatt from her inept biography was a form of detective game that Woolf connected with the process of reading and imagining character: 'Our reading is always urged on by that instinct, [to] complete what we read . . .

to complete, to supply background, relationship, motive . . . this is nothing but a random game, like that we play in railway carriages with people who leave us at Putney . . . [? it is creating living people] . . . a game too perpetually interrupted by life . . .'[39] The unknown, silent woman, seated in the corner of a railway carriage (as she so often is), flitting about London as in 'The Mysterious Case of Miss V.', glimpsed through the window of the house opposite,[40] or left dusty and unread upon a library shelf, fascinated Woolf; the invention or realization of such fugitive figures was a way of using a 'fact', a person or a book, as a starting-point for the flight of imagination.

One such figure whom Woolf rescued from oblivion, or at least from the indifference of the *DNB*, was 'Miss Ormerod' (1919),[41] a Victorian entomologist who had pioneered the use of the chemical 'Paris Green' as an insecticide in Britain; her father, a historian of Cheshire, had an entry of his own, but despite her significant contribution to agriculture, there was no account of her. Woolf's biographical sketch takes the form of a series of scenes from her life: she is first shown in a high chair, absorbed in the contents of a tumbler full of pond life, and correcting her father's assumptions from her own already sharp observation; receiving the gift of a rare locust; and finally (and significantly) sitting up in bed to discuss with her doctor what she would be remembered for. Woolf seems to have known of the collection of her letters and writings, and yet she resuscitated the forgotten entomologist by reinventing her, supplying the scenes she described from her imagination.

The result was a hybrid, neither fiction nor biography, and as such Woolf had difficulties in placing it. Originally conceived as the first of a series of lives of eccentrics planned for the *Athenaeum*,[42] it did not appear there, nor in her collection of short stories *Monday or Tuesday* (1921), being, perhaps, too fictional for the former, too factual for the latter. It was eventually published in the American edition of *The Common Reader* (1925), where it joined two other 'Lives of the Obscure' (thus maintaining its anomalous status by remaining outside the British canon). It was not the only biographical sketch to combine history and fiction: at such moments Woolf's reading became re-creation, and the boundaries between biography, reverie and fiction (and, perhaps, between the processes of reading and writing) threatened to disappear altogether. But the generic indeterminacy of 'Miss Ormerod' was particularly appropriate for a woman who had firmly defined herself as an outsider.

In the case of Eleanor Ormerod, her existence within her letters or in her father's *DNB* entry had provided the fact that occasioned the fantasy, but its freewheeling nature remained suspect. In two short stories, Woolf explored biographical fantasies occasioned by facts and subsequently dissipated by them ('a game . . . perpetually interrupted by life'). In 'Sympathy' (1919),[43] the starting-point is that most literal of facts, a newspaper record. Reading the announcement of the death of a friend, the narrator drifts into a reverie in which she pictures the young man's death-bed and a country walk with his widow; the brevity of his life is mourned in elegiac terms that point forward to those other lost lives, of Jacob Flanders, Septimus Smith, and Percival in *The Waves* ('his silence is profound. He has laid his life down like a cloak for us to tread over').[44] The final paragraph suddenly reveals all this to have been based on a simple misapprehension: it is the friend's father who has died; thus further fact dismisses fiction. While the power of the imagination and its enactments are celebrated in the study, they also generate a distrust that makes it necessary to call back the narrative and resubmit it to the claims of 'truth'.

While 'Sympathy' imagines a death, and some of its consequences for the living, 'An Unwritten Novel' (1920) creates an imagined life for Woolf's first archetypal anonymous middle-aged woman in a railway carriage, a woman invisible to historians and novelists alike, and thus the precursor of Mrs Brown in Woolf's essay 'Mr Bennett and Mrs Brown'.[45] The woman's nervous movements and anxious expression stimulate the narrator to imagine a life of poverty and loneliness in graphic detail, as an object of pity and contempt to her brother's family. But, as in 'Sympathy', the life imagined for her is abruptly interrupted, and effectively cancelled by the appearance of her son, come to meet her at the station. The narrator's initial distress at the collapse of her story is succeeded by pursuit of the new narrative, as mother and son walk away together, and the intervention of fact is recognized as the occasion of pleasurable shock, and the renewal of creativity: 'Wherever I go, mysterious figures, I see you, turning the corner, mothers and sons; you, you, you. I hasten, I follow . . . adorable world!'[46]

'An Unwritten Novel' recalls 'Memoirs of a Novelist' in its use of a 'fact', a moment of reality as a touchstone to dissipate fantasy or self-deception. And, as in the earlier piece, the story's deployment of the processes of fiction-making makes it more difficult to accept that moment as reality. The unwriting of the title is never really effected, since the most memorable part of the story is the imagined narrative of a life, and its status as speculation had in any case been established at the outset. The life-writing that is disposed of by an inconvenient fact is closer to biography than to the novel, where the writer should enjoy comparative freedom. And as in biography, facts may invalidate one line of thought, but they are likely — as they do at the end of 'An Unwritten Novel' — to engender another.

Woolf's earliest writings can be read as a series of attempts to reconceive biography, by focusing on the kinds of material and technique that it had traditionally avoided — mundane reality or imaginative flight — while at the same time hankering after its characteristic virtue, its claim to truth. Yet this process had brought her steadily closer to fiction, whose greater freedom involved a consequent loss of conviction. Her second novel, *Night and Day* (1919), transforms the material of biography — the lives of her father, her aunts, Vanessa, Clive Bell, and Leonard Woolf — into fiction. It also examines the problems of fiction-writing in terms of the difficulty of writing a particular (imaginary) biography. Inevitably, this is the novel most directly concerned with the weight of the past, with literary ancestor-worship and its impositions. In it, Woolf set out to exorcize her own literary inheritance — it may be a measure of her success in doing so that its critics have consistently dismissed it as an 'exercise in classicism'.[47]

Her determination to master the traditional novel form and at the same time to break away from it is directly reflected in her heroine Katharine's commitment to help her mother finish her grandfather's biography:

The glorious past, in which men and women grew to unexampled size, intruded too much upon the present, and dwarfed it too consistently, to be altogether encouraging to one forced to make her experiment in living when the great age was dead . . . sometimes she felt that it was necessary for her very existence that she should free herself from the past . . .[48]

Both Katharine's parents are biographers: Mr Hilbery, working away in his study on the lives of the Romantic poets, recalls Leslie Stephen, while Anne Thackeray Ritchie was the main model for Mrs Hilbery. Life at Cheyne Row is full of echoes of life at 22 Hyde Park Gate, and shares the same physical focus: 'The tea table, the very hearth and centre of family life'.[49] The Sunday tea party, its literary status guaranteed by the presence of Henry James (Mr Fortescue), provides the opening scene of the novel.

The novel's heroine combines characteristics both of Woolf herself and also of Vanessa: like Vanessa, Katharine has acquired 'the reputation, which nothing in her manner contradicted, of being the most practical of people'. Like Vanessa, she has rejected the family preoccupation with the 'manufacture of phrases', and turned instead to pure form, in her case, of mathematics rather than painting. Katharine acquired her name from another fictional treatment of biographical material, Leonard Woolf's second novel *The Wise Virgins* (1914), which re-enacts his courtship of Virginia, giving it a disastrous outcome. The Stephen sisters are here figured as Katharine (Vanessa) and Camilla (Virginia), the latter the brilliant but cool and unattainable object of the hero's unrequited love.[50] In Woolf's righting and rewriting of Leonard's narrative, her heroine comes to recognize the attraction of the outsider (a version of Leonard) and surrenders to the world of the imagination by falling in love.

Mrs Hilbery is writing a life of her father, the great (albeit imaginary) Victorian poet Richard Alardyce. She has all the facts (i.e. documents) and a fertile imagination, but she is unable 'to face the radical question of what to leave in and what to leave out':[51]

no one with the ghost of a literary temperament could doubt but that they had the materials for one of the greatest biographies that has ever been written. Shelves and boxes bulged with the precious stuff. The most private lives of the most interesting people lay furled in yellow bundles of close-written manuscript. In addition to this Mrs Hilbery had in her own head as bright a vision of that time as now remained to the living . . . she had no difficulty in writing . . . but nevertheless . . . the book still remained unwritten . . . there were twenty pages upon her grandfather's taste in hats, an essay upon contemporary china, a long account of a summer day's expedition into the country, when they had missed their train, together with fragmentary visions of all sorts of famous men and women, which seemed to be partly imaginary and partly authentic.[52]

The steady proliferation of material for the life and Mrs Hilbery's sense of its limitless possibilities carry implications not merely for traditional biography, but also for the over-formal structure of the novel as a whole. By contrast, this primal scene of creation, with its uncounted tales, memories, and discourses is at once fertile and hard to control: in its freedom, it has affinities with the short stories Woolf was writing concurrently, stories such as 'The Mark on the Wall' (1917)[53] that develop extravagantly from a single object, and resist the tyranny of logical or chronological structure, as the unwritten biography seems to do. The study is cluttered with potentially relevant material, replete with suggestion, yet Mrs Hilbery cannot contemplate the diminution and exclusion that a single narrative would inevitably impose.

Mrs Hilbery is at once the model Victorian daughter, piously assembling her father's relics, as so many literary daughters had done (Anne Thackeray Ritchie among them),[54] and the woman writer, questioning her culture's orders of value and its inherited narratives. She is absent-minded but inspired: everything is potentially exciting to her and she is a powerful and generative figure at the heart of the novel, associated with the freedom of the imagination, while Katharine, in her self-imposed role as the practical one (for, paradoxically, she too is a secret dreamer), tries vainly to discipline her mother, organizing her to work by the clock and trying to sort her endless new beginnings into an ordered sequence. Later, a more subversive side of Mrs Hilbery emerges as she abandons the biography and sets out for Stratford to prove that Anne Hathaway wrote Shakespeare's sonnets, thus challenging 'the safety of the heart of civilization itself'[55] and searching for a new, and more compelling version of the 'truth' about Shakespeare. It is as if, having failed to write the new (i.e. totally frank) biography of her father, she turns to the fantasy version, the biography of what might or should have been, the biography that, like *Orlando*, will free itself altogether from conventional constraints.

Mrs Hilbery's impatience with traditional methodologies (such as had determined Miss Linsett's approach), and her eagerness to supplant Shakespeare with a convincing woman rival anticipate the woman writer of *A Room of One's Own*, yet in one vital respect she is utterly different, for she is essentially a writer of traditional romance, a historian of love and marriage. She would prefer to represent her father's life as an ongoing romance (the love-affairs of Victorian poets were favourite subjects for sentimental biography, as *Flush* reminds us), but doing so inevitably leads back to the extremely inconvenient 'fact' of his failed marriage. Not only is she unable 'to face the radical question of what to leave in and what to leave out. She could not decide how far the public was to be told the truth about the poet's separation from his wife.'[56]

The question of 'what it is that you can write', what can and cannot be said in biography, had been crucial, interrupting the life of Vanessa and silencing Miss Linsett at a moment of imminent revelation in 'Memoirs of a Novelist'. It continued to be a more general problem for Woolf as a woman writer, and it made for particular difficulties when she wrote her biography of Roger Fry, since Fry's own sexual honesty seemed liable to offend the sensibilities of the average reader. *Night and Day* initially introduces the problem of sexual scandal in terms of the Alardyce biography: the poet's marriage had turned sour after three months of passion. He and his wife had lived apart, and she had taken other lovers. This mishap has repercussions throughout the rest of the novel, since it calls in question the assumption that romantic love finds its natural outcome in happy marriage, an assumption fundamental to the type of novel Woolf was writing. Katharine's cousin Cyril is introduced to amplify the point: quoting Ibsen and Samuel Butler,[57] he deplores marriage as an institution and refuses on principle to marry the woman who lives with him and bears his children. When those guardians of public morals, the aunts, discover this, they descend on the Hilberys, insisting that the family honour is at stake and the family head must intervene (their behaviour recalling the reaction to Vanessa's relationship with Jack Hills).

Katharine herself is eager to marry, if only to escape from the problems of the biography, and to find the freedom and independence she longs for; but when her aunt warns her against marrying if she wants to have her own way, its attractions begin to fade.[58] The apparently passionless marriages of the older generation seem to justify Katharine's own distrust of passion, as well as her recognition that, when it comes, marriage is not the only scenario available: '"Why, after all, isn't it perfectly possible to live together without being married?"'[59] When Mrs Hilbery fails to rewrite the plot of her father's (or Shakespeare's) biography without concealing or altering the known facts, she turns instead to rewriting the plot of 'life' (that is, of course, of the rest of the novel). She urges her daughter towards marriage as 'the happiest life for a woman' (later she corrects this to 'the most interesting').[60] But Katharine and the novel's more thoughtful characters do not share Mrs Hilbery's blind confidence that marriage offers women the greatest happiness; this was to be the conviction of Mrs Ramsay in *To the Lighthouse*, but by that stage Woolf's creative women, artists or writers such as Lily Briscoe or Miss La Trobe, had decisively rejected it.

In this way Woolf uses the device of Alardyce's unwritten biography to cast doubt on the assumptions of social comedy that had determined the shape of her novel. The problems it raises, of the limitation of genre and the constraints on what can be said, suggest a critique of the novel she was writing and an impulse to escape, with Katharine, from an obligation to fulfil the social expectations of her day. *Night and Day* is the only novel that uses marriage as a conventional closure, but the biography of Alardyce enables Woolf to set up a dialogue between the fiction she is writing and the wider truths ('facts'?) about marriage that Mrs Hilbery and the novel's structure cannot allow for. Mrs Hilbery's hesitation as to 'how far the public was to be told the truth about the poet's separation from his wife' exposes the nature of the reader's expectations in old-fashioned biography, and this in turn leads to a questioning of marriage as a 'happy ending', the literary convention characteristic of the type of novel that Woolf is writing, and, beyond that, of our social myths of marriage in the actual world. Thus this biographical quandary opens up a line of questioning which serves to introduce an element of much-needed scepticism into a novel centrally concerned with the nature and power of fantasy and romance.

The novel makes no attempt to close the unwritten biography, which has been used to articulate structural and social problems that haunt the novel as a whole. It remains, like the grit in the oyster, the starting-point for the critique of 'Modern Novels' that followed,[61] silently acknowledging that the traditional ordering of the novel, its social and literary rules, can no longer accommodate the experiences and desires of Katharine's generation. In terms of Woolf's own development, she had reached the point where she would abandon conventional form altogether. Though biography gradually ceased to provide a model for thinking about the nature of imaginative writing, the issues it raised remained potent for her: *Jacob's Room* contrasted the *DNB* view of the lives of great men with a more mundane reality, and saw heroic ideals as simultaneously fulfilled and destroyed by the War; *Mrs Dalloway* and *To the Lighthouse* are both forms of imaginative life-writing, that drew on biographical material; *The Waves* and *The Years* epitomize the lives of individuals outside and inside history; *Orlando* and *Flush* revise the traditional concept of biography; and late in the 1930s, Woolf wrote a life of Roger Fry and began her own autobiography. In her essays on the subject, she continued to draw a contrast between the granite of truth and the rainbow of personality, associating truth with scientific fact (in 1927, she compared it to radium).[62] Even in 1940 she was still opposing the facts of biography to the freedom of fiction, while making the crucial admission that the status of facts could change.[63] But the fertility of the marriage she had effected between them had long since precluded so stark an opposition.

Notes

1. VS to CB, *The Letters of Virginia Woolf*, ed. Nigel Nicolson and Joanne Trautmann, 6 vols. (London, 1975–80), i. 325 (15 Apr. 1908).
2. Virginia Woolf, *Night and Day* (1919; repr. Harmondsworth, 1992), 27.

3. *The Diary of Virginia Woolf*, ed. Anne Olivier Bell and Andrew McNeillie, 5 vols. (London, 1977–84), ii. 277 (3 Dec. 1923); letter from V W to Ethel Smyth, *Letters*, iv. 145 (27 Feb. 1930).
4. 'A Sketch of the Past', *Moments of Being*, ed. Jeanne Schulkind (1976; 2nd edn., London, 1985), 120.
5. *Night and Day*, 26.
6. 'The Art of Biography', *Collected Essays*, ed. Leonard Woolf, 4 vols. (London, 1966–7), iv. 222.
7. 'The Art of Biography', 221–8 ('the accent on sex', 226); 'The New Biography', 229–35, both in *Collected Essays*, vol. iv.
8. Repr. in *The Essays of Virginia Woolf*, i, *1904–12*, ed. Andrew McNeillie (London, 1986), 127–9.
9. 'A Sketch of the Past', *Moments of Being*, 158.
10. Ibid. 158–9.
11. 'The Art of Biography', *Collected Essays*, iv. 226.
12. The friend was Jack (John Waller) Hills, according to a letter to Violet Dickinson, *Letters*, i. 151 (Nov. 1904).
13. 'Sterne' (1909), *Essays of VW*, i. 281.
14. Virginia Woolf, *The Voyage Out* (1915; repr. Harmondsworth, 1992), 200.
15. *Diary*, i. 23 (18 Jan. 1915); 'The Eccentrics', *Essays of VW*, iii, *1919–24* (London, 1988), 38–41.
16. See 'Lady Hester Stanhope' and 'The Duke and Duchess of Newcastle-Upon-Tyne', *Essays of VW*, i. 325–9, 345–9, and 'The Duchess of Newcastle', *The Common Reader: first series* (1925; ed. Andrew McNeillie (London, 1984), 69–77). For Julia Margaret Cameron, see below, n. 21.
17. 'The Journal of Mistress Joan Martyn', *The Complete Shorter Fiction of Virginia Woolf*, ed. Susan Dick (1985; new edn., London, 1989), 33–62; '"Anon" and "The Reader": Virginia Woolf's Last Essays', ed. Brenda R. Silver, *Twentieth Century Literature*, 25 (1979), 356–441.
18. See, e.g., VS to Violet Dickinson, *Letters*, i. 146 (24 Oct. 1924), which describes her aunt Caroline Stephen showing her family letters and diaries.
19. *Sir Leslie Stephen's Mausoleum Book*, intro. Alan Bell (Oxford, 1977); for Jem Stephen's memoirs, see Noel Annan, *Leslie Stephen: The Godless Victorian* (London, 1984), 7.
20. VS to Violet Dickinson, *Letters*, i. 163 (6 Dec. 1904).
21. The essay (a brief life) in *Victorian Photographs of Famous Men and Fair Women* by Julia Margaret Cameron (London, 1926), and recently repr. in S. P. Rosenbaum (ed.), *A Bloomsbury Group Reader* (Oxford, 1993), 81–8; *Freshwater*, ed. Lucio P. Ruotolo (London, 1976); (cf. Queenie Colquhoun in *Night and Day*, 95).
22. According to Quentin Bell in his biography *Virginia Woolf*, 2 vols. (London, 1972), i. 122, the life of Vanessa was begun when she was staying at Playden, near Rye (Aug.–Sept. 1907). It is reprinted under the title 'Reminiscences' in *Moments of Being*, 34–68, though referred to in her

letters as the 'life of Vanessa'. The life of Violet Dickinson was completed shortly before Virginia went to Playden, and so was actually written before that of Vanessa, but they were closely contemporary. I have discussed them in the reverse order of composition in order to follow Woolf's developing interests outside the family.

23. *Moments of Being*, 35.
24. Ibid. 43.
25. Ibid. 40, 46.
26. V S to C B, *Letters*, i. 325 (15 Apr. 1908).
27. 'Friendship's Gallery', ed. Ellen Hawkes, *Twentieth Century Literature*, 25 (1979), 270–302. The note to Violet Dickinson accompanying the life is undated, though written early in Aug. 1907 (*Letters*, i. 303).
28. Bell, *Virginia Woolf*, i. 82.
29. 'Friendship's Gallery', 279.
30. Ibid. 282.
31. 'Sterne', in *Essays of VW*, i. 281.
32. Ibid. 281.
33. 'Memoirs of a Novelist', *Complete Shorter Fiction*, 70.
34. Ibid. 69.
35. Ibid. 73.
36. Ibid. 79.
37. Ibid. 74.
38. Bell, *Virginia Woolf*, i. 153–4.
39. 'Byron & Mr Briggs', App. 2, *Essays of VW*, iii. 482, 483, 485. This incomplete and heavily corrected essay was intended to introduce a book on 'Reading'.
40. For example, Mrs Brown, in 'Mr Bennett and Mrs Brown', repr. as 'Character in Fiction', *Essays of VW*, iii. 420–36; Mrs Norman in *Jacob's Room* (1922; repr. Harmondsworth, 1992), 23–4; 'The Mysterious Case of Miss V.' (1906), *Complete Shorter Fiction*, 30–2; *Mrs Dalloway* (1925; repr. Harmondsworth, 1992), 203–4.
41. *The Common Reader: first series*, 122–33.
42. 'I open this book today merely to note that Miss *Eleanor Ormerod*, destroyer of insects, promises well for Murry: should he take kindly to my first (Eccentrics: I myself rather liked it)', *Diary*, 260 (30 Mar. 1919) (John Middleton Murry was currently editor of the *Athenaeum*). 'Miss Ormerod' first appeared in the American periodical, *The Dial* for Dec. 1924. Its subsequent appearance only in the American edn. of *The Common Reader* may be an assertion of (or otherwise connected with) the American copyright.
43. 'Sympathy', *Complete Shorter Fiction*, 108–11.
44. Ibid. 110.
45. 'An Unwritten Novel', *Complete Shorter Fiction*, 112–21 (for 'Mr Bennett and Mrs Brown', see above, n. 40).
46. Ibid. 121.

47. E. M. Forster, 'The Early Novels of Virginia Woolf', *Abinger Harvest* (1936; repr. Harmondsworth, 1974), 122.

48. *Night and Day*, 29, 32.

49. 'A Sketch of the Past', *Moments of Being*, 130 (Woolf compares the tea table with the bedroom: 'the double bedded bedroom on the first floor was the sexual centre; the birth centre, the death centre of the house').

50. After reading *The Wise Virgins* (see *Diary*, i. 32), Woolf adopted Leonard Woolf's unusually spelt 'Katharine' as the name of her heroine (she had previously been called 'Effie'). She later used the name 'Camilla' with reference to herself, in *To the Lighthouse*, for Mrs Ramsay's youngest daughter, whose role in the family corresponded to her own.

51. *Night and Day*, 30.

52. Ibid. 29, 32.

53. 'The Mark on the Wall', *Complete Shorter Fiction*, 83–9.

54. Like Mrs Hilbery, Anne Thackeray Ritchie had written biographical accounts of her father, in her case in the form of introductory memoirs to individual novels. She would have had comparable difficulties in writing about her father's marriage, since her mother had been classified as insane while she was still a child.

55. *Night and Day*, 364.

56. Ibid. 30.

57. Ibid. 85, 87.

58. Ibid. 177–8.

59. Ibid. 411.

60. Ibid. 179.

61. See my Introduction to *Night and Day* (Harmondsworth, 1992), p. xxxii. 'Modern Novels', *Essays of VW*, iii. 30–6, later became 'Modern Fiction', in *The Common Reader*, 146–54.

62. 'The New Biography', *Collected Essays*, iv. 229, 235.

63. 'The Art of Biography', ibid. 221, 225–6.

❧ 17 ❧

Learning about Ourselves: Biography as Autobiography

HUMPHREY CARPENTER
in conversation with Lyndall Gordon

LG. Well, Humphrey, can you remind me what was the title of your talk at the Newcastle conference?

HC. 'What discretion forbids: the unprintable parts of a biography.' And then I decided that the talk was unprintable too!

LG. So — does that involve some sense that there is a biographer's duty to a subject's family? Do you feel actually that the biographer has really more duty to the audience, who will expect you to tell the truth about the life?

HC. I think in the end your duty as a biographer is to yourself, because you've clearly got some motive for writing the book. The obvious one is financial, if you're doing it as a means of making a living, as I am. But there should be a deeper motive. And I've thought a lot about this recently, for all sorts of reasons, and it seems to me that biographies are likely to be either acts of worship or acts of destruction. And the best ones have elements of both.

LG. Yes. I suppose Victorian biography was notable as acts of worship, and on the whole in our century we've reacted against that. We want very much to know the whole truth. But what I wanted to ask you is, are there limits to the truth?

HC. You can only tell certain kinds of truth in a biography, can't you? You can only, if you're being purely factual, in the end put together an A-followed-B picture. And you're always going to leave out another dimension of complete truth. I think I've felt that with all the biographies I've written. But at the same time you've got this drive to try not to be put off by reticence, by people's assumptions. I always feel in each life I tackle that there is some hidden story or fact, some clue, which when you get hold of it begins to unravel the whole thing. You still won't get the *complete* truth about that person, but you'll get a kind of truth, which works within its own terms.

LG. Of course, if you think of your own life, there's no way you could tell the whole truth, even if you wished to.

HC. Exactly. At the moment I'm finding this, because I'm working with a living subject, Robert Runcie, the former Archbishop of Canterbury. And that's a strange experience for both of us, because he's never sat down to consider his life as an objective entity. And I'm clearly prompting him to do that. The danger is that he starts producing ideas which I think are wonderful — until I remember that they were implied in my questions to him. This has taught me a lot about biography: the extent to which we work within concepts, within matrixes of ideas. You can't really follow the story of a life, when you come to deal with an archive, with letters and diaries, with orally collected memories, unless you have some sort of preconception of what you're looking for. Otherwise you won't *know* what to look for. The people who come to grief writing biography — who get seriously stuck — are those who start researching without any idea of what they're looking for.

On the other hand, what you're looking for is going to say more about you than about the subject. You're always bringing your own agenda to it. My particular agenda (as I said in the original lecture) is that of a rather naughty small boy who was discouraged by his mother from a natural tendency to open other people's drawers and read their letters. But I could sense that she was really egging me on. She was a very anecdotal mother, who always discussed everything in a kind of *ad hominem* way, so that I gradually discovered my own cultural background and place in the world via a series of short narratives about other people. And this, I think, is probably why, when (as a grown-up spoilt only child) I decided to please her by writing books — it was all motivated by that, I'm sure — I actually wrote the kind of books that related most to the way she'd talked to me.

LG. Did she have a great interest in lives?

HC. She had a great interest in people. I felt at the outset of my
writing that she was my ideal audience, in general social terms
— a typical upper-middle-class Englishwoman, quite well educated, not reading anything terribly demanding, knew her Jane
Austen and so on, but not somebody who went beyond the
Oxford English syllabus of her generation (she read English at
Somerville in the late 1930s). But I realize now that I was
writing *specifically* for her, as somebody who had this magpie
curiosity about individuals. To give you an example, the very
first biography I wrote wasn't a book; it was a play about Father
Ignatius of Llanthony, a very camp Victorian who believed
himself to be the first practitioner of the monastic life in England
since the dissolution of the monasteries. And he worked his own
miracles (or believed that he had), and even hired his own
biographer to write them down — a colourful lady calling
herself the Baroness de Bertouch. Ignatius (whose real name was
Joe Lyne) has been a great source of camp amusement to people
who like that sort of thing. But I was fascinated by him not
because of the campery, but because of the sheer eccentricity of
the whole story. My mother, who I suppose had read Arthur
Calder-Marshall's superb biography of him, kept telling me the
story about the time he went abroad, accompanied by a nun of
his own invented religious order, and a child called the Infant
Oblate. And in Milan station the Father was taken poorly, so the
nun went to the engine driver carrying a hot-water bottle, and
asked for 'l'eau chaud'. Well, if my mother told that story once,
she told it twenty times.

She was a Trevelyan before her marriage, and almost a late
Victorian in outlook. She came from a large Victorian vicarage
family (Victorian in character if not quite in date), and I think
that's rather the way they all thought — anecdotally, I mean;
certainly my aunt Mary Trevelyan, who had a long romantic
friendship with T. S. Eliot, was just the same. So in a sense I've
inherited that part of the Victorian mind.

LG. One's very struck — I'm saying this to you as an outsider, a
foreigner — by the taste for eccentricity in the English, a delight

in eccentric stories. Would you have been drawn, in choosing subjects for biography, to people who had slightly curious stories attached to their lives?

HC. Absolutely. This very English taste for eccentricity carries the implication that if somebody's eccentric then he or she is all right. I think I set out with that assumption at the beginning of my career as a biographer. The first biography I did in book form was the life of Tolkien, and I thought, here is this rather comic Oxford academic — the stereotype absent-minded professor — who would be lecturing on Beowulf with a parcel of fish from the fishmongers sticking out of his pocket. And the first draft of the book was written very much in that mode, treating him as slightly slapstick. At least it began that way. But as the book went on, I realized he wasn't like this at all. He had had a very strange childhood. His mother had died early (his father was already dead) and he was brought up by a Roman Catholic priest — an unlikely parent-figure. Consequently he acquired certain uptight Pauline moral values. And my caricature of the Oxford academic clashed with his, and I never resolved it properly.

The first draft of that life was a long sprawling thing, and was deemed unacceptable by the Tolkien family, or by the member of it who controlled permission to quote previously unpublished material. I went away and rewrote it, and it was then deemed acceptable. What I'd actually done was castrated the book, cut out everything which was likely to be contentious. I've therefore always been displeased with it ever since.

LG. Yet it was a great best seller.

HC. Given Tolkien's enormous popularity, almost anything would have been. I wasn't so silly as to ruin it completely, but Margaret Drabble's review called it 'polite', which I think was a very good word for it. I learnt my lesson then. I ought to have learnt it before, because even my play about Father Ignatius had run into difficulty with the family living in his monastery in South Wales, who felt I was being disrespectful towards him. But after the Tolkien book I learnt that one doesn't jump straight into the water without testing the temperature first. You've got to take into account the vested interests and assumptions of the people who control the copyrights, who are always in a potentially adversarial position towards the biographer.

LG. And yet they've chosen you, or at least accepted you. But you feel they're still very wary of what you will write?

HC. It never ceases to surprise me the way that people go on selecting biographers for tasks without looking at their track record, and saying 'Well, look what he did to so-and-so — we're not likely to get a book which is terribly polite; he's bound to ask awkward questions'. It's a bit like inviting a private detective to investigate your family secrets and then being upset when he unearths something unsavoury. (I've always wanted to write a series of whodunits in which the detective is a biographer. The two roles are very, very similar.)

LG. I've never had to approach a family about writing a biography, so what I'm curious to know is, when you plan such an approach, does candour, discretion, or charm work best?

HC. What a wonderful question. Definitely charm. I haven't got much of it, but I pull every bit out of the locker. With the Tolkien family, I went to them one by one and said, 'Look, I don't know much about writing biography, but I did know your father a little, and I know Oxford, I know the milieu in which he operated, and I think if you don't get somebody who has those advantages, you'll probably find a worse biographer coming along.' Sure enough, not long after I'd started, somebody got to work on a crazy book about Tolkien, which when it was published consisted of bits of mine patchworked into a lot of silly nonsense.

LG. But you have to be a bit thick-skinned if you're going to go through with a biography written under the eye of the family?

HC. Your skin has to be incredibly thick. And the vital question is always, who is actually in charge of the literary estate? Who controls the permissions? Now, you'd have thought that W. H. Auden would be a hornet's nest for a biographer. He said he didn't want a biography written, and his private life was full of incident, to put it mildly! Yet there was an extraordinary openness about Auden, a transparent honesty about the way he went about that private life, which left my book on him curiously free of any hothouse nervy atmosphere. Also, he appointed a very sensible, dispassionate man, Edward Mendelson, who was teaching at Columbia University and was an Auden scholar without being a close friend, to control his literary estate after his death. Mind you, Ed and I had a very aggressive relationship for the first six months. Ed is a New Yorker, and we fought! He used to write me furious letters, and I'd write stubborn ones back. Then we met, and immediately became great friends, and he let me write my book without any interference whatever — except that some of the best ideas in it are actually his! I had no sense with Ed that I was dealing with a keeper of the shrine.

LG. Was there such a keeper in the case of Ezra Pound?

HC. The Pound estate is immensely complicated. I can't give you a candid history of it here — it might result in legal action! But the actual permissions were then being handled by James Laughlin, the poet who was Pound's publisher from the 1920s. When they first met, Laughlin was a rich WASP student at a time when anti-Semitism was very much in the air in such circles. And the only things Laughlin asked me to cut out of the book were references to his own racial views in those days. So the book was pretty easy from the censorship point of view. Indeed, the Tolkien style of difficulty didn't occur again until I tackled Benjamin Britten, and had to steer the book past somebody who was passionately concerned to protect Britten's reputation.

LG. I wanted to ask you about that. The sad fact about many great creative people is that corners of their lives are very questionable. And I wanted to ask how you coped with Britten's predilection for young boys?

HC. It wasn't really just a murky corner of Britten. It was, to my mind, the principal source of creative tension, the breeding-ground of his best musical ideas. Actually, I haven't come across a single instance — neither writing nor reading biography — where the murky areas of an artist's life *aren't* part of the creativity. Charles Williams, about whom I wrote in *The Inklings*, is very good on this. In his Arthurian poetry there's a place called Broceliande, which is Williams's name for what Kenneth

Grahame called 'The Wild Wood': a kind of dark night not of the soul but of the psyche, in which awful passions and sexualities rage away, but *making* goes on. Remember that in *The Wind in the Willows*, Badger's home, the still point of Grahame's turning world, is at the heart of the Wild Wood. I don't think you'll find a single creative artist whose personal danger areas aren't right at the centre of the creative personality.

LG. I remember Christopher Ricks saying of Eliot's anti-Semitism that it provides some of the most brilliant lines in his poetry.

HC. Exactly. And Pound also. I mean, one can simply dismiss the whole of Pound (or certainly a great deal of later Pound) on account of the anti-Semitism. And I wouldn't say it produced poetry on the level of Eliot's. But it is one of the driving forces of the *Cantos*, and a biographer — unless he or she is writing with some very clear political or other external agenda — will have to tackle it uncensoriously, accepting it as an important part of the poet.

LG. It would be no good if a biography had an agenda, would it?

HC. But I think all biographies have them. Is there such a thing as a completely dispassionate biography?

LG. Maybe they have hidden agendas.

HC. To my mind, the principal agenda is always the personality of the biographer. For example, Richard Holmes is always finding books to write which are really about him, about his own analytical sensitivity, while I'm always looking for idols to demolish, because I'm that sort of person. And it always strikes me as significant that Michael Holroyd's photograph on the back of his Shaw books has more prominence than that of Shaw on the front! No, we're all really writing about ourselves. That's the hidden agenda. And if we ourselves are a mass of contradictions, we'll produce rather contradictory biographies. I've spent the last two decades trying to discover who I am through the people I've been writing about. I suppose you could call it living your own life at second-hand. It sometimes feels that way. Maybe it's time I had some first-hand experience of the world!

LG. It's curious, isn't it? We go to enormous lengths to prove to the reader that everything is properly researched, that we're scrupulously accurate and objective. And yet it's all really about a meeting between the biographer and the subject.

HC. Of course it is — the personal interaction of two people, one living and the other (usually) dead. And you know as well as I do that, while we pretend to complete objectivity and accuracy, in reality there's the most enormous amount of selection, and therefore, by definition, distortion. I mean, having finished writing a biography, one could go back to the source material and write several completely different lives of the same person, which would be just as long, and which used different material to tell a very different story.

LG. In some ways we're talking about gaps in lives, and what we put into those gaps certainly comes from our own 'meeting' with the subject.

HC. Now that you mention gaps, one thing I want to touch on — more discreetly than in the original lecture — is the tricky question of the people who can't be mentioned in a biography, or whose role and importance can't be identified clearly. I'm talking chiefly about sexual relationships, of course. This caused me problems with Auden and Britten. Both had relationships with teenagers in the 1930s, physical relationships, and in both cases the people in question eventually married and put this homosexual past behind them. They didn't want it revealed in the biographies. Yet these relationships were terribly important to both my subjects, and they were reflected in their work. What I did was rather unsatisfactory. Both people are named, but the nature of the relationship isn't specified. Intelligent readers should be able to spot the truth, but it requires a close reading.

LG. That's a solution.

HC. Not a very good one. Another would have been to say, quite specifically in the narrative, when I reached this point, 'I'm going to pull down the blinds here. There's something I can't tell you.' But we don't usually do that. It would break up the perfect flow — would be untrue to the belletrist principle that biographies have to be seamless narratives. Of course, lives aren't seamless, are they? So really it's a pretty silly principle.

LG. I've been tempted to do this. I actually have, indeed, in my book on Charlotte Brontë. I've said, 'There's a gap here. It could be this — it could be that.' Because I've felt there's something almost wrong in making it so seamless.

HC. But that was a gap in your own understanding, something that you couldn't be certain about, rather than something you were deliberately suppressing?

LG. Well, a lot of material had been destroyed at her death because it conflicted with the image people wanted to present. So there are gaps. But there was something you said a few minutes ago which has remained in my mind: that you picked up the idea of telling stories about real people from your mother, and that she was in a sense your audience for your books. Do you have an audience in mind when you write?

HC. O yes. When A. N. Wilson was writing his life of C. S. Lewis, he would tell me how the book was going. He produced a very convincing theory that Lewis was essentially, all his life, trying to expiate the unfortunate and embarrassing sexual relationship he'd had at an early age with a friend's mother, Mrs Moore. That seemed to me the most persuasive explanation of Lewis's strange personality which I'd come across. (I'd written about Lewis myself in *The Inklings*, and was certain I hadn't got the whole story about him; this seemed to be it.) Well, Wilson had had to put it together from very slight evidence, and when he showed me the first draft of the book, I found that he'd left this theory out. I asked him, 'Where is all that vital stuff?' And as I recall, he said he'd left it out because he didn't want to upset the loyal Lewis following who he envisaged would be the principal audience for the biography. And I realized that for me, upsetting the loyal fans is one of my main aims. I've always explained this aggression to myself by saying that around each figure there's an absurd cult of admirers, people who want the great person to remain untarnished. And it's a challenge to try and tarnish them, to prove to these rather silly people that human beings *aren't* perfect, least of all if they're great artists. But I think it goes much deeper than that. I think it's actually my resenting my mother, resenting having been given this rather limited and limiting task by her, of writing about other people's lives anecdotally. I'm responding by trying to shock her.

LG. Most biographies are quite voluminous. Do you think some details are superfluous? Do you think biographers go into too much detail sometimes?

HC. Certainly in a really good biography, nothing will seem superfluous. But of course style changes with generations. From the end of the Second World War till the mid-1960s, the fashionable style of English biography was brisk, dramatic, and wry — a typical late example is Arthur Calder-Marshall's splendid life of Father Ignatius, which I mentioned earlier, *The Enthusiast* (1962). Then it all changed, and we began to get the heavyweight lives, which at their worst descended to the level of the laundry list. But length and inclusiveness don't in themselves make for a bad book, providing there's a real narrative drive. Of course, you can convince yourself that you've written a really tight narrative, in which no detail is superfluous, and then read a review accusing you of having published a mere card index! American reviewers tend to make that accusation to me, much more than British. And I think I know why. I used to lodge in the house of an Oxford don's widow, a very, very English person, who once described her own verbal style as 'the language of understatement'. A brilliant phrase! It's that very British notion that you don't need to spell things out. You tell things by means of sketched-in stories. You let the reader *think* — you don't build any enormous construction of interpretation — you don't say, 'What I think this meant was . . .' But that, generally speaking, is not the American style of writing. Actually it can be — Hemingway rather worked in that deadpan, pointillist way. But certainly where non-fiction is concerned I think American readers are inclined to want to have things spelt out. So I get quite frequent accusations from American reviewers that my books are card-index jobs without a powerful narrative, and that there's too much detail, not enough analysis or authorial comment. Actually those things, the analysis and the comment, are going on all the time, but only by implication, by the way I've selected my material. So the American critics are not reading me in the way they're meant to.

LG. There's a great cultural difference, yes. But you don't have any particular kind of person in mind when you write?

HC. My audience is myself. We all, surely, write for ourselves. We ourselves are the only readers we really know properly, and can cater for. And it's worth emphasizing, in this context, that I've rarely written about anyone I really knew about before I started researching. The biographies, for me, have always been an exercise in self-education. Surely all good books are. The writer who knows the subject intimately before starting work is often handicapped — he or she has no idea what the reader needs to know. But if you know nothing, you're full of curiosity, and that's the perfect motive.

LG. That's what makes it so interesting — you're venturing into a new field.

HC. And I'm sure one's excitement at discovering communicates itself to the reader. You're taking the reader on the same journey.

LG. You're obviously a biographer who aims at a much broader audience than mere academics.

HC. Is there such a thing as a pure academic biography? If there is, I've never read it. I think it's a contradiction in terms. Obviously there are pure academic studies of literature, but once you go into biography you're automatically moving into an area of general understanding. Even literary theorists write clearly when they have to narrate lives!

LG. I come from academe towards biography, and my tendency is often to treat the *work* a lot. And getting that proportion right seems difficult.

HC. I don't think one can overdo the emphasis on the subject's work. I mean, why else are we bothering to write about these people? But I agree that it's never quite clear how a biographer should approach the work. There are so many different ways. I find you've got to be much more assertive when you're slipping from narrative fact into literary criticism and analysis. You're going from statement to hypothesis, and that can involve an uncomfortable gear change. On the other hand I frequently read biographies where there's a complete cop-out on the work. The

277

recent life of Malcolm Lowry is not a bad book (though it's far too long), but it contains no literary discussion of *Under the Volcano* or his other writings. That's a mistake, purely from the point of view of information. I had never read Lowry before I began reading the biography, and I wanted to discover about his writings. And I didn't. I didn't get any sense of what his work was like. At the very least, a biography must take you on a lightning tour of the work. And the best possible reaction a biographer can get from a reader is, 'Oh, it made me want to go away and read all the works.'

LG. That's it! I've always felt that's the best compliment.

HC. And I was upset when Paul Fussell wrote of my life of Auden that the man was more interesting than the poetry. (Which I don't agree with at all.) You know, in the end I would probably rather write more about the work than the life. Even with someone like Britten, though I was fascinated by the man, in the end what I wanted to do was use the life as a way of illuminating the music, of making the listener to his music aware of all that was crammed into it.

LG. In choosing a subject, do you feel that there is something that has drawn you to them on a personal level?

HC. There's got to be some sort of personal relevance. With Tolkien, the personal agenda was my own childhood. I'd lived in the same culture as him, in an Oxford academic family. I wanted to portray that milieu, about which I had very mixed feelings.

LG. What about your short book on Jesus?

HC. Well, that was about my loss of faith. That's about resenting being the son of a bishop (which my father became when I was in my teens). I became an atheist at 21, when I started to experience the world, but later, when I was happily married, I felt there ought to be an afterlife, because life was good and should go on. And just then I was writing about C. S. Lewis and Charles Williams, in *The Inklings*, and I found their theology very persuasive, so that book is about almost regaining my faith. But I hadn't become quite sure. And then by chance I was asked to write a Past Masters book on Jesus — not really a biography, but a study of the texts. So I spent six months reading New

Testament theology, and came out of it a complete unbeliever — though with certain questions in my mind which I couldn't resolve. So it was very much a personal journey. And I could never write a book if I didn't feel I had some sort of journey to make in it myself. I tackled Evelyn Waugh and his circle, in *The Brideshead Generation*, because part of me had always wanted to be the kind of writer who earns enough to live in a Georgian manor-house. By the time I'd finished, I felt like moving to a council flat — I deplored everything that Waugh and his friends stood for. The only biography which doesn't immediately suggest a personal quest is my life of Ezra Pound. And then I remember that, when I wrote it, I was suffering from severe depression, alternating with fairly manic fits (exacerbated by a vicious sleeping-pill which I believe has now been banned from the market), so that, as I wrote at the very end of the book, while rushing round America researching it I was at least as mad as Pound was ever supposed to have been! Yes, that book is really about being on the edge mentally, about taking risks with one's personality.

LG. George Eliot's theory was that, if you've got enough sympathy in you, you can make some imaginative connection with anybody.

HC. Yes. But essentially the real subject is always going to be yourself, some aspect of your own personality, some reflection of what's happening in your life at the time you're writing the book. Actually I've generally found that my books anticipate what's going to happen in my life. So in future I'm going to be rather more wary about choosing my subjects!

NOTES ON CONTRIBUTORS

LINDA ANDERSON is a Senior Lecturer in English at the University of Newcastle upon Tyne. She is the author of *Bennett, Wells and Conrad: Narrative in Transition* (1988), has edited *Plotting Change: Contemporary Women's Fiction* (1990), and has a forthcoming book *Remembered Futures: Women and Autobiography in the Twentieth Century*. She is an editor of the creative writing magazine *Writing Women*.

JOHN BATCHELOR is Joseph Cowen Professor of English Literature at the University of Newcastle upon Tyne, formerly Fellow and Senior Tutor of New College, Oxford. His books include *Mervyn Peake: A Biographical and Critical Exploration* (1974), *The Edwardian Novelists* (1982), *H. G. Wells* (1985), a study of Conrad's *Lord Jim* (1988), *Virginia Woolf: The Major Novels* (1991), and *The Life of Joseph Conrad: A Critical Biography* (1994). He is General Editor of the World's Classics edition of Conrad (Oxford University Press) and has edited *Lord Jim* and *Victory* for that series.

DAVID BRADSHAW graduated from the University of Newcastle upon Tyne in 1978 before going on to Lincoln College, Oxford. Since 1987 he has been a Fellow in English at Worcester College, Oxford. He has written on Yeats, Conrad, and Lawrence, and is at work on a biography of Huxley. His edition of *The Hidden Huxley* appeared in 1994.

JULIA BRIGGS is a Fellow in English of Hertford College, Oxford, and has published *Night Visitors* (1977) a history of the ghost story, *This Stage-Play World* (1983), on the context of Renaissance literature, and a biography of E. Nesbit, *A Woman of Passion* (1987). She has recently edited the works of Virginia Woolf for Penguin and is currently writing an intellectual biography of Woolf.

HUMPHREY CARPENTER became a full-time writer in 1975, after several years as a BBC staff producer and presenter. His many books include biographies of J. R. R. Tolkien (1977), W. H. Auden (1981), Ezra Pound (1988), and Benjamin Britten (1992). He also writes children's books, has created musical shows performed by children, has been a bandleader, and plays jazz on a variety of low-pitched instruments.

LYNDALL GORDON was born in Cape Town and is a Fellow in English of St Hilda's College, Oxford. Her first three biographies, *Eliot's Early Years* (1977), *Eliot's New Life* (1988), and *Virginia Woolf: A Writer's Life*

(1984), are all in the series Oxford Lives. Her more recent biographies are *Shared Lives* (1992) and *Charlotte Brontë: A Passionate Life* (1994).

RICHARD HOLMES is a biographer and travel writer. His works include *Chatterton: The Case Re-Opened* (1970), *Shelley: The Pursuit* (1974), *Footsteps* (1985), *Coleridge: Early Visions* (1989), and *Dr Johnson and Mr Savage* (1993). He is a Fellow of the Royal Society of Literature and was awarded the OBE in 1992.

PARK HONAN is Emeritus Professor at the School of English, University of Leeds. His books include *The Book, the Ring, and the Poet: A Biography of Robert Browning* (1974, with William Irvine), also *Matthew Arnold: A Life* (1981), *Jane Austen: Her Life* (1987), and *Authors' Lives: On Literary Biography and the Arts of Language* (1990). He has held Guggenheim, Huntington Library, and Folger Shakespeare Library fellowships, and is working on a life of Shakespeare.

HERMIONE LEE is Professor of English at the University of York. Her books include studies of Virginia Woolf (1977), Elizabeth Bowen (1981), Philip Roth (1982), and Willa Cather (1989), and editions of works by Stevie Smith, Bowen, Cather, Woolf, Kipling, and Trollope. She is working on a new biography of Virginia Woolf and the *Oxford Book of Women's Verse*. She is a Fellow of the Royal Society of Literature.

CATHERINE PETERS is the author of *The King of Inventors: A Life of Wilkie Collins* (1991) and *Thackeray's Universe* (1987). She taught English at Somerville College, Oxford, 1981–92, and is currently teaching for the Department of Continuing Education at Oxford. She is a Fellow of the Royal Society of Literature.

KEN ROBINSON was formerly Head of the School of English at the University of Newcastle upon Tyne. He has published widely on later seventeenth-century literature and is working on a biography of Rochester. Trained as a psychoanalytic psychotherapist, he now works in private practice. His interests in psychoanalysis and literature combine in his forthcoming book, *Valuable Allies*.

JÜRGEN SCHLAEGER is Professor of English and Comparative Literature and Director of the Centre for Literary Anthropology at the University of Konstanz. He is chairman of the German Association of University Teachers in English. His works include *Imitatio und Realisation: Funktionen poetischer Sprache von Pope bis Wordsworth* (1972) and *Kritik in der Krise* (1986). He has published extensively on early English diaries and autobiographies.

JON STALLWORTHY is a Fellow of the British Academy and a Professor of English Literature at Oxford. His books include seven collections of poems (most recently, *The Anzac Sonata: New and Selected Poems* (1986)); two critical studies of Yeats's poetry (1963 and 1969); translations (with Peter France) of Alexander Blok (1970) and Boris Pasternak (1983); and biographies of Wilfred Owen (1974) and Louis MacNeice (1995).

ANTHONY STORR is a Fellow of the Royal College of Physicians, Honorary Fellow of the Royal College of Psychiatrists, and a Fellow of the Royal Society of Literature. He is also Honorary Consulting Psychiatrist to the Oxfordshire Health Authority, and an Emeritus Fellow of Green College, Oxford. His publications include *The Integrity of the Personality* (1960), *Human Destructiveness* (1972), *The Dynamics of Creation* (1972), *Jung* (1973), *The Art of Psychotherapy* (1979), *Solitude* (1989), *Freud* (1989), *Churchill's Black Dog* (1989), and *Music and the Mind* (1992).

ANN THWAITE, who graduated from St Hilda's College, Oxford, has published *Waiting for the Party: The Life of Frances Hodgson Burnett* (1974; reissued 1994), *Edmund Gosse: A Literary Landscape* (1984, winner of the Duff Cooper prize in 1985), and *A. A. Milne: A Life* (1990, Whitbread Biography of the year). She has taught at two different periods at Tokyo Women's University (Joshi Daigaku), but has spent most of her time as a writer.

NORMAN WHITE, formerly Leverhulme Research Fellow, University of Liverpool, and now Senior Lecturer in English at University College, Dublin, founded and edited *The Hopkins Research Bulletin* and has published very extensively on Hopkins. His *Hopkins: A Literary Biography* (1992) was shortlisted for the Whitbread Biography prize for 1992.

JOHN WORTHEN is Professor of D. H. Lawrence Studies at the University of Nottingham. He has produced four volumes in the Cambridge edition of Lawrence, is series editor for the new Penguin edition of Lawrence, and is the author of *D. H. Lawrence: A Literary Life* (1989) and the first volume of the Cambridge biography of Lawrence, *D. H. Lawrence: The Early Years 1885–1912* (1991).

Index

Abercrombie, Lascelles 151
Ackroyd, Peter 20, 210, 235
Aldington, Richard 238
Alexander, Peter 13
Anderson, Linda 1, 5, 173–83
Apsley, (Sir) Allen 103
Arbuthnot, Dr 17
Arnold, Matthew 193–4, 199
Auden, W. H. 221, 271–2, 274, 278
Austen, Jane 189–91, 199

Baines, Jocelyn 117
Bair, Deirdre 209
Balzac, H. de 85, 187, 188
Barnacle (Joyce), Nora 38, 115, 116
Barnes, Julian 33, 34, 36, 210–11
Barroll, Leeds 189
Batchelor, John 1–11, 48, 115–27
Bate, W. Jackson 85
Beadnell, Maria 85
Beckett, Samuel 209
Beer, Gillian 134
Beer, Thomas 18
Bell, Clive 131, 245, 250
Benfey, Christopher 18
Bennett, Arnold 131
Berger, John 132
Berryman, John 84
Binney, Cecil 166
Binyon, Laurence 151
Bishop, Elizabeth 5, 173–83
Blacker, C. P. 165, 166–7
Blake, Robert 188
Blunt, Wilfred Scawen 209
Bobrowski, Tadeusz 117, 118–19, 126
Boswell, James 15–16, 27, 62, 188, 203
Bowlby, Rachel 134, 143
Bradshaw, David 1, 5, 151–71
Bridges, Robert 216, 220
Briggs, Julia 1, 4, 245–65
Britten, Benjamin 272–3, 274, 278
Brock, (Sir) Lawrence 165–6
Brogan, Hugh 7
Brontë, Charlotte 87–90, 96, 97, 275
Brook, Peter 199

Browning, Elizabeth Barrett 48
Browning, Robert 48
Buckingham (George Villiers, second
    Duke of Buckingham) 105
Bullitt, William C. 75–6
Burgess, Anthony 132, 217–18
Burnet, Gilbert 103, 104, 109
Burrows, Louie 229, 232, 237–40
Butler, Samuel 208
Byatt, A. S. 7, 17, 27, 32–3, 35–6

Calder-Marshall, Arthur 269, 276
Callil, Carmen 209
Carey, John 4, 9, 131, 135–6, 146–7
Carlyle, Thomas 8
Carpenter, Humphrey 1, 267–79
Carpenter, Mrs U. M. 268–9
Carroll, Paul 191
Caute, David 159–60
Chambers, Alan 227
Charles II 102–3, 105, 106
Chatterton, Thomas 84
Chesterton, G. K. 167
Church, A. G. 165
Clare, John 84
Clarendon (Edward Hyde, first Earl of
    Clarendon) 108
Claude, Mary 193–4
Clough, A. C. 193
Clough, Anne 193
Cockshut, A. O. J. 6, 8, 202
Coleridge, S. T. 3, 5–6, 84
Collins, Harriet 50–1
Collins, Wilkie 49–56
Collins, William 84
Compton-Burnett, Ivy 6, 206
Conrad, Jessie 117
Conrad, Joseph 117–27
Cowper, William 84, 85
Crane, Hart 84
Crane, Stephen 18
Crayle, Benjamin 105
Curll, Edmund 17

Darwin, Leonard 164

Defoe, Daniel 21, 22, 23, 24
de Man, Paul 191
DeMaria, Robert, Jun. 3
Derrida, Jacques 189–91, 197
Diana (Princess of Wales) 15–16
Dickens, Charles 47, 52, 53, 54–5, 57, 64,
    85, 235, 241
Dickens, Fanny 85
Dickinson, Emily 87, 90–1, 96–7, 173
Dickinson (Elliott), Frances 51–4
Dickinson, Violet 250–3
Disraeli, Benjamin 7–8
Diston, Marshall 153
Donaldson, Frances 209
Donaldson, Ian 197
Donne, John 84
Dostoevsky, Dr 74–5
Dostoevsky, F. 74–5
DuBrow, Joan, 191
Duncan-Jones, Katherine 189
Dworkin, Andrea 133–4

Eagleton, Terry 1, 3
Edel, Leon 3, 6, 76, 192, 204, 210, 231,
    233, 234
Egg, Augustus 55
Ehrenpreis, I. 188
Eissler, K. R. 76
Eliot, George 55, 97, 218, 279
Eliot, T. S. 7, 191, 192, 194, 269, 273
Elliott, Gilbert 53–4
Ellis, Havelock 160
Ellmann, Richard 2, 3, 6, 20, 27, 37–9,
    76, 77, 115–6, 192, 193, 203
Empson, W. 191
Erikson, Erik 76

Fanshaw, William 103
Ferris, Paul 209
Fisher, R. A. 164–5
Flush (E. B. Browning's spaniel) 48–9
Forster, E. M. 160
Foster, Margaret 20, 48
Frank, Joseph 74
Freud, Sigmund 73–6, 77–9, 112, 122,
    179, 187, 188
Froude, J. A. 8
Fry, Roger 136–7, 260, 262
Fussell, Paul 278

Gadbury, John 103
Garnett, David 160
Garnett, Edward 120–1

Gaskell, Elizabeth 46, 88
Gay, John 23
Gay, Peter 77
Gittings, Robert 47, 208
Glendinning, Victorian 20, 62, 67–8, 69,
    70, 207, 208, 209
Goldensohn, L. 134, 139–40
Golding, William 7, 17, 30–2
Gordon, Lyndall 1, 7, 87–98, 210, 267–78
Gorman, Herbert 214
Gosse, Edmund 62, 205, 207, 208, 210,
    214, 215
Grahame, Kenneth 272–3
Graves, Caroline 51
Greenblatt, Stephen 196, 198–9
Greene, Graham 209
Grosskurth, Phyllis 206
Gurevitch, M. G. 160
Gurr, Andrew 195

Halifax (George Savile, Earl of
    Halifax) 104
Hamilton, Ian 7, 17
Hardy, Thomas 34, 214
Harrod, Roy 77
Harsnett, Samuel 196
Hartley, L. P. 29–30
Hayman, Ronald 209
Hayter, Alethea 46
Haywood, Eliza 21, 22
Head, Henry 154
Heard, Gerald 155, 161–2
Heger, C. G. R 87, 89
Hemingway, Ernest 276
Hilton, Tim 117
Hobhouse, L. T. 160
Hobson, J. A. 160
Hogarth, Georgina 55
Hollander, Paul 159
Holmes, Richard 1, 2, 5–6, 15–25, 45, 66,
    70, 273
Holroyd, Michael 2, 20, 27, 62, 69, 77,
    208, 210, 273
Homer 27
Honan, Park 1, 2, 6, 8–9, 187–99
Honigmann, E. A. J. 195, 197
Hopkins, G. M. 78, 84, 213–25
Hughes, Ted 17
Hunt, John Dixon 117
Huxley, Aldous 5, 151–71, 238
Huxley, Julian 156, 160, 163, 165,
    168
Huysmans, J. 105, 111–12

Index

Isherwood, Christopher 155

James, Henry 3, 17, 28, 76, 87, 91–2, 95–6, 140–1, 210, 214
James, William 91
Jarrell, Randall, 84
Johnson, Edgar 192, 235–7
Johnson, Samuel 15–16, 18–19, 20–5, 62, 85, 188, 208
Jones, Ernest 76
Jonson, Ben 195
Joyce, James 17, 37–9, 115–16, 151, 195, 214
Jung, C. G. 79

Kafka, F. 82–4, 209
Karl, Frederick 117
Ker, Ian 188–9
Kermode, Frank 101
Keynes, J. M. 77
Korzeniowski, Apollo 118–19, 126
Kristeva, Julia 179–81

Larkin, Philip 19–20, 36–7, 132, 201–2, 235
Lasch, Christopher 65–6
Laski, Harold 160
Laughlin, James 272
Lawrence, D. H. 9, 151–2, 209, 227–44
Lear, Edward 84
Leavis, F. R. 191
Lee, Hermione 1, 4, 129–50
Lees-Milne, James 209
Leonard, Tom 46
Lewes, George 55
Lewis, C. S. 275, 278
Lindsay, Kenneth 155, 156, 157
Lockhart, R. 235–7
Longford, Elizabeth 209
Lowell, Robert 84, 173–4
Lowry, Malcolm 278
Lurie, Alison 35–5
Lyne, Joe (Father Ignatius) 269, 276
Lyons, Paddy 104

MacBeth, George 205
MacCarthy, Desmond 137–8, 188
MacDonald, Ramsay 153, 163
Maclean, Norman 191
MacNeice, Louis 27–42
Maddox, Brenda 47
Maitland, F. 247, 249–50
Mann, Thomas 219

Manton, Jo 47
Manuel, Frank E. 76
Marchand, L. A. 192
Marcus, Jane 133
Mariani, Paul 233–4
Marlowe, Christopher 195
Martin, Jay 234
Martin, Robert Bernard 78, 84–5
Mendelson, Edward 272
Mepham, John 134
Meyers, Jeffrey 229, 233, 240
Meyers, Jeffrey 6
Middlebrook, Diane Wood 17
Millais, J. E. 116
Miller, James 23
Millgate, Michael 7, 28, 36, 204, 206
Millier, Brett 175–6
Milne, A. A. 205, 207, 210, 211
Milne, Christopher 204
Milton, John 16
Moore, H. T. 232, 233, 238, 239
Moore, Jerrold Northrop 79
Moore, Madeline 133
Mortimer, Raymond 155
Morton, Andrew 15–16
Mosley, Cynthia 154, 162
Mosley, Oswald 154–5, 159, 162
Motion, Andrew 19–20, 132, 209
Moyer, C. R. 191
Mulryne, Ronnie 195
Murray, J. Middleton 142, 143

Nadel, Ira Bruce 6, 188, 209
Najder, Zdzisław 117
Nehls, Edward 239
Newbolt, (Sir) Henry 151
Newmans, J. H. 189
Nichols, Robert 154
Nicholson, Max 155, 156–8
Nicolson, Ben 136
Nicolson, Harold 141, 209
Nicolson, Nigel 209
Nokes, David 188

Ostwald, Peter 234–5
Owen, Wilfred 36, 39

Painter, George 192, 193
Parsons, Robert 103–4, 110–11
Patterson, Rebecca 173
Paulin, Tom 130–1, 143
Pear, T. H. 133
Peters, Catherine 1, 2, 3, 43–56

Pinto, Vivian de Sola 103–4
Plath, Sylvia 17, 84
Poe, Edgar Allan 84
Pollack, Max 112
Pound, Ezra 272, 272, 273, 279
Proust, M. 192, 193, 195

Ragan, Larry 191
Ray, G. N. 192
Reid, Christopher 213
Richards, I. A. 191, 193
Ricks, Christopher 134–5, 129, 140–1, 273
Robinson, Ken 1, 2, 101–14
Rochester (see Wilmot)
Roethke, Theodore 84
Rolfe, F. (Baron Corvo) 208
Rosenberg, John 117
Rossetti, D. G. 116
Rudd, Martha 51
Runcie, Robert 268
Ruskin, John 116–17
Russell, Bertrand 160

Sackville-West, V. 141, 209
Salinger, J. D. 17
Sartre, J.-P. 76
Savage, Richard 18–19, 20–5
Schlaeger, Jürgen 1, 2, 4, 57–71
Schreber (Judge) 75
Schreber, Daniel 75
Schreiner, Olive 87, 92–3
Schwartz, Delmore 84
Scott, Walter 235–6
Sexton, Anne 17, 84
Shakespeare, William 2, 27, 194–9
Shaw, G. B. 27, 160, 210, 273
Shelden, Michael 228
Sherry, Norman 209
Shewring, Margaret 195
Shove, Fredegond 141
Showalter, Elaine 133
Sinclair, Andrew 69
Skidelsky, Robert 8, 154, 162, 202
Smart, Christopher 84
Smith, Agnes 137
Smith, George 87–8, 89
Smith, Reginald 254
Smyth, Ethel 143–4
Snowden, Philip 153, 154
Spurling, Hilary 7, 144, 206
Stallworthy, Jon 1, 3, 27–42
Stephen (Bell), Vanessa 249, 250, 258

Stephen, Julia 249–50
Stephen, (Sir) Leslie 142, 245–7
Storey, Graham 53
Storr, Anthony 1, 6, 73–86
Strachey, Lytton 8, 27, 74, 77, 79, 215, 253
Sutherland, John 116
Swift, Jonathan 188
Symonds, J. A. 206
Symons, A. J. A. 208
Symons, Julian 208

Taylor, A. J. P. 155
Taylor, Mary 88
Temple, Minny 90–2, 95
Tennyson, Alfred (Lord) 33–4, 78, 84–5, 201, 210
Tennyson, Emily 201–11
Tennyson, Hallam 33–4, 206
Ternan, Frances 53
Ternan, Nelly 47, 53, 241–2
Thackeray, W. M. 54–5
Thomas, Dylan 209
Thomas, Edward 84
Thwaite, Ann 1, 201–11
Tillotson, Kathleen 192
Tolkien, J. R. R. 270–1
Tomalin, Claire 20, 47, 241–2
Treglown, Jeremy 104
Trevelyan, Mary 269
Trevor, Meriol 189

Uglow, Jenny 46

Vieth, David 104

Wagner-Egelhaaf, Martina 57–8, 70
Wain, John 216
Walker, Keith 104
Walpole, Hugh 160
Watt, Donald 161
Waugh, Evelyn 209, 279
Weekley, Frieda 229–30
Weiser, D. K. 198
Wellek, René 192
Wells, H. G. 160
White, Norman 1, 3–4, 213–25
Whitman, Walt 217
Wilde, Oscar 27, 115–16
Williams, Charles 272–3, 278
Williams-Ellis, Clough 156
Wilmot, Henry (first Earl of Rochester) 102–3, 108–9

Wilmot, John (second Earl of
 Rochester) 101–14
Wilson, A. N. 275
Wilson, Charles 151
Wilson, Lily 48
Wilson, Richard 187
Winnicott, D. W. 107–8, 110
Wodehouse, P. G. 209
Woolf, Leonard 137, 138, 143–4, 160, 258
Woolf, Virginia 4, 35, 43, 48–9, 87, 93–5,
 96, 97, 129–50, 160, 177, 203–4,
 245–65
Wordsworth, William 214
Worthen, John 1, 209, 227–44
Worthington-Evans, Laming 153

Yeats, W. B. 164, 223

Ziegler, Philip 7
Zwerdling, Alex 134